YEAR OF THE KING

For my parents and Jim

Antony Sher

YEAR OF THE KING

An Actor's Diary
and Sketchbook

Limelight Editions

Limelight Editions
512 Newark Pompton Turnpike
Pompton Plains, New Jersey 07444

First published in 1992 by Limelight Editions
Fourth printing, 2006

Originally published in 1985 by Chatto & Windos

Printed in the United States of America

Library of Congress Cataloging-in-Publication Data

Sher, Antony, 1949–
    Year of the king : an actor's diary and sketchbook / Antony Sher.
    —1st Limelight ed.
        p.   cm.
    Originally published: London : Chatto & Windus, 1985.
    ISBN 0-87910-165-2 (pbk.)
    1. Sher, Antony, 1949– —Diaries. 2. Shakespeare, William, 1564–1616.
King Richard III. 3. Shakespeare, William, 1564–1616—Stage history—
1950– 4. Royal Shakespeare Company. 5. Richard III, King of England,
1452–1485, in fiction, drama, poetry, etc. 6. Actors—Great Britain—Diaries.
I. Title.
[PN2598.S47A38   1992]
792'.028'092—dc20
[B]

                                                          92-21034
                                                               CIP

www.limelighteditions.com

Contents

Fool, of thyself speak well. Fool, do not flatter.

Richard III, v. iii

Introduction

Last Saturday night saw the final performance of *Othello* at the RSC's Swan Theatre in Stratford, prior to its Japanese tour and London run. To mark the occasion, my dresser Keith Lovell gave me a farewell gift: a small framed photograph. I stared at it in astonishment. It showed me twenty years earlier, backstage at the main house, in the middle of a performance of *Richard III*. It must've been taken just before or after the Coronation sequence which we invented for our production, since I am wearing the vast red silk robe with the special clasp that allowed us to reveal Richard's naked deformed back during the annointing ritual. Mal Storry, who played Buckingham, is posing for the camera behind me, and to one side is my then dresser, the foul-mouthed, good hearted Black Mac. Both Mal and Mac look rather deadpan, while I have a strange sideways smile on my face.

What strikes me first is not how young I look – though this is fairly alarming – but how relaxed. For the journey towards *Richard III*, told in the pages of this book, was a difficult one, full of anxiety, self-doubt and struggle. Back in 1984 it felt like my whole life depended on the attempt to conquer this one great role. Yet the photo shows someone just larking about in the wings. It looks like just another show, just another part.

And here I am now, in 2004, still working for the RSC – my love for the company undimmed – and indeed playing another of Shakespeare's villains, Iago, a man so thoroughly disturbed and disturbing that he makes Richard III look like the good guy. So what's changed? Everything. Twenty years might seem like a long time, but it doesn't feel long

enough for some of the differences between the world I was describing
in *Year of the King* and the world now.

Most extraordinary is what's happened to my birthplace, South
Africa. At the time of writing the book, the system of apartheid seemed
immovable, and its brutalities knew no bounds. And yet now, in this very
month of this very year, South Africa is celebrating the tenth anniversary
of its first democratic elections. Democratic elections? In South Africa?
Ask the thirty-five-year-old in the photograph and he'd have told you it
was impossible, at least not without the streets running with blood. Yet
that didn't happen either. Instead a miracle did. A miracle that began
with one remarkable man walking out of prison to freedom.

On a personal front, much has happened too: as a gay man I've
come out publicly (in this book I'm afraid I'm still very coy about my
relationship with my then partner, Jim Hooper), and my father has died,
my funny, difficult Dad, and I've been knighted, and I was in a clinic for
cocaine dependency, and . . . well, if the reader is interested, they could
look at *Beside Myself*, my autobiography. *Year of the King* was my first
book, but I've since published seven more, as well as a stage play, *I.D.*
Writing is now a serious rival to acting in my professional affections, and
I'd be hard pressed to say which occupies the place of first love.

Re-reading *Year of the King* I was surprised by my obsession with
Olivier's Richard III. At the time I genuinely thought there was such a
thing as a definitive performance of a Shakespeare role or play. Yet since
playing the role myself, I've seen two other Richard IIIs that are certainly
as good as anyone might hope for: Ian McKellen's chillingly sour
Blackshirt at the National, and Simon Russell Beale's glorious poisoned
toad at the RSC. I now believe that a significant part of Shakespeare's
genius, and one of the reasons why his work has lasted four hundred
years, is that he constantly yields himself to re-interpretation. God
knows what he himself would make of our endless and busy explorations
of how to stage his plays. An all-female *Shrew* or an all-Yorkshire *Antony
and Cleopatra*, a circus *Dream*, the roles of Henry V and Henry VI played
by black actors, a Hamlet who vomits up his father's Ghost, or indeed a
Richard III on crutches . . . would he be dismayed by these portrayals? I
hope not.

For me another big difference between 1984 and 2004, and one which
is vital to record here, lies in my approach to speaking Shakespeare's
language. There's a very significant diary entry on page 228 of *Year*

of the King, dated Sunday 10 June, the weekend before we opened the show: 'Time to stop and think, which I don't really want to do. Refuge in the Gielgud book, *The Ages of Gielgud*, only to come across John Mortimer's lament on modern verse-speaking. I snap it shut as if killing a bug.' The truth of the matter is that I was terrified of the verse, ashamed of my inexperience with it, and nursing a secret fear that I was trespassing anyway. Wasn't classical theatre the territory of handsome, rich-voiced British giants like Gielgud and Olivier, and out of bounds for little Cape Town nebbishes like me?

I now feel bold enough to answer that question with a resounding no. Shakespeare belongs to us all.

Richard III was my first attempt at one of the great roles, and Iago is my latest. In between there's been Macbeth, Leontes, Titus and Shylock, as well as several other classical parts, like the eponymous heroes of *Tamburlaine the Great* and *The Malcontent*, Caesar in *The Roman Actor*, Vindice in *The Revenger's Tragedy*. In fact, I believe it's the experience of playing Shakespeare's contemporaries that has made the speaking of Shakespeare himself easier for me. The other writers don't have Shakespeare's gift with the verse – despite all their strengths they don't have, let's face it, his genius – and so they are much harder to speak. After you've battled with, say, the monotonous thump of Marlowe's mighty lines or Tourneur's awkward, twisting mouthfuls of words, you come back to Shakespeare with such relief, such joy. He's done all the work for you. All you have to do is breathe it in and speak it out; just let it live in the air. This is, of course, easier said than done. But only by doing it, by practising the skills, will you eventually learn to master them. In the meantime the problem remains, and you can read about it in this book. I think it's only right for me to confess here that the search for a spectacular physical shape for Richard was partly to compensate for my feeling of inadequacy with his language. You could say there was something symbolic about the eventual use of crutches.

These days I believe that performing Shakespeare begins and ends with the speaking of the verse, and no amount of physical bravura can make up for it. The brains of his great characters are more interesting than their bodies, and their brains are revealed in their manner of talking. Sometimes I sense there's a public conception that all of his creations talk the same way, and that the *Collected Works* simply represent a great generalised wash of Shakespeare-speak. Far from it. Leontes's neurotic, fractured utterances, Macbeth's dangerously measured tone, Iago's sick sex-fuelled images, and the sheer energy and wit of Richard's speeches: these are all very different from one another. And it's only by observing the individual ways these men express their thoughts that you can really get to their hearts.

My conversion to this new approach has been hugely helped by the most important change in my life between 1984 and 2004, and that is the relationship – seventeen-years-old next month – with my partner, the director Greg Doran. Just recently, Greg has been enjoying a terrific run of success with the RSC, conceiving and producing the Jacobethan Season (for which he won the 2003 Olivier Award for Outstanding Achievement), the double of *The Taming of the Shrew* and *The Tamer Tamed*, *All's Well* with Judi Dench, and now *Othello* – and the press has repeatedly hailed him as one of the best Shakespeare directors in the country. Quite apart from all the other riches of our partnership, I feel I've been remarkably lucky to share my life with someone who knows and loves Shakespeare quite like he does, and who can communicate this passion with such vitality.

The Swan Theatre didn't even exist in 1984 – it was still our rehearsal room then, the Conference Hall often mentioned in this book – but it is now the best auditorium I know, both as performer and audience member. It creates the illusion, essential for a good classical space, of functioning like a camera: switching from close-up to wide shot, from intimate to epic. It's where I've done all my recent work with the RSC, and I always feel intense excitement when I arrive there to open a new show, and then intense sadness when it closes. So at last Saturday night's performance of *Othello* I was already rather emotional when Keith suddenly presented me with the photograph of backstage life during *Richard III*.

Looking at it, I remembered that for all the struggle and doubt of the journey, and for all my inadequacy at verse-speaking, the role of the 'bottled spider' turned out so well for me that it's been quite a hard act to follow. (Who was it that said, 'Be careful of getting what you want'?) I also remembered that one of the other men with me in the photo, Black Mac, is no longer with us – he died in 2001 – and I miss him. As I hope this book reveals, he was a tremendous, larger-than-life character: originally from the North-East, working both as an army sergeant and a theatre dresser, rude, funny, kind, aggressive, full of contradictions, the sort of character Shakespeare would've loved. I like it when, in the

diary entry dated 18 June, the day before our opening, Mac overhears me practising my speeches and says 'Clever, henny, clever, must be clever to remember that fokkin bollocks.' But then later he confides in me: 'The shows I've seen here, mate, the memories I've got, and I've viewed them from angles no other bugger has ever seen, no fokkin critic, not even the directors have seen them like I have, from my special places in the wings.'

So it is with Black Mac in mind – and other departed figures who haunt the pages of this book, like Dad, and indeed Olivier – that I now invite the reader to go on a twenty-year-old journey with me, in search of one of Shakespeare's most dynamic and original creations, King Richard III.

Antony Sher, London

1. Barbican 1983

August 1983

Summer.

To be more precise, my thirty-fourth summer in all, my fifteenth in England away from my native South Africa, my eleventh as a professional actor, and my second as a member of the Royal Shakespeare Company.

These last two years have been eventful, a time of change. Last year, a successful season in Stratford playing the Fool in *King Lear* and the title role in the Bulgakov play *Molière*. Then, in November, an accident. In the middle of a performance as the Fool one of my Achilles tendons snapped and I suddenly found myself off work for a period that was to last six months.

Unexpectedly, this proved to be a happy time. Apart from anything else, the enforced rest was a chance at last to do all those paintings and sketches I'd long been planning. With my leg encased in plaster I'd sit for hours at my easel, just managing now and then to hobble a few steps back to get a better view. If anything, time passed too quickly. After years in a profession where you're on public display, it was a relief to be a recluse for a change. My temporary disability made any journey from my home in Islington difficult and vaguely humiliating, so few were worth it. There was one exception.

The Remedial Dance Clinic in Harley Street is so-called because it serves as repair shop to most of the dance companies. Each day I would have to make my way there for long sessions of physiotherapy. This was a new experience for me. Strange, invisible currents of electricity, ultra-sound and deep-heat were passed into my leg and somehow started it working again. The process was slow. When the plaster first came off, the white shrunken leg revealed underneath was virtually useless. But gradually, stage by stage, my crutches could be exchanged for a walking-

stick, then that was abandoned for boots with stacked heels, and eventually
I was walking again in ordinary shoes. Now the process accelerated in the
other direction. Running, then jumping, even trying a cautious cartwheel
. . . preparing to go back into *King Lear* for the London run at the Barbican
Theatre.

Another treatment of a very different sort, which I decided to try while
I had the free time, was psychotherapy. Here the currents are stranger,
but just as impressive. A man called Monty Berman has been listening
patiently to the story of my life, yawning only occasionally. He makes
comments like 'Let's validate that', when I relate certain chapters, and
'Bullshit!' to others. I sit there, peering at him through my large, tinted
specs, nodding in agreement, and then hurry away afterwards to check
words like 'validate' in the dictionary.

So the Achilles incident has been a kind of turning point. Invisible
mending from head to heel. Now I also pay regular visits to the City Gym,
the Body Control Studio, and various swimming pools. I have developed,
along with new muscles and energy, that brand of smug boastfulness on
the subject of physical fitness: the kind that makes other people – and I
remember this well from being on the other side – want to slap you around
the mouth.

Going back into *King Lear* after six months away was like climbing on
to the horse after it has thrown you. But its short London run is already
over and I escaped uninjured. I have since opened in a new production of
Tartuffe, playing the title role. This has been directed by Bill Alexander
(as a companion piece to his production about its author, *Molière*) and has
been a great hit with audiences, although less so, I believe, with the critics.
My uncertainty stems from the fact that, along with a whole string of
unwanted habits ditched since going to Monty, I have stopped reading
reviews. I never thought I could do it, never thought I could live without
them. But now, apart from the occasional twinge, I hardly miss them at
all. Rather like giving up cigarettes, I suppose. Unfortunately, I still smoke
quite heavily. Which is just as well, as I'm required to do so in the new
David Edgar play, *Maydays*, which is about to go into rehearsal . . .

In the meantime, at the Barbican, *Tartuffe* and *Molière* continue in the
repertoire.

JOE ALLEN'S Dining with a friend one evening, I notice Trevor Nunn
[RSC Joint Artistic Director] at another table. He's been on sabbatical
ever since I joined the RSC last year, so I haven't met him properly. Yet

Self as Molière and Tartuffe

he *is* the RSC, so a social gesture might be required. Is it just a little nod? Or a little wave? Or a little of each with a mouthed, 'Hi, Trev'? Or as much as popping over to his table and using the more formal, 'Trevor, hello'? Luckily, his back is to me at the moment, so none of these decisions will have to be taken till my exit. For the moment I can concentrate on my Caesar Salad.

Hours later, my companion goes to the loo and almost instantly, as if by magic, Trevor Nunn is leaning forward on to my table.

'Tony.'

'Trevor!'

'I did enjoy *Tartuffe* the other evening.'

'Ah. Good. Thank you.'

'I thought Bill Alexander got a perfect balance in the production between the domestic naturalism and the black farce.'

'Yes, hasn't he? It's a –'

'You really ought to play Richard the Third soon.'

'Oh. Well. That would be nice.'

I look up at him hopefully. He smiles politely, a touch of enigma, and retreats, disappearing into the smoky, gossipy crowd . . .

Back at home, Jim [Jim Hooper, RSC actor] says, 'Beware. It's only Joe Allen's chat.' He's quite right, of course, so I try not to think any further about it. Which is like trying not to breathe.

There was something unfinished in what he said. 'You really ought to play Richard the Third soon –' what might he have said next? 'And I shall direct it'? Or, '– but not for us'? In the next few days these nine words, this innocent piece of Joe Allen's chat is subjected to the closest possible scrutiny. It is viewed from every possible angle, upside down and inside out, thoroughly dissected, at last laid to rest, exhumed, another autopsy, finally mummified.

I try not to tell people about it, but it does have a peculiar life of its own, this ghost, and will keep slipping out.

I make the fatal mistake of mentioning it to Mum on one of my Sunday calls to South Africa. She instantly starts packing.

Another mistake is to mention it to Nigel Hawthorne (playing Orgon) at the next performance of *Tartuffe*. He twinkles. From then on the shows are accompanied by comments like, 'Thought I noticed Tartuffe developing a slight limp this evening', or, overhearing me complaining about putting on weight, he says, 'Can't you just edge it up for the hump?'

This successfully helps to shut me up, so apart from Mum's weekly question, 'And Richard the Third?', as if we were about to open, there is no further mention made of it.

Time passes. Now it is winter.

Thursday 3 November

BARBICAN Paranoia is rampant these days, down in our warm and busy warren, miles below a chilly City of London. The end of the season, and for many their two-year cycle, is in sight. Rumours are rife about world tours of *Cyrano* and *Much Ado*, videos of *Molière* and *Peer Gynt*. Many are keen to return to Stratford where, rumour boasts, Adrian Noble will direct Ian McKellen as Coriolanus and either David Suchet or Alan Howard will be giving an Othello. But will people be asked back and, if they are, will good enough parts be on offer? It is widely believed that planning meetings are already in session in those distant offices above street level. As the directors pass among us for their lunches, suppers and teas, actors perform daredevil feats of balance in order to eavesdrop on conversations half a room away.

I am not above these feelings of unease myself. These years with the company have been the happiest of my career and I too don't want them to end.

CANTEEN Terry Hands [RSC Joint Artistic Director] suddenly at my elbow in the lunch queue. Is it because he's re-rehearsing *Poppy* at the moment that he seems even more oriental than usual? Dressed in black, smiling slightly and knowingly from hooded eyes, a sense of immense energy and power in repose.

Terry Hands

He says, 'We really ought to have one of our meals soon.'

'Absolutely. When?'

'Well, I'm busy with *Poppy* technicals till the week after next. Has Bill spoken to you?'

'No.'

'Bill hasn't spoken to you?'

'No. What about?'

'Oh, you know . . .' He smiles. 'Life and Art.'

'Ah. No. Definitely not.'

'We'll let Bill speak to you first.' He starts to go. Actors leaning towards us at forty-five degree angles quickly straighten, ear erections drooping. Terry turns back to me and smiles.

'Oh, and don't sign up for anything else next year. Yet.'

Friday 4 November
Bill Alexander rings. We arrange lunch for Monday.

MAYDAYS After the show, Otto Plaschkes comes round to my dressing-room. He's a film producer, the latest in a long line to try to finance Snoo Wilson's screenplay, *Shadey*. I was first approached about playing the eponymous hero (a gentle character who possesses paranormal powers and wants to change sex) over a year ago. I tell him I'm about to be talked to by the RSC, presumably about returning to Stratford. If he could be more definite about dates I could ask the RSC to work round them. He can't, but it's an encouraging meeting.

Sunday 6 November
Wake in the early hours. Meeting Bill tomorrow. It's got to be Richard III. Got to be. Alan Howard's was about three, four years ago, so it's due again. And it's the obvious one if they're going to give me a Shakespeare biggy. Sudden flash of how to play the part – ideas are so clear in the middle of the night – Laughton in *The Hunchback of Notre Dame*. Very misshapen, clumsy but powerful, collapsed pudding features. Richard woos Lady Anne (his most unlikely conquest in the play; I've never seen it work) by being pathetic, vulnerable. She feels sorry for him, is convinced he couldn't hurt a fly.

The Nilsen murder case – the Sunday papers are full of the trial of this timid little mass-murderer. The sick, black humour seems to have a

Nilsen

flavour of *Richard III*: Nilsen running out of neckties as the strangulations increased; a head boiling on his stove while he walked his dog Bleep; his preference for Sainsbury's air fresheners; his suggestion to the police that the flesh found in his drains was Kentucky Fried Chicken; even his remark that having corpses was better than going back to an empty house. The headlines squeal 'Mad or Bad, Monster or Maniac, Sick or Evil?'

Spend hours sketching him, looking for some signs in that ordinary, ordinary face. The newspaper editors compensate for its ordinariness by choosing photos that are shot through police-van grills, or where the flashlights have flared on his spectacles to make him look other-worldly. But his ordinariness always seeps through. Isn't it that which makes him really frightening?

I ask Jim whether he believes we all have a Nilsen within us. He says, 'Well, certainly not *you*. You can't boil an egg, never mind someone's head.'

Monday 7 November
TRATTORIA AQUILINO Over lunch, Bill offers me Richard III. Although I've been expecting it, my heart misses a beat.

I don't know whether Bill is any younger than the other directors, but he is somehow always regarded as such. After seven years with the company he is the only one titled Resident – rather than Associate – Director, his missing qualification being a Shakespeare production in the main auditorium at Stratford. In fact the only Shakespeares he's ever done for the company were the *Henry IV*'s for the small-scale tour a couple of years ago. But after his successes this year with two classics (*Volpone* and *Tartuffe*) in The Other Place and The Pit this next step is inevitable.

We complement one another curiously, pulling in opposite directions – him towards the naturalistic, me towards the theatrical – and, I hope, stretching one another in the process. Almost the only thing we do have in common is a serious commitment to scruffiness. We both seem to find our days too short to waste time on shaving, brushing hair, or doing anything with clothes other than washing them and jumping into a familiar, unironed assortment hurriedly.

He is quite frank about next year's Stratford season. They did try to get Howard and McKellen, but failed. So they have resolved instead to introduce a new, younger group of Shakespearian actors. Roger Rees has been mentioned as well as one or two others whom he won't name yet.

I am flattered to be thought of in these terms, but am keen to know what else they have in mind for my season. Last year in Stratford convinced me it is no place to spend a whole year unless you're constantly employed or a devoted ruralist.

He says *Henry V* is being considered and wonders aloud what I feel about playing him. He stresses that this is not part of the offer, hasn't even been mooted at the directors' meetings. I reply that it's a part that would be challenging rather than wildly attractive. We also talk briefly about *Othello* (Iago, obviously), *Troilus* (he mentions Thersites but, as he's deformed, that seems too close to Richard III; I steer towards Pandarus – does he have to be older?), *As You Like It* (Jaques? Yes please. Touchstone? No thanks), *Merry Wives* (Ford? Yes, absolutely).

We talk briefly about Richard. I feel he should be severely deformed, not just politely crippled as he's often played. Bill says one should identify with him: a man looking in from the outside and thinking, 'I'll have some of that.'

I mention meeting Trevor in Joe Allen's and how I'm worried by the immediate association of Tartuffe with Richard. He smiles. 'I'm not asking you to play Richard like Tartuffe, or because of Tartuffe.' But it's a happy opportunity at last to discuss the inexplicable transformation that show made from the unhappiest rehearsal period (a major cast change, a mistaken lack of faith in the new translation, days of unremitting gloom) to this highly popular success we have on our hands. Have we just had a lucky escape? My own performance certainly feels like a survival kit rather than bricks and mortar. Bill feels that, although by accident rather than design, the mixture has turned out to be an exciting one – bourgeoisie invaded by gargoyle. I'm still not sure.

Coming to the end of the meal he asks, 'So how would you like me to report back at the next directors' meeting?'

'Well, ideally I'd like to be in four shows, no less than three, the majority to be Main-House Shakespeares, let's say two biggies and one supporting, and then perhaps one new play at The Other Place.'

'And coffee to follow?' the waitress is saying at the next table.

We leave the restaurant and Bill jumps into a passing taxi. We've only had one bottle of wine, but I'm left standing unsteadily on Islington Green, my head spinning. All I can think of is Michael Gambon telling me about driving up the M1 to Stratford to do a show last year: 'There's all these cars gliding past, Tone. Men in shirtsleeves, jackets hanging neatly from those little hooks in the back, eyes glazed, commuting back and forth like zombies. And then this thought suddenly hits me, like for the first time, and I say to myself, "Michael, you're driving up to Stratford-upon-Avon to play King-Fucking-Lear!" '

Tuesday 8 November
MONTY BERMAN SESSION He's pleased by the Richard III news, but as soon as I mention I would find Henry V more difficult to play he pounces on this and won't let go. By the end of the session I am totally convinced that unless I play that part my mental health will be in the gravest danger; then I remember and say, 'But Monty, that's not the one that's been offered.'

Phone my agent, Sally Hope, who's very laid back indeed about the news. I know she wants me to leave the RSC, feels I've been there long enough.

So I'm left to rejoice on my own. Buzzing around the house with the text, doing the speeches. This is almost the best time with any part, when it's on offer but you haven't said yes. You can have an unadulterated, indulgent wallow in it.

An image of massive shoulders like a bull or ape. The head literally trapped inside his deformity, peering out. Perhaps a whole false body could be built, not just the hump, to avoid having to contort myself and the strain or risk of injury that would entail.

Already dropped the Laughton image. Or maybe that's how he starts – an unkempt mess. Then, after 'a score or two of tailors / To study fashions to adorn my body', his grossness is transformed into some very impressive image – in the same way Nazi uniforms were so flattering that all sorts of odd-looking men, the undersized, the obese and the club-footed, all looked sensational in them.

My copy of the play is rather irritating for a wallow like today's. It's full of scribblings and sketches. I've been in the play before, playing Buckingham to Jonathan Pryce's brilliant Richard (a natural, born Richard) in Alan Dossor's 1973 Liverpool Everyman production. Following hard on Brook's *Midsummer Night's Dream*, it was set in a circus lions' cage, everyone was in track suits (different colours for the different factions) and had white faces. We all had to learn acrobatics, aiming for back-flips and eventually settling for forward-rolls. In retrospect the production was vintage Golden Age Everyman. Anarchy ruled. After Tyrrel reported the successful murder of the princes, Jonathan used to slip in a 'Nice one,

Pryce, Hill and self in <u>Richard III</u>, Liverpool Everyman, '73

Tyrrel' between some immortal couplet. In his tent at Bosworth he used to bring the house down by referring a line about 'soldiers' to the strips of toast on his breakfast tray. Hastings' head was passed like a rugby ball, each of us screaming as it landed and passing it on. In the hands of brilliant, dangerous actors like Jonathan and Bernard Hill (who played a succession of murderers and mayors) the clowning was inspired, departing from the rehearsed scenes and taking cast and audience on a magical mystery tour which, more often than not, proved to be the highlight of that night's show. I had no such courage and remember feeling woefully inadequate. I settled instead for a careful, detailed caricature – Buckingham as a smooth-talking, suave aristocrat with a copy of *The Times*, a monocle and solidly sleeked-back hair which I relied on for my biggest laugh: 'My hair doth stand on end to hear her curses.'

Sunday 13 November
Dickie [Richard Wilson, actor and director] phones from Bangalore where he's filming *Passage to India*. So at last I can shout it halfway across the world – 'They've asked me to play Richard the Third!'

'Good,' comes the polite reply, brimming with sub-text. Of all my friends Dickie has been the least reticent in suggesting that my work has deteriorated with the RSC – particularly in *Tartuffe* – and the most genuinely concerned that it shouldn't be allowed to continue.

Next, Mum phones from South Africa. But her response is muted as well. After all, she's known since August.

Monday 14 November
MOLIERE An alternative future presents itself. In the audience tonight sit two film producers, one American, one British. They're going to make a film about Albert Schweitzer and are looking for someone to play the part. Tonight's performance was sold out, but I managed to have them squeezed in by selling part of my soul. Could this be my *Gandhi*? My *Lawrence of Arabia*? Sure it'll be tough spending two years filming in the leper colonies of Central Africa, but then there are the premières, the Royal Command Performances, the Oscar ceremonies . . .

I hurry to the stage door afterwards, a hue of mascara and stage blood still glistening around my hopeful eyes. The American producer looks exactly like an American producer, rather like Orson Welles. He steps forward to greet me:

'Bravura performance, Mr Shw . . . Sht . . .'

'Sher.'

'Yup. But let me give it to you straight. You are not our Schweitzer. The one thing that Schweitzer was, was tall!'

Tuesday 15 November

MONTY SESSION He sits looking at me, all folded round himself, long limbs so relaxed they seem to bend anywhere like elastic, a little cushion sometimes held within the spiral. A red sweater is sometimes draped round the shoulders. The face is long; it has great wisdom; the eyes are tired, doctor's eyes – they've seen a lot of what there is to see. He works as a G P (at the age of sixty-one cycling daily from his Highgate home to the Lewisham practice), an acupuncturist and psychotherapist, is on the council of European Nuclear Disarmament, writes the occasional book, goes mountain climbing in the Himalayas in his spare time.

His phrases: 'Let me posit . . .', 'Let me share with you . . .'; 'I hear you', to reassure; his favourite form of refutation – 'Bullshit!' His toughest rule: you are never allowed to answer, 'I don't know.' And you don't half make some progress when you can't hide behind that one. At our first meeting back in March he said, 'You'll go through various attitudes towards me. You'll mistrust me, then you'll love me like a father, then I'll be a guru, then you'll hate me, and then with any luck you'll see me as just another person.' I don't think I ever got past the guru stage.

And he's South African. Or was. Originally from good Communist Jewish stock, he was imprisoned after Sharpeville for distributing leaflets (in prison he claims to have given a notable Lady Bracknell), exiled and can never return.

It is South Africa that we discuss today. Recently I've had this yearning to go back to visit and see my family. But this feeling is most uncharacteristic – I've been back only once in the fifteen years away; that was eight years ago. For so many years I was a closet South African. Having to say 'I was born in South Africa' stuck in my throat like a confession of guilt.

Monty is delighted. Thinks it is an excellent idea to go and have a grub round in my roots, rub that soil through my fingers; he sees it as an encouraging development in our work together.

I confess to him (so much of this is like Confession, I wonder if there's less call for therapy in Catholic circles) that another reason in the past for not returning is that I wanted to wait until I could step off the plane to the crackle of exploding flashbulbs. This seems silly now. He says it is a common syndrome – people who've left home to make good elsewhere want to return as heroes.

'Anyway,' he says, 'maybe there will be photographers at the airport.'

'There won't. I'm not famous.'

'You're well known.'

'There won't be photographers, Monty.'

'So, all right, maybe *one* photographer.'

I leave the session very uplifted, very excited. Going home.

Wednesday 16 November

Today is a special day. The first anniversary of my accident in Stratford . . .

Halfway through the evening performance of *King Lear*. We'd done the first storm scene. I was alone on stage, coming to the end of the Fool's soliloquy. Goosestepped to the front of the stage, 'FOR – I – LIVE – BEFORE – HIS – TIME', aware that I was slamming my feet down harder than usual . . . swung into the little dance – BANG! My first thought as I fell was, 'Fucking floorboards!' I looked round. No hole in the stage. No floorboard sticking up. Then what had hit the back of my leg? What had made that noise? A bullet? Dazed, I looked towards the audience for the assassin or some explanation. Realised I was sitting on the floor, had missed several cues, the music was unwinding round me, I tried to rise, fell again. Hopped off stage and fell. Lear, Kent and Fool have to go back on almost immediately. To Gambon (King Lear): 'Mike, I can't walk!' He, thinking this was part of our patter, said, 'Well then you'd better crawl, hadn't you? Stupid red-nosed tit.' Cue light. They ran on. I crawled after. The audience probably thought it was intentional – Lear, Kent, Poor Tom running round the heath, the Fool flagging, crawling behind . . .

End of that scene. Crawled into the wings. A crowd of stage-managers had gathered. 'Tony, what's the matter?' 'Don't know, can't stand up.' 'Are you in pain?' 'Don't know, don't know what's going on.' The next entrance was from under the stage, down several flights of stairs. Mal Storry (Kent) picked me up in his arms and carried me like a child . . .

For the Fool's death I had to step into a dustbin. Impossible to do without transferring the full weight from one leg to the other. This was the worst moment. For weeks afterwards this was the moment that I couldn't think about without going cold, the moment of stepping on to this soft dead leg, the nauseating pain as it took the full body weight . . .

Interval at last. Carried into the wings. A St John Ambulance man from front-of-house said, 'Might be the Achilles tendon.' Ian Talbot, my understudy, was staring down at me white-faced . . .

Carried up to the dressing-room on a chair. The St John Ambulance man and Steve Dobin, the stage-manager, puffing and struggling like Laurel and Hardy getting that piano up those stairs . . .

Sat in my dressing-room with a crowd of actors at the doorway peering in, Sara Kestleman saying, 'I think it might be the Achilles tendon, my darling, it happened to me at the National.' Left alone to change. Took off the red nose, saw myself in the mirror – my face a Francis Bacon smear of sweat and clown colours . . .

Pete Postlethwaite [RSC actor] drove me to the hospital. At first we couldn't find it, then when we did, couldn't find Casualty. The little country hospital looked closed for the night. At last, a weary nurse on duty. She said no one could see me till lunchtime the following day, gave me a bandage, painkillers, two mogodons and an unofficial diagnosis: 'Achilles tendon, I would have said.'

'The tendon has ruptured completely,' said the surgeon who operated a week later, 'up the back of your leg like a venetian blind.'

A mysterious accident that befalls sportsmen in top condition, little old ladies stepping off the curb, and a surprising number of actors: Judi Dench, Tim West, Nick Grace, Brian Cox, Paul Hertzberg, Sara Kestleman and I, all part of the Achilles mythology.

Friday 18 November
An unsettling dream during the night: The first read-through of *Richard III* on the balcony of a Tuscan villa overlooking a town square. Roger Rees playing Clarence. The moment comes to start. Everyone looks towards me. I know the play begins 'Now is the winter . . .', but cannot say it. Everyone waits, staring. A crowd starts to gather in the square below. Someone says, 'Oh don't mind them, they're the same old assassins that gather every time a Pope is elected.'

Unable to get back to sleep, I find my copy of the play and have a proper look at the speech.

'Now is the winter . . .'

God. It seems terribly unfair of Shakespeare to begin his play with such a famous speech. You don't like to put your mouth to it, so many other mouths have been there. Or to be more honest, one particularly distinctive mouth. His poised, staccato delivery is imprinted on those words like teeth marks.

I sit in shock, in the middle of the night, staring at the text.

'Now is the winter . . .'

God. It's as hard as saying 'I love you', as if you had just coined the phrase for the first time.

Has Olivier done the part definitively? Surely not. Surely the greatness of the play is lessened if such a feat is possible? Surely contemporaries thought the same about Irving, Kean, even Burbage? The trouble is, Olivier put it *on film*.

To cheer myself up on the subject, I dig out my 1980 diary to read this entry: 28 January. The Roundhouse. With Dickie and the actor Philip Joseph to see the Rustavelli *Richard III*. A stunning production by this Russian company. Ramaz Chkhivadze plays Richard like a species of giant poisonous toad. And he touches people as if removing handfuls of flesh. I will never forget the moment of Accession. As the crown landed on his head it seemed to squash the face beneath it like in an animated cartoon. You knew it was going to be downhill for Richard from then on. Dickie thought it was a definitive production, but I'm not so sure. How can we know when so much of the experience was slightly dream-like, that is, in a foreign language? But Dickie was undeterred.

'It makes me very envious,' he said. 'Mind you, they do have two years to rehearse.'

'Yes,' said Philip Joseph, 'but think of the two-month Technical.'

Saturday 19 November
This letter has been pinned up on the Green Room notice board, concerning the moment in *Tartuffe* when I pull down my tights to commence the assault on Elmire, and my bum is exposed; it's from a College of Higher Education:

'Dear Sirs,

I attended a performance of *Tartuffe* with my Sixth Form pupils last night and we were all rather offended by the totally unwarranted nudity in Act IV. We have tickets for *Cyrano de Bergerac* on 2 December and I would therefore be grateful if you could let us know if there is any nudity in that, and if so, how much?'

They're lucky it wasn't more than just my bum: the rest is contained in a posing-pouch hidden under the smock, following a conversation in rehearsals that went, 'Bums are funny, breasts funny-ish, but pubes, penises, testicles and vaginas are definitely not funny at all.'

Chkhikvadze in Russian _Richard III_

Some thoughts on *Richard III*.

In several copies I've looked at it's called *The Tragedy of King Richard the Third*. Yet a tradition has evolved of playing it as black comedy. I've never seen anyone play Richard's pain, his anger, his bitterness, all of which is abundant in the text.

Literature and drama are full of angelic cripples, deformed but kindly and lovable: Quasimodo, Smike, the Elephant Man, Claudius in *I, Claudius*. It seems to me that Richard's personality has been deeply and dangerously affected by his deformity, and that one has to show this connection.

But the problem in playing him extremely deformed is to devise a position that would be 100 per cent safe to sustain over three hours, and for a run that could last for two years. Play him on crutches perhaps? They would take a lot of the strain off the danger areas: lower back, pelvis and legs. And my arms are quite strong after months at the gym. Also I was on crutches for months after the operation so they have a personal association for me of being disabled. They could be permanently part of Richard, tied to his arms. The line, 'Behold mine arm is like a blasted sapling wither'd up', could refer to one of them literally.

The crutches idea is attractive, too attractive at this early stage. Must keep an open mind on the subject.

Worrying silence from Bill. It's about two weeks since we met. I ring him. He sounds evasive. I sense that something's wrong. He says that Richard III is still the only offer. Roger Rees has been talked to about a Hamlet and Ken Branagh about a possible Troilus.

But good news about the videos. Both *Molière* and *Tartuffe* are to be done. Bill will direct them himself with the aid of a technical director.

Monday 21 November

A DAY AT THE BARBICAN Walking through the foyers first thing in the morning, it's like some futuristic city mysteriously depopulated. A pair of automatic doors have quietly gone mad during the night and can't stop opening and closing.

At the top of the main staircase there is a plaque unveiled by the Queen at the Gala Opening on 3 March 1982. I was present and had an encounter which now seems to have a curious significance.

I was leading a little group to this staircase for the arrival of the Queen. Apart from Jim, the group consisted of RSC stalwarts Adrian Noble and Joyce Nettles. They knew the building much better than I did, as I hadn't even joined the company, so why I should have been leading is something of a mystery. At the time I put it down to drunkenness – champagne had been flowing freely – but now I suspect it was more to do with A Greater Scheme Of Things. Anyway, leading I was. The Royal arrival was imminent. DJs and evening gowns shimmered and rustled; the lights tickled over jewellery and hair lacquer; the smell of exclusive scents, the sounds of sophisticated gossip and discreet champagne burps.

I turned back to beckon my flagging group and almost immediately crashed into someone heading in the other direction. I say crashed, but it was as soft and cushioned as befits a collision with Destiny. The recipient of my careless shoulder was an old man with a white beard and rimless spectacles. The face was vaguely familiar, the voice even more so.

'Are you trying to kill me?' he asked with the gentle humour of someone who has looked Death properly in the eye.

'No,' I replied with certainty. And then as an afterthought, 'Sorry.'

And that's all there was to it. That's all that was said. It was puzzling that a little circle had cleared around us, me and Father Time, but not unduly worrying. He smiled and passed on. I joined my group who now stared at me with an assortment of strange expressions, as if they had witnessed some miracle. I smiled, nonplussed, a little drunk, and made to lead on.

'Do you know who that was?' demanded Jim.

The urgency of his voice caused me to swing round and stare after the retreating figure. Suddenly I recognised him, or rather recognised his wife – she was holding his arm now and steering him, to avoid further collisions with drunken actors in hired DJs – Joan Plowright.

The Queen arrived, but my encounter had so stunned me that I was pointing in the wrong direction, expecting her to come down the stairs instead of up them, and missed seeing her altogether.

It didn't matter, for I had just brushed shoulders with Richard III.

This morning, almost two years later, a cleaner is hard at work, polishing the plaque. I arrive at the stage door. This is run like the reception desk of a modern hotel. Usually there are a few people standing around clutching briefcases (journalists, members of the government doing financial surveys) and a queue of members of the public who think they're at the box-office.

I will be greeted either by Irish Shamus, large and friendly, 'Hillo Towni,' or by Cockney Ron with tomahawk head, 'Aw'ri' Toan?'

Into the corridors where Radio 3 is piped during the day: it gets
everywhere. The uninitiated may be alarmed, going into a loo to find the
1812 playing. They pee, glancing nervously over their shoulders as canons
explode in the cubicles behind them. On Saturdays *Critics Forum* might
be on and if you've just opened in something, *you* might be under
discussion. You hurry along the corridors then, hands clasped over ears,
in an Orwellian nightmare, as disembodied voices tell you what they think
of you, and it's being broadcast all round the building!

In the evening the show is relayed, Main House or Pit depending on
which corridor you're in. It can change from *The Tempest* to *Molière*, *Cyrano*
to *Tartuffe*, with the slapping of a swing door.

Today it is *Maydays*, so I move into the Number One dressing-room.
This involves carrying my large cardboard box (containing shampoos,
deodorants, aftershaves, vitamins, glucose, Rennies, Kaolin & Morphine,
dressing gown, towel and little cushion for the quick zizz) from the
communal Pit dressing-rooms down several floors to the individual Main
House dressing-rooms on street level.

The Number One dressing-room (its number is actually Fifty-One, but
that doesn't have the same ring to it) looks rather like something out of a
motorway motel. Characterless functionalism. Its main feature is a pay
phone fixed on to the wall in a plastic module of almost alarming yellow.
Otherwise there's a sofa, three chairs, work-surface, wash-basin and a
window. Through this you can watch legs and wheels going down the
ramp to the car-parks. You cannot see the sky, but by twisting down and
sideways you can just see a reflection of the sky in the glass building
opposite. This is not to be sneezed at when you're underground for most
of the day.

Despite all, I love it, the much maligned Barbican. In a hundred years
they will look on it with such affection. 'Why can't they build theatres like
the Barbican nowadays?' they will sigh.

Tuesday 22 November
MAYDAYS Neil Kinnock in the audience. The play was very moving as
a result, like when George Harrison came to *John, Paul, George, Ringo and
Bert* (in which I played Ringo). This fiction you're playing is someone
else's reality, you hear the lines through their ears, as if for the first time,
and they suddenly come out quite fresh. I didn't want my character to
defect to the Right tonight.

Afterwards I'm summoned to meet Kinnock. The corridor is full of men – Secret Service? Surely not. He is small, has instant charisma, and is very cheerful; in fact he positively glows with enthusiasm; the light he gives off is orangey, from his hair, freckles and gums. His wife tells us how she couldn't get twelve decent seats for the performance. 'They probably thought,' she says in a Welsh accent even stronger than his, 'that I was someone from the sticks bringing in a little charabanc for a night on the town.' So they all sat right at the back. It seems they go to the theatre a lot – they recognise Stephanie Fayerman from a feminist fringe show.

Ron [Ron Daniels, RSC director] asks him whether he's enjoying his new role as leader of the Labour Party. 'Enjoying it!' he laughs, an orange firecracker going off, 'Enjoying it! Enjoyment doesn't come into it. Enjoyment is for afterwards, when it's all over and you can discuss your memoirs on television.'

When they've gone, Ali [Alison Steadman], Shrap [John Shrapnel] and a friend of his have a drink in my dressing-room. We're all very star-struck, like schoolgirls at the stage door.

'Wasn't he *nice*!'

'And so ordinary and easy to talk to.'

'And so little.'

'Seems much bigger on the telly.'

Discussion about power. Shrap's friend says that you can't want to lead any party without desiring power, which actually makes you unsuitable for the job. Like actors, politicians must have a basic flaw in their personality, or at least a peculiarity, that makes them want to do the job in the first place.

Richard III?

Wednesday 23 November
Molière has always been a strangely jinxed play. Right from the original 1935 Moscow production when, in order to get it on, Bulgakov had to do battle with everyone from Stanislavsky to Stalin. Last year it finally got its British première, ran about three months, and then my accident occurred, threatening to take it out of the repertoire – there are no understudies at The Other Place. Pete Postlethwaite volunteered to take over and was rehearsed into it. On the Saturday before he was due to open he hit black ice driving out of Stratford after a show and found himself upside down in a field, the car a write-off and his back injured. The show came out of the repertoire for the rest of that season. Sadly, in the following months

Derek Godfrey, who had been playing Louis XIV, has died. And now David Troughton has to have a knee operation and will be out for six weeks. We're rehearsing John Bowe into the part he plays, Bouton.

KING'S HEAD PUB, BARBICAN With Bill after rehearsals. Still no news. I've made a private resolution not to discuss any Richard III ideas. I must play down my enthusiasm for the part, even with Bill, if I am to get a full season out of them. As casting now gets under way they will have so many people to keep happy that I will quickly be put to one side as soon as they think they've got me. This resolution lasts as long as the first round of drinks. Then we both gleefully plunge into the subject uppermost in both our minds.

A discussion about the play as Tragedy or Black Comedy. Example: the line 'Chop off his head' is bound to get a laugh, partly because of its Medieval B-Picture associations. But would the line have been funny to Shakespeare's audience for whom decapitation had a grislier reality? Probably yes, possibly more so. To some extent a modern audience's attitude to violence is similar to then, bombarded with maimings and slayings (real and simulated) on television and in films. On the other hand they faint nightly down in The Pit when Bob Peck's eyes are gently, clinically removed by David Bradley's doctor in Bond's *Lear*. A score-sheet is kept backstage.

I read Bill some extracts from an interesting *City Limits* article on the Nilsen murder case: 'The Yorkshire Ripper story is usually treated with extreme wariness these days, even by the press. Not so with Nilsen. People who would no more tell a racist joke than a Sutcliffe one can be heard tittering over the latest Dyno-rod story.' The author suggests this is due to the character of Nilsen himself: articulate and droll. Richard's own tendency towards flippancy seems also to steer the gruesome events of the play away from Tragedy. Bill believes a tragic element is reclaimable in the play.

Against my better judgement I outline the crutches idea. He listens carefully – he is an excellent listener – then at the end says, 'But would one be able to go into battle if one relied on crutches?'

'Well, absolutely. It could be rather moving. We bring on a real horse and show him having to be lifted on to it. Then they take away his crutches. The next time you see him the horse has been killed and he can only crawl.'

'The trouble with bringing on a real horse is that is distracts an audience.

They sit there thinking, "That's a real horse which might shit any moment", instead of listening to the lines.'

'Not if you brought on one heavily armoured, like at the bullfight.'

'Like a tank.'

'A huge walking war-machine, a monster.'

'Of course the idea of lifting him on to it comes from Olivier's *Henry V* film.'

'Does it? Oh . . .'

The unmentionable. Bill leans forward now, and in hushed tones confesses that he's never seen the *Richard III* film, and wonders if we should hire it to have a secret look so as to avoid overlapping. I tell him that I have already seen the film far too many times and that I would no sooner see it again at this point in my life than play the part in a black page-boy wig, long false nose and thin clipped voice.

'However,' I say, 'I think it would be an excellent idea for you to have a look at it to help guide us in a different direction.'

'Thanks a bunch. I think I'll remain in ignorance.'

Friday 25 November

MOLIERE John Bowe's first night after only four days' rehearsal. He does magnificently well. A very different Bouton from the sad-eyed peasant that David Troughton plays; John's is like the fussy, bespectacled dwarf in Disney's *Snow White*.

KING'S HEAD PUB, BARBICAN Another hushed conversation with Bill, heads close together, while actors around us strain to eavesdrop. He reports on the latest directors' meeting. To mark the tenth anniversary of The Other Place the season there will be exclusively new plays. In the Main House the plays in Slots Three, Four and Five are currently *Richard, Hamlet* (Ron directing) and *Love's Labour's* (Barry Kyle directing, with Roger Rees as Berowne). Apparently I am only available for these three slots anyway, because the *Tartuffe* and *Molière* videos will happen at the same time as the first two Stratford plays rehearse. Very disappointing news. Nothing for me in *Hamlet*, nor, as far as I can remember, in *Love's Labour's*. Bill says the latter could still change to *Merry Wives*.

'Ford would be of interest,' I say, 'but is still not going to make it worthwhile going back for another two-year cycle.'

'I know. Everyone knows. Nothing is settled yet. We're all trying to sort something out for you. At the last meeting Terry said, "You know, this whole problem with Tony could be solved if it wasn't for the *Molière* video in March. What would you say Bill, if I asked you to postpone or cancel it?" To which I replied, "I would say, Terry, get stuffed." And then Trevor said, "Well that's the shortest and most effective statement anyone's yet made at this meeting." '

Ron Daniels has asked me to lunch on Tuesday. That might throw some new light. *Is* there a part for me in *Hamlet*?

Sunday 27 November
A quick glance at *Hamlet*'s Dramatis Personae confirms that there isn't.

Try to read *Love's Labour's*, looking for something in that. Costard? God, Shakespeare's Fools are tedious. They joke in code and their characters are all interchangeable. Costard could be Touchstone could be Feste could be Gobbo could be . . .

The thing that made Lear's Fool fascinating to me is that his unintelligible jokes *add* to the nightmare. In the comedies the Fools are usually the least funny people on stage. The best Feste could never make you laugh as much as the worst Malvolio.

Give up on Costard, look at the King of Navarre. Hasn't he been played by character men? Jacobi at the Old Vic, Richard Griffiths in the last RSC production. Don Armado?

Get nowhere. Abandon the play. Cross with myself for not trying harder or understanding better. Reading Shakespeare is sometimes like looking through a window into a dark room. You don't see in. You see nothing but a reflection of yourself unable to see in. An unflattering image of yourself blind.

Walk across Highbury Fields. Slush and wind. The sky is a cold white with harsh bits of grey and black. A season of Shakespearian parts does not look likely. If I go back to Stratford I will end up spending four years with the company, during which time they will have done thirteen Shakespeares and I will have been in two – yet I joined the company to play Shakespeare. The situation is absurd.

A punk vagrant is stuck in a tree, having tried to climb into a deserted property. High off the ground, his long coat caught among the branches like wings. He tries to free himself occasionally, listlessly, then gives up again. His hair is a rainbow of the most vibrant colours. From a distance bright and beautiful. A tropical bird. But as I pass underneath, close to, the hair is matted and filthy. His eyes are closed. He seems to have fallen asleep.

Tuesday 29 November
MONTY SESSION He talks about Fritz Perls and the Gestalt theory. The here and now is the only time that exists. And being yourself. Not accepting yourself, not taking yourself for granted. *Being* yourself. Your self. Monty defines 'normality' as a contentment with who you are.

The sunlight is weird at this time of year – an insistent silver light. This morning as I shave it falls on the water and throws a strange light on my face. Instantly Richard III. I stare at him for a moment, then quickly fetch a sketchbook to put down what I've just seen. But it's a difficult drawing.

The strange light can only be indicated by leaving one eye unfinished and beaming out of the darkish face. So difficult to avoid cliché. What I find myself recreating is straight out of Hammer Horror. And worse of all, the lips I have drawn are not my own, but Olivier's. Again that giant shadow falls across the landscape and I dart around trying to find some light of my own. My Richard is in its infancy; barely that, it is still struggling to take form, uncertain even *whether* to take form. And there's this fully formed, famously formed, infamous child murderer leaning over the cradle . . .

DUO FRANCO RESTAURANT Lunch with Ron Daniels. I developed a great affection for Ron during *Maydays*, partly because we're both Anglicised foreigners – he's from Brazil.

'Servants do make life easier,' he says wistfully as we settle at our table.

'Oh God, don't they just? Being brought up with them finishes you for life. I find it impossible to do any domestic work at all. It just seems the most appalling waste of time.'

The restaurant is run by a swarthy brotherhood of Italians. They play opera instead of muzak and sing along loudly as they pass among the tables. The specialities of the day are told to you in aggressively thick Italian accents, followed by a dark-eyed stare which challenges you to ask them to repeat. This Mafia once-over is worth it for the calves' liver which is the sweetest in the world. I urge Ron to try it.

We are on to our desserts before he says, 'Right, let's talk business.'

'Yes please.'

'Channel Four are interested in a mini-series of *Maydays*, possibly in four parts . . .'

Clever tactics. I was expecting the Stratford season, get a *Maydays* telly instead. But I'm not going to bite: 'Sounds wonderful. It's a pity negotiations aren't further ahead. It might help me sort out next year. I'm so disappointed you've all failed to find anything else for me.'

'Paranoia, PARANOIA!' Ron yells in delight, disturbing one of the waiters as he was reaching for his big moment in *Otello*; the man glares murderously, but Ron is still laughing, 'We didn't even finalise the Main House season till last night.'

The plays will be *Henry V* (Adrian Noble directing Ken Branagh), *Merchant of Venice* (John Caird directing Ian McDiarmid), *Richard*, *Hamlet*, *Love's Labour's*.

'First of all,' says Ron, 'I must urge you to have a play out after *Richard*.

I know you're a workaholic, but it is a terribly taxing part, vocally, mentally, physically. Richard is notorious for crippling actors. They spend years afterwards on osteopaths' couches. Trust me – you'll need a rest.'

'But isn't Roger going straight from Hamlet to Berowne?'

'Not the same thing at all.'

'Oh come on – Hamlet?'

'Not at all. Hamlet tends to stand there while things happen round him, to him. Richard is doing, doing all the time, making everything happen.'

'All right, let's say I have a play out. What then?'

'A Robert Holman play. To be written specially for you. In Slot Five. At The Other Place.'

I decline immediately. In the past I have not enjoyed having plays written for me. The process is nerve-racking and seems to cramp everyone's style. 'Also,' I say, 'I joined the RSC to do Shakespeare, not new plays. I've spent my whole career doing new plays . . .' The old refrain, growing feebler by the day.

Ron thinks for a moment, then, 'I'm wearing two hats now. One as RSC director, the other as the producer of this *Maydays* series. If that works out, we'll need every minute after *Richard* opens. We can film it up in the Midlands if necessary. If that works out –'

'*If*, Ron. It's an "if", not a reality. It can't enter into this discussion.'

He thinks again. 'Tony, we are setting up a season to introduce the actors we believe are going to be the next generation of leading Shakespearian players. You must be there. Your Richard must be in that line-up.'

Not a lot I can say to that. Feel I'm losing ground all the time.

We leave the restaurant and Ron climbs into his car. 'Well, I'll go back and report,' he says cheerfully. 'Don't worry. It'll work out. Just keep reading *Richard*.'

'I'm resisting that actually. I haven't read it at all yet. Don't want to get all excited if –'

'Get excited, get excited!' He grins and drives off.

Back at home I look at this morning's self-portrait again. It's better than I thought. And it does have some of the oddity of that original moment. This is a familiar syndrome. There is a stage with every drawing or painting when it looks banal and clumsy. It's worth pushing through that, working through the cliché to find out what made it a cliché in the first place.

And the lips don't look even remotely like Laurence Olivier's.

Wednesday 30 November

All morning spent wrestling with myself: should I go and buy a new copy
of the play and read it properly? The Liverpool Everyman copy is useless
for anything other than dipping into. But buying a new copy is a kind of
commitment. It means I'm definitely going to do it. Am I not definitely
going to do it? I truthfully believe I could still forego it at this stage (and
must if negotiations continue as non-productively as they have been so
far) without it hurting too much.

Nevertheless . . .

CANONBURY BOOKSHOP

'Do you keep plays?'

'We do. What are you looking for?'

'Shakespeare.'

'But of course. Which one?'

Speaking the title aloud, particularly to a stranger, seems like a further
commitment. I play for time. 'You do keep the Arden editions, do you? It
must be the Arden edition.'

'Ah. No. We only keep Penguins. They take up less room.'

'Oh.'

I stand staring at the row of Penguins, *Richard III* pulsating ever so
slightly among the Histories.

'Moving on from Molière to Shakespeare?' asks the bookseller suddenly.

'Ye-e-es!' I laugh too loud, startled that he's recognised me.

'We could order an Arden. But I expect you need it immediately?'

'Uhm. Yesss . . .'

'Which play is it?'

'Oh look, not to worry, thank you.'

I hurry from the shop. Reprieved.

Thursday 1 December

RUDLAND & STUBBS FISH RESTAURANT Yellow light, wooden
panelling, sawdust on the floor. After *Maydays*, dinner with Shrap, Ali
Steadman and the director Mike Leigh.

The head waiter tells us that after Richard Gere ate here a few nights ago
many of the waitresses, and some of the waiters, made a bee-line for his
chair – which has since disappeared.

Mike is just back from Belfast where he's been researching for his latest
film. He looks tired and grey. 'Northern Ireland bears as much relation

to life here as ancient Tibet.' We all get worked up about the recent attack on a church, where the congregation were mowed down by machine guns.

'Murder, murder!' cry Ali and I.

'It's not murder, it's war,' says Mike, with the weariness of one who's had it drummed into him for weeks and weeks.

'Murder,' says Shrap, 'is a bespectacled civil servant walking his dog in Muswell Hill while a human head simmers on his stove. There is no cause, no logic. It's just loopy.'

I find myself drifting in and out of the conversation. Images from a recent television programme which featured interviews with Belfast teenagers, boys of about fifteen with puffy eyes and shorn heads. The first thing that struck you was that they didn't behave like other adolescents in front of a camera, they didn't blush or try to show off; they just talked very openly about death and looting, setting fire to buildings or cars. 'It doesn't matter,' they kept saying, in those accents which are themselves like blades held gently against your cheek.

'Why not?' persisted the well-trained, well-spoken BBC investigative reporter.

''Cause we've grown up with it. It's what we know'– which could be Richard III talking. He's grown up in a period of fierce civil war, the Wars of the Roses, and has never known anything else. It seems very important this. Growing up watching street battles, people being maimed, yet another funeral passing. It takes the character out of the Hammer Horror world of ghouls, away from Mickey Mouse words like Evil, and towards something that is recognisable.

'. . . and that's the only relevant point that's been made so far in this discussion. With respect.' Mike Leigh is proclaiming, finger held in the air. He is an extraordinary man. Dauntingly articulate. A merciless sense of humour, reminiscent of his work. His large, bearded head is sunk into small shoulders, around which his little hands constantly dart, as if warding off insects and fools, or conjuring, or working puppets. A favourite word of his is 'clairvoyant', and indeed he often knows what you're going to say as you start a sentence, which can make conversations a little one-sided.

But tonight he is subdued by Belfast. I ask his advice about the Stratford business. He hints that he doesn't think it a good idea. I know he didn't like the *Molière* or *Tartuffe* productions. 'Look, Richard's clearly a part that you can play, that you will play, but are conditions right at this point in time?'

We leave the restaurant at about half one. Smithfield Market is coming noisily to life. Giant lorries trundle into the floodlights. Men in bloody aprons, breath steaming in the cold night air, carry carcasses into the great halls. Inside I glimpse the rows of meat hooks and a man stirring a boiling cauldron, stripping the flesh off a few heads.

Friday 2 December

BARBICAN Terry Hands, in black bomber jacket, kneading a piece of blue-tak in one hand, chain-smoking with the other, talking about *Richard III*:

'No one has really cracked the part since Ian Holm in 1964.' Terry has done four productions of his own, and believes it is the play in which Shakespeare made all his mistakes. 'For a start he doesn't give Richard a rest. Macbeth has the England scene, Hamlet has all that Ophelia stuff, Lear's got the whole Edmund sub-plot, but Richard is on throughout. With the terrible physical strain, of course, of sustaining a crippled position all evening.' Tells me that when Robert Hirsh did it for him in his Comédie Française production, he limped on alternate legs from night to night, with two sets of costumes. 'You might like to think along similar lines. I've been advised by an osteopath that irreparable damage can be done to the pelvis otherwise. It's a little known historical fact, but apparently after the original production Burbage said to Shakespeare, "If you ever do that to me again, mate, I'll kill you." '

'Terry, is this meant to help me decide about next season?'

'Oh but I love that play,' he says, suddenly serious (I think), 'there is more pleasure in one broken-backed Richard than in ten perfect Hamlets. I hate Hamlet.'

It only occurs to me afterwards that it was all a dare. He was saying to me: never mind what else we might offer you, I *dare* you to try a Richard III. What a cheek. Especially because, as tactics go, it has been the most effective so far: I head off to the gym, determined to get myself even fitter than ever.

CITY GYM Oh, the puffing and heaving and clanging of muscles and weights, the bending and squatting and cycling and lifting and lowering. Squeezed eyes, bared teeth, streaming faces, matted hair, clammy clothes . . .

'. . . eigh' . . . ni' . . . te' . . . elev' . . . twel' . . .' is the strained mutter from the man in the mirror.

An unfair contest between puny wet flesh and those iron bars, so sleek, so smooth, so cool.

'. . . twenny-si' . . . twenny-se' . . . twenny-eigh' . . . twenny-ni' . . .'
as Hawaiian favourites play in the background.

And the row of sit-up contraptions where men clutch their ears and
drag themselves forward to head-butt their own knees, heaving back and
forwards. And those strange exercises for the elderly, little bowings and
prayings and paddlings in the air and delicate steppings like stick insects.

And always that man in the mirror, thinking: I'll show you Terry Hands,
I'll show you RSC, '. . . foy-fi' . . . foy-si' . . . foy-se' . . . foy-eigh' . . .'

Saturday 3 December

SAVOY TEA-ROOM Today is dedicated to thanking Charlotte Arnold,
the physiotherapist who bullied me back to full strength and health after
the operation. I treated her to the matinée of *Tartuffe* this afternoon, which
she's loved, and now insist on buying her the Savoy's formidable Full
Tea. 'For giving me my leg back,' I say, having to use an American
soap-opera accent, but meaning it with all my heart.

The Tea-room is high and wide, all in rose and beige, and full of
chandeliers, mirrors, palms and nostalgia (although it doesn't actually
relate to anything in my own past at all). An elderly violinist in white jacket
and bow-tie, and a lady pianist in evening dress play old tunes. We should
all waltz and quick-step, but instead sit heavily, working our way through
these interminable and almost sickening Full Teas. Above us on the
balcony, a Mediterranean gentleman of considerable years and poundage
slumps into a cane chair and starts to spread over its edges as if there's
yeast at work, while staring at Charlotte through sleepy oily eyes, a bubble
of saliva popping on his slightly parted lips.

Charlotte is very pretty in a very English way. Blonde hair, large eyes,
cheeks like Worcester apples, and a naughty turn to her smile.

We discuss *Richard III*. If I do it, will she help? Research the deformity
and devise a safe way of playing it. I tell her I'm thinking of using crutches.
She thinks I'm joking and laughs. (Perhaps the idea is simply ludicrous.)
But she is keen to help. When she saw *Molière* she was impressed by how
thoroughly I'd researched his heart condition, so she knows I am serious
about this aspect of the work. She has various contacts and says she could
arrange visits to homes for the disabled. 'I know this sounds awful,' she
says, 'but it all depends if they've got what you're looking for on the day
we're there.'

Whenever the subject of research comes up I always think back to an
argument with the playwright David Hare a few years ago, when we were

both on the Royal Court Seminar at Louisiana State University. I had just finished playing the Arab in Mike Leigh's *Goose-pimples*. There had been strong protests from the Arab community and I felt I had betrayed those Arab contacts who had helped me research the part.

'I know,' David had said, 'we all feel that. And yet we take what we need.' A smile that might have been self-parodying. 'Perhaps it's a licence we have as artists.'

I argued that Mike Leigh was devising the play, that it was his responsibility, not mine, at which point David had suddenly lost patience and said, 'Well, all right, if that's how you prefer it. He's the artist, you're just the actor. Passive and dumb.'

I reeled away from the encounter, stung and challenged by his honesty. Later that evening I resolved to research in the future with a new unsentimental rigour and ruthlessness, and thus reinstate myself as An Artist . . .

The Full Tea lives up to its name. I stagger back to the Barbican for the evening show, several sizes larger than when I did the matinée. A slight air of sadness in the dressing-room – it's Nigel Hawthorne's last stage *Tartuffe*, although Bill is still hopeful of persuading him to do the video.

The familiar routine. Put on the posing pouch, tights and smock. Into the small lift, squeezed into a cocktail of characters from French literature, *Cyrano* and *Tartuffe*, down six floors to The Pit (shedding Rostand's lot along the way) where the Orgon household are gearing themselves up for the first scene. Into the wings to do the Overture (an intoned Latin prayer duelling with a frivolous harpsichord) and to sniff the audience. Back into the lift, alone now. Always at this point, over the tannoy, Jacobi going 'Balloon, buffooon, baboooon'. Into the dressing-room and the long wait now, almost an hour, for my first entrance: the most delayed first entrance of an eponymous character in the whole of Drama – until Beckett wrote *Godot*. Put on the wig and make-up. Warm up on a few speeches. Can't help noticing in the mirror that he's here again: the long black wig together with my own pointed nose have turned me into a first cousin of that famous crookback.

Out into the corridor, stooping into character, having to go down the stairs now, not the lift because it wouldn't have been invented yet, muttering Ave Marias, winding the giant wooden rosary like a knuckle-duster round one fist, settling into a pious creeping stalk . . . Over the tannoy, Cyrano has gone to visit some pastry chefs.

Into a corridor where neither show is relayed, imagining a silent crypt now, drifting along close to the side, one hand trailing behind on the wall, insect-like.

Through a door into a secret corridor, a back entrance to The Pit, where Ali Steadman waits in character and we do a brief Mike Leigh warm-up improvisation, never planned and never referred to, passing one another slowly, her fan nervously fluttering, my sighs growing more and more explicit.

Alone into Rehearsal Room One, adjoining The Pit, to do the distant Ave Marias which will herald Tartuffe's first entrance; the room is a surrealist's lair with dismembered giants strewn about, Louis XIV's head from *Molière* over here and those colossal boobs from *Custom of the Country* over there.

I can smell incense being lit. My cue-light goes red, green, my nerves go taut. Into the wings where John Tramper as Laurent, dressed and bewigged identically to me, slides alongside mirroring my walk and stoop. Stage-managers stand poised on either side of the curtains. We mark time, all the while Ave Marias looping endlessly. Another green light. They whip open the curtains, our marking time turns back into a walk and we slope into the light . . .

An excellent show. There's been a queue for returns all day so the audience are even more enthusiastic than normal; their hysteria is quite thrilling and occasionally catching. During the rape-on-the-dining-table scene (or the inter-course intercourse) everything just stops for about thirty seconds while Ali and I join the audience screaming with laughter. A most peculiar event, breaking all the rules. The more we laugh, the more they do. At last we struggle back on to the text and the audience seems as shame-faced as we are for having misbehaved so badly, which leads to further sporadic outbreaks.

Why is an actor's unintentional giggling called a 'corpse'? It seems to me quite the opposite. It proves that he's very much alive, and can still tell how silly this all is: him dressed up as someone else speaking words written by a third party.

Speaking of whom, Chris Hampton turns up in the dressing-room afterwards, a little startled that his translation was subjected to that unscheduled interruption, but since he spends much of life on the verge of corpsing, not too bothered.

As we're leaving the theatre we pass a group of *Cyrano* players trooping into the main lift which is huge; a neon-lit garage filled with Koltai's monochrome people. Black velvet and lace. White faces. The only colour: some gold, and red tongues.

They look exhausted. It's 10.30 and they're only just starting Part Three.

'Ta-ra, we're off to the pub,' I call into them.

'PISS OFF!' they yell in unison.

Chris giggles behind me.

'Have you seen it yet?' I ask.

'Life's too short to see *Cyrano*.'

KING'S HEAD PUB, BARBICAN Interesting discussion about the difficulties we had in rehearsal with *Tartuffe*. It's going to be excellent trying it again now for the video, now that we trust the play more and our ability to perform it. The problem with Molière's writing is the deceptive thinness of it. There's no poetry, no sub-text, just a very basic situation, like sit-com. Chris says, 'All there is is what is there, but that happens to be brilliant.' He says the French find Shakespeare difficult for the opposite reason. Why is he so oblique? they cry in Gallic confusion, why doesn't he just say what he means?

Norma, a girl who works in the Stratford box-office, comes over and says, 'Congratulations. I hear you're coming back to play Richard the Third.'

'Oh, but it's not definite.'

Chris leans in. 'What was that?'

'Don't ask. It's a long story.'

Monday 5 December

OXFORD STREET A steady procession of Christmas shoppers: faces so determined, so concentrated, round and round we go, the Hajj in Mecca.

Spot two disabled men and can't stop myself from staring. One has his pelvis so twisted that his feet point away at ninety degrees from his torso. Walks with two sticks. The impression is of a skier negotiating a difficult turn.

Strange how, ever since Richard III was suggested, I keep crossing paths with the disabled. Did I just not notice before or are there vibes at work?

The other day in Euston Road, a dwarf dodging through the traffic, one shoe massively built up like a clanging black anchor on his leg. He reached a traffic island and shouted at the world. My car passed close. The face was red, unshaven, in pain.

And yesterday, a black couple leaving the local church. Both young and good-looking. In their Sunday best, but jazzy as well. He had one thin, very withered leg and had to hobble along on the tip of that foot, in its white patent-leather shoe. It made his walk seem even more dude-like. She strolled at her normal pace, making no concession. He kept up with her. They smiled at one another. After they passed, people stared.

SELFRIDGES 'Hello Tony.' David Hare, towering above me. He always looks at me slightly sideways, as if not quite sure about me yet, and speaks slightly from the corner of his mouth. 'Congratulations. I believe you're playing Richard the Third.'

'Thank you, but it's not decided yet. Who told you?'

'Oh, someone . . .' He gestures vaguely, blaming a passing shopper, and quickly changes the subject. 'I'm Christmas shopping for my kids.'

'I'm shopping for holiday presents. Going to South Africa on Sunday.'

'You're going to South Africa. Blimey.'

'I know. Very mixed feelings.' (I'm still doing it: apologising for where I was born. *Must stop*.)

I ask him about his TV film *Saigon*, which has just been shown, and he says, 'Well, of course it's been mercilessly hammered by the critics.'

'Critics? But you don't read them.'

'Didn't use to.'

'Oh no. You're back on them?'

' 'Fraid so.'

I stare at him, shocked. Along with Jacobi and Peter Gill, David has been a guru for me in my own new-found abstention.

'But . . .' I stammer, '. . . but . . . when we did *Teeth 'n Smiles*, if anyone so much as came near you with a newspaper, they took their life in their hands.'

'I know . . .' he says, nostalgically.

'What made you start again?' Gently, as to an alcoholic.

'They get through somehow. So what's the point in not reading for yourself? I mean, after *Saigon* someone phoned and said, "How d'you feel about your battering?" I mean, you know, what does one do?'

Later at home it occurs to me that he's the second outsider to congratulate me on Richard III. Who's broadcasting it? Someone at the RSC obviously regards it as a foregone conclusion that I'll do it.

Is it?

Tuesday 6 December

Bill phones. 'God, Tony, I didn't realise you were leaving so soon. We must meet. Tonight after the show?'

MOLIERE There is a moment at the beginning of the show when Molière's troupe are posed on the upper level, frozen in the backstage frenzy before a curtain-call. On the back wall little cardboard cut-out chandeliers light up through a red gauze, a sound effect of distant applause creeps in and a cello starts to play. It is a low-budget, small-stage compromise for Bulga-kov's spectacular description: 'We can see the stage now from one of the wings. Candles burn brightly in the chandeliers – we can't quite see the auditorium, the nearest gilded box is empty, only sense the mysterious watchful blue haze of the half darkened theatre.' Quite a sad compromise really, but it always moves me. The tattiness and magic of theatre are very close.

And the lunacy . . . During a break in the show I stroll into the Green Room. Caliban, wearing only a loincloth and red island mud, is contorted over the pool table aiming a difficult shot. Elsewhere around the room, Ariel's sprites sit reading the *Standard* or chatting to Louis XIV's mus-keteers.

Molière finishes long before *Tempest*. I am showered and changed and on my way out, heading down one of the long faceless corridors, when I suddenly hear Jacobi over the tannoy:

'Ye elves of hills, brooks, standing lakes, and groves;

And ye that on the sands with printless foot

Do chase the ebbing Neptune . . .'

It can stop you in your tracks, those words in that voice, make you put your head back, close your eyes, and try, as with beautiful music, to hold it a moment longer. Cocteau talks about the speed of beauty . . .

ISLINGTON Bill comes back to the house to talk. Slot Five at The Other Place is now a play by either Nicky Wright or Peter Barnes. Adrian would direct – that's a plus. Bill wants to sound me out about both writers, but I tell him I'm more interested in reading the plays in question. He says these are still being written and he's not sure when there'll be anything to read. I ask whether Richard could be moved later in the season to enable me to do the Snoo Wilson film in the summer (Plaschkes has almost got the money together). Bill thinks not, because of Roger Rees' availability. He asks what plays I'm dying to do, suggesting we could make a deal for the Barbican '85 season. I can't see how that would help a thin time in Stratford '84, but trot out the old favourite, *Arturo Ui*, which is probably too close to *Richard III* to be a good double anyway.

Bill leaves with the obligatory, 'Well, I'll go back and report.'

It is quite clear now – the offer is *Richard III* with one new play at The Other Place, and that having to be taken on trust. So far from what I wanted.

For the first time I think seriously about not doing Richard. Apart from a vague notion that I could play the part, there hasn't been a single good sign for the project. Friends give it a hearty thumbs-down, the RSC appears not to want to employ me more than they absolutely have to.

Lie in bed unable to sleep, these same thoughts plodding round and round the exercise yard. The darkness looks the same if you open or close your eyes.

Wednesday 7 December

But I can't leave Richard alone. Driving with Jim; he puts on a tape of Boris Godunov and the grotesque, baroque sounds instantly bring Richard limping out into the light again. We talk about how, after he is crowned, he could be carried around to this triumphant music. Borne aloft on a bier, the Henry VI funeral bier, this black lump on a tray, deified.

And we talk about how he might get on rather well with the Princes. He could mimic his deformity and act an ape (I'm thinking of Brando's death scene with his grandchild in *Godfather*) to make them laugh. The famous insult from young York ('little like an ape ... bear me on your shoulders') is just part of their rapport; and so we by-pass the famous moment from the film – the leering turn, shot from the child's point of view. Only when they are gone does he show his true feelings for them. Presumably a true psychopath behaves like that. Presumably Nilsen's victims had no warning; they were sitting there happily drinking and listening to music, he was smiling and chatting, making them feel pleased to be there.

As the music thumps about in the car I become very inspired again. It is more than just a notion that I could play the part. I *know* that I could do something special with it.

And yet – the memory of last year in Stratford; one or two performances a week, endless days and nights to fill in between.

What to do, what to do?

Thursday 8 December

KING'S HEAD PUB, BARBICAN Pete Postlethwaite: eerie wisdom, eyes like blue boulders.

'I hear you might do Dick the Shit. Be a very brave move, very dangerous.'

'Really? I think it's type-casting.'

'Exactly. You can play the part standing on your head. But if you could go past that stage, eschew all that, go beyond, surprise *yourself*, that would be very dangerous. Worth travelling up to Stratford to see. Otherwise it'll just be, "Oh Tony's playing Richard in Stratford, I don't need to go all the way up there, I can just run it through in my head." It would be like me playing Iago.'

Friday 9 December

A thank-you card from Charlotte Arnold with this P S: 'I have started the ball rolling re Richard III. Should have news in January about homes and centres for the disabled that we could visit. Did you mean what you said about crutches? It's just that I've been thinking they might actually be the *safest* way of you playing extreme disability. Can't think of anything else that would take the strain off *you* in the same way. It's what they're designed to do. But were you serious?'

FOYLES Finally buy an Arden edition of *Richard III*, to read in South Africa. (And leave behind there perhaps?) The cover is very strange – hollow eye sockets and gaping mouths, all rather vaginal.

BARBICAN CANTEEN Two of the directors, Adrian Noble and Barry Kyle, have a little light supper at my table before another planning meeting. Neither say anything about Stratford or the current situation. Instead Adrian starts talking about aeroplane crashes and the recent case of a woman suing one of the airlines for shattering her nerves. The plane had started to plummet and only at the last moment did the pilot regain control and yank it back up into the air.

'So there are all these people,' Adrian says, munching at his supper, 'who have felt what those last few minutes are like. That fall. Can you imagine? And who've lived to remember it.' He always discusses matters like this with a kind of bright-eyed, yet detached, fascination. Perhaps it's because he's an undertaker's son.

They go off to their planning meeting and I sit viewing Sunday's flight in a new light.

Saturday 10 December
In this morning's *Guardian* a full-page advertisement for the Free Nelson Mandela Campaign. Hundreds of signatures, mine among them. Bad timing. Hope the South Africans don't go through this with a fine tooth comb, which of course they will. Image of being frog-marched out of the airport lounge and shot against the nearest wall.

Howard Davies [RSC director] rings. *He's* doing the Nicky Wright play now and says there's a terrific part in it for me.

'What's it about?'

'Well, it's set in Cairo –'

'Oh God. Another Arab.'

'No, no. British Intelligence, Second World War. An officer with a Napoleonic complex . . .'

The play sounds very exciting. It's now scheduled for Slot Four. The Peter Barnes play is in Slot Five, with Adrian directing, and apparently it also contains a terrific part for me. 'Adrian's been itching to talk to you all week,' Howard says.

I tell him that Ron had advised me to have a play out after *Richard.*

'Yes I know. He relayed that conversation to us and I got rather angry. I said to them, if we want Tony in the season, and we do, what's the point in having him do as little as possible?'

'Well actually Ron made some rather good points about osteopaths' couches . . .'

But this news is too good to start worrying about minor details like health. Two new plays are a decent compromise. I ring Bill to tell him, 'It all sounds very promising.' He says that he's definitely going to offer Buckingham to Malcolm Storry. It will be a powerful image: the small deformed Richard with this giant as right hand man. And our rapport as actors and friends will be a corner-stone for the whole production.

Last minute packing, feeling very excited about everything, not least that now is the winter and on Monday the summer . . .

The thing I keep remembering is Monty seeing me to the door after our session on Tuesday. He suddenly said, 'I envy you. I'd love to see South Africa again. Christ, I can't watch a programme on TV about that bloody country without crying.'

2. South Africa 1983

Sitting next to me on the plane is a ten-year-old boy. He looks up and says with great excitement, 'We're going to live in South Africa!' He's called Leon and is from Manchester. Points across the aisle to where his parents sit, restraining lap-fulls of his little brothers and sisters. As the eldest he has volunteered to sit on his own.

As we are about to take off, I offer him the window seat. He says, 'Ooo, could I?' He has never flown before and the take off is intolerably exciting. In fact he can hardly bear to watch this miracle and keeps turning back to me blushing and grinning.

Monday 12 December
Dawn. The round window is a milky blur of pink, orange, blue. Gradually it focuses into one of these endless fields of clouds.

'Is it ice on the sea?' asks Leon as he wakes and clambers over for a good peer. He stares in wonderment. 'The air must be thin up here, so close to outer space.'

An hour later the clouds are more mountainous, erupting. They break dramatically, disappear, and there below is a red land with soft black hills that look as if they're melting in extreme heat, and one long, white, perfectly straight road. Africa.

I point it out to Leon who shouts, 'It's Africa, it's Africa! Look Dad, it's Africa!'

The father looks at me wetly and shrugs, apologising for his son. I've taken a dislike to this man, primarily because he's emigrating to South Africa.

As we are coming in to land at Jo'burg I say to Leon, 'Come on you'd better move over to the window seat.' He's looking glum and says, 'My

Dad has said not to bother you anymore.'

'Oh don't be silly.' I turn to the father. 'He must see the landing in his new country. Something for him to remember in years to come,' wondering if the man perceives any double meaning at all.

Leon presses his face to the window again and remains glued there as we descend and South Africa turns into reality with a gentle bump from below.

During the connecting flight to Cape Town I become very emotional. Different feelings and memories welling up, settling, welling up again. As the plane begins its descent they start playing schmaltzy music which makes it all much worse. Bits of me, dormant for years, coming to the surface. Excitement and fear.

Stepping off the plane, the blast of dry heat, the baking afternoon with its brilliant blue sky, is all familiar and calming.

Monty and I were both right about the photographers: there aren't any, yet there is one – my sister Verne clicking away on an Instamatic as I walk into the airport lounge. Everyone is there, brown and glowing: the men have taken the afternoon off work. Mum is presiding, looking glamorous in the simplest of summer frocks and with a film star's instinct for when the shutter is going to click. My older brother Randall says, 'Hi, howzitt?' as if he saw me yesterday, and hugs me; he's rounder and greyer than I remember. Dad pops up from behind a group to go 'Haah', which is his shorthand for 'Hello and how are you?' Esther, my drama teacher (we called it 'elocution') from way back, flies into my arms, crying. The nephews and nieces all come up shyly to shake hands and be kissed, grown into new shapes, new people. Everyone keeps saying, 'You look terrible. Don't they feed you in England? So white, like a ghost.' They ask about my dreadfully short hair cut (to go under *Maydays* wigs). I tell them I'm thinking of catching up with some National Service while I'm here.

Driving back from the airport, nothing is familiar until Green Point Common and the Sports Stadium. Memories of walking back with Tony Fagin from Saturday afternoon bioscope, discussing The Art Of The Motion Picture. And then more memories as we drive along the beachfront – certain blocks of flats, the Pavilion, the Aquarium – but distantly, sensations rather than clear pictures.

The house in Alexander Road is transformed. They've split it down the middle and sold the other half. It's hardly recognisable, but I find my way through to the back yard calling, 'Katie, Katie.' She comes out of the maid's room. Still wearing those little aprons and linen caps, but older, shorter, squatter. Her shy smile showing gold among the white teeth. We hug. 'Oh, Master Antony, oh, Master Antony,' she keeps saying.

The house is like it would be in a dream. A familiar place put together wrongly. A few things have survived the rebuilding. The stair rail. A cupboard door. I round a corner and there's a piece I recognise, the rest strange. Even the smell is quite new. A different furniture polish I suppose.

I'm on display everywhere. Every inch of wall space is covered in photos of me or my paintings or posters of plays. It makes me feel rather uncomfortable; as if I've died and this is the shrine.

I'm taken on a grand tour. Mum watches my reactions closely, keeps asking, 'Well, what d'you think?' and I keep replying, 'I don't know, it's very strange.'

Their bedroom. Blinds drawn against the strong afternoon sun which still saturates the room and makes the blinds glow. Little strips and squares of sunlight have got through and fall across the bed, and across the soft pale carpet. A radio plays quietly. This feeling of a hot afternoon indoors, with the radio a tiny, constant comforting sound – that's the closest feeling to what it was like being a child here.

Tuesday 13 December
Wake to that smell of the sea . . . Dad and Katie in the back yard chatting away in Afrikaans.

Breakfast. Both Mum and Dad have capsules to take with their coffee. His are thick, black things like slugs. When I ask what they're for, he says, 'Lord alone knows, but if I was ten years younger I'd've had triplets by now.'

Mum's are prettier, little opaque golden baubles. 'They are very expensive,' she says, 'a natural extract made from the oil of Evening Primrose, for the skin, for circulation and so much more. Apparently the entire population of Russia are given these free for one month each year.'

'That's why their Premiers keep dying,' mutters Dad as he heads off to work.

'Tsk,' goes Mum, and settles down with Katie to plan the day's menus; there's meat to be taken out of the deep freeze, recipes to be checked through. That done, she begins her own notes for the day; careful lists written in her curving elegant handwriting (so familiar from those blue airmail envelopes that drop through the letter box back in Islington) concerning shopping and appointments.

Katie starts washing up the breakfast things. She is rather proud of the batch of bagels she baked for my homecoming.

'Were they all right, Madam?'

'Haven't tasted one yet,' says Mum concentrating on her list.

'But do they look all right?'

'Look fine.'

'I burnt a few for Madam, Madam mos' likes them burnt.'

'Mmm.'

Katie smiles secretly to me, almost winks, as if to say 'I keep her happy and she stays out of my hair'.

Their relationship seems to have mellowed over the years. In my childhood I remember stormy rows; Katie was always packing and leaving, often did. One or the other would eventually apologise sulkily, all would be well again until the next time.

I wonder if either have ever realised the deep affection they have for one another. They're both in their early sixties now, having spent forty long years together. They see more of one another than they do of their husbands, and yet all the time leading very different lives.

Mum's day is made up of her shopping, her beauty treatments, massages, manicures and pedicures, her classes in keep fit and philosophy, her spiritualist meetings, her visits to theatre, cinema, ballet, variety shows, anything to fill the long hours of leisure.

Katie's day begins at five o'clock in the coloured township Bonteheuwel; she cooks breakfast for her husband, catches the six o'clock bus to Sea Point, works here from seven till five, back home to make supper and do the housework there, then to bed at midnight. She says to me, 'I thank God that I've still got my health so I can work hard for Madam and myself.'

SAUNDERS BEACH Astonishing to see the beach mixed. Black men in the briefest swimsuits sunbathing next to Jewish princesses, who lie face down with bikini-tops discreetly untied. And yet the Immorality Act still officially exists. So they lie there inches away from one another, very nearly naked, watching with interest and wariness, sensing, smelling, stirring one another, but not permitted to touch.

The sea is choppy, the wind strong and cold. As soon as you are protected from it, baking heat. Clouds tumble over the Seven Apostles. I notice how magnificent Lion's Head is, as if for the first time. This ex-volcano dominates Sea Point; our school anthem was called 'Beneath

Katie and Mum

the Lion Bold'. The mountain was so familiar that I stopped noticing it, but seeing it now, it has tremendous power. Richard III is in there somewhere. But which bit is the head, which the hump?

'Haah.' Dad back from work. He goes into the kitchen to nibble at the supper Katie is preparing, and to chat in Afrikaans. I think they both look forward to these moments of their day.

'How was work?' I ask.

'Every day, same day,' says Dad, pouring a large Scotch. He keeps rubbing his hands which have developed bad arthritis and gout. 'They're changing,' he says, 'look at these dents and bumps. First the right was worse, now the left; half time all change. Growing old is like keeping a bloody car you wish you'd got rid of years ago. Just get one bit right and another bit goes.'

He puts on the television. Today it is Afrikaans till eight o'clock, then it changes over to English. Tomorrow vice versa. The West Indian cricket tour is on. He points to it gleefully. 'And they were here last year also.'

'I know. And criticised for it.'

'Yet here they are again.'

'Money.'

'Money, my boy, money talks in a language that is out of this world.'

I have made a resolution not to get involved in any political discussions, so concede the point without further comment.

'Now is the winter . . .'

I start to read *Richard III* properly, cover to cover. First impression: the world of the play is a superstitious one. A man is imprisoned because his initial is G, a corpse bleeds. The other thing that strikes me is that Richard *is* funny. This is a danger area for me. In *Tartuffe* rehearsals I remember saying, 'I don't think it's funny at all what he does in this household. It disturbs me.' But at the first preview, at the first whiff of the audience's delight in this bloodsport, I was off; inventing snorts, hops, dancing eyebrows before their very eyes. The irresistible drug of laughter. It will be so predictable playing Richard like that. Must root his wit in self-defence. Everything comes from his deformity, his pain.

Interesting that the first two encounters happen *to* him. He's just sitting there when Clarence and Hastings pass. Almost as if he's in a wheelchair – he's been pushed out into the sun and left there.

Play him in a wheelchair?

Wednesday 14 December

Coming out of the gym I stop to memorise the surroundings for future visits. I realise with a shock that I'm a block away from Sea Point Boys' High School. All the shops have changed over the years and nothing is familiar. Then I round the corner and there's the parade ground and the school, exactly the same. Lean on the fence and stare hard. A flash of me and Tony Fagin walking during Break, talking, talking, dreaming of going overseas and becoming famous.

The gates are open. I wonder whether to go in but the signs 'Trespassers will be Prosecuted' intimidate, particularly in Afrikaans.

Walking along the fence staring up at the windows. Those classrooms. In one I glimpse a world globe, almost black with dust. That must be the Library. A book of photos – Alec Guinness in all his roles and disguises – pored over endlessly.

I have to pass through a group of Coloured women. They are very drunk, their eyes and mouths ugly; they sway viciously. Maids off duty still dressed absurdly in those pink uniforms. One looks at me horribly through bloodshot eyes. She is rake thin, her bony arms flailing around in the air; toothless, her thick lips flapping like her jaw has no hinges, shouting a stew of Afrikaans and English, swearing and spitting as she staggers down the street. These are the people who will murder us in our beds, we thought as children. They still frighten terribly.

Reading *Richard III*. For a play so famous for its mass-murders, there's surprisingly little violence on stage, but a constant sense of danger which I like. When the violence does erupt (the stabbing of Clarence, Hastings' head being brought on) I think it should be done very realistically and shock immensely.

Leafing through piles of old *Time* magazines that Dad has collected over the years, on cue I come across a fascinating article on murderers and capital punishment.

A mass-murderer called Henry Brisbon Jnr, twenty-eight, Negro, from a family of thirteen children, his father a strict Muslim, says: 'I'm no bad dude, just an anti-social individual. I was taught to be a racist and not like whites. As I grew up I decided I didn't like nobody.'

Different methods of capital punishment through the centuries. One of the oddest is from nineteenth-century India, where the culprit was tied to the hind leg of an elephant which was then forced into a fast trot, bouncing the man along behind. He was untied, given a glass of water and then had to put his head on a stone. The elephant was made to step up and crush it.

Not that modern electrocution is any less bizarre; the way the jury have to take their seats as at the theatre, the executioner invisible behind a two-way mirror. (Lermontov's line from *Maydays*: 'I have always thought the condemned are blindfolded not for themselves, but for the executioner. So he can't see their faces.') When the electricity is pumped through, the victim's eyeballs bulge from their sockets and burst. Then his brain boils alive. The state boiling brains, Nilsen boiling heads . . .

And my current fear is making Richard too funny.

Thursday 15 December
As I'm going out to sketch, Katie makes a big fuss about locking the door behind me. She says she's scared to be in the house alone.

'It wasn't like that when I lived here.'

'Oo Master Antony, it's terrible what goes on here now.'

Sketching Lion's Head. More and more alive. Massive shoulders with a terrible growth (hump?) on one of them. That growth, a rock formation with great slabs and chunks, is so like animal or human muscle; the surface

Lion's Head — view from Sea Point

has a smoothness, a silkiness, the folds are very soft – there are crevices you want to run your fingers over and into – but within there's this enormous hard power. Feminine and masculine.

STEAK HOUSE The family has gathered in force. As the men arrive they plonk down bottles of wine or whisky. Both will be drunk freely throughout the meal.

Despite an agreement that there should be no political discussions, everyone is spoiling for a fight, particularly the more liberal – my sister-in-law Yvette and her brother Ashley. 'You've diagnosed the sickness,' they say, 'now suggest a cure.'

My younger brother Joel (a giant walking wall of muscle, but gentle-natured – Hercules in specs) says with a kind of regret, 'I am selfish. This is my country. I've nowhere else to go. So I must stay in power. And live with my guilt.' He runs an off-licence (or 'bottle store' as they call it). I ask him why I've seen so many Coloureds pissed out of their brains. He says it's Government policy to keep the price of cheap wine as low as possible. 'To anaesthetise the population.'

Discussion rages about the recent referendum granting the vote to Coloureds and Indians, but not to blacks.

Back at the house, Joel and I stay up drinking – another bottle of Scotch plonked down between us. We talk about school days and teachers; several have died including my mentor, the art master McCabe. God, when did I last have a conversation like this? Joel talks about how I dominated his childhood (because of the fuss made over me as a child artist), cramped his style, left him no space. But this is said without any bitterness. He's the most centred of us all.

Behind his head the black window panes turn navy blue, start to lighten.

At about five o'clock in the morning, Dad staggers downstairs blinking, his hair a little storm around his ears. 'Hell's bells!' he says seeing us, 'I'm going to the lav.'

Saturday 17 December
Lunch with Esther. She still lives at No. 303, Shoreham Flats, where I used to come week after week for classes. Who would have thought *Elocution* could be so thrilling?

Her skin is tanned, turquoise splashed around those jet-black eagle eyes, her hair a sculpture in vanilla ice. She is flamboyantly theatrical – a cross between Ethel Merman and Sybil Thorndike – but this is deceptive.

In this modest living room with its sunny balcony overlooking the beach front, Esther was a pioneer in the experimental and the avant-garde. At that time, the mid-Sixties, South African theatre had just caught up with *The Chalk Garden* by Enid Bagnold, but we were poring over Beckett, Osborne, Wesker and above all Pinter. We even did *improvisations*. In most of these I would play either Oscar Werner in *Ship of Fools* or Harry Andrews in *The Hill*, both favourite performances at the time. My inventiveness was endless: whatever the subject or setting of the improvisation, I would contrive to turn up as either a sadistic British RSM or a bleary Viennese ship's doctor spouting gems like, 'Life is a zhip and ve are merely foolz.'

Today we wallow. Remembering events that happened and some that didn't.

It's a cold night; the wind is wild and buffets the car as we drive to Randall's home in Camps Bay. From this side of the coast Lion's Head looks even more like a Richard shape viewed slightly from behind – hunched on his tray as he's carried from the coronation. The mountain is a terrifying silhouette against midnight blue.

Watch a video (the national pastime because the telly is so bad) of *Fitzcaraldo* with Klaus Kinski, not at his best: he tells us he's bonkers from the first shot. Mad eyes roving, crooked smile. Nowhere to go. That face though – like something melted by Dali.

Lose interest and find myself thinking of Lion's Head and lions. Remembering images from a trip long ago to the Etosha Pan Game Reserve – lions lying in the sun breathing heavily, short heavy pants, mouths slightly open. Great strength resting. I try it out discreetly as Kinski goes interminably up the Amazon. You also see severely deformed people do this – breathing with heavy little gasps.

Sunday 18 December
Another family day. A barbecue (or 'braai') and then a steady stream of relations popping in for drinks and to have a look at the prodigal son.

Granny has turned eighty-seven and has been very ill; she looks half the size I remember, but still maintains her legendary independence. Great difficulty walking but refuses to use her metal walking stick, carries it instead under her arm like a brigadier. She has a problem climbing the few steps to the patio and I'm about to help her when Joel restrains me and whispers that her elbow jabs are lethal. She sits in the shade of a tree.

'I can't run around like I used to, but you learn to accept it.' Her greatest regret is that she's no longer fit enough to work in the Old Aged Home where she used to help the *really* aged. She tells me about one old woman whom she used to look after. They discovered they were both from the same town in Russia, Plumyan. They'd not seen it for over eighty years but by putting their heads together they could build up images of streets and shops and a water pump on a corner. She looks at me very steadily and says, 'To think I should see you again.'

Rona and Jack, a favourite aunt and uncle. Puzzling over Northern Ireland, she wonders why the British don't just pull out. He says it's because Britain doesn't want an enemy on her doorstep. 'Be overrun with Communists in no time, man.' The world through South African eyes.

Dad's sister Rosie is a wonderful eccentric. Deep throaty chuckle, oriental eyes, and a single grey streak in her hair like Diaghilev. She's seventy-five, loves travelling, but is increasingly scared to go overseas in case she dies there: 'I'd be so embarrassed. Nobody would know what to do with me.' As she leaves she says to me, 'Well so long, probably won't see you again, don't have much longer to go. Anyway, nice knowing you and keep up the good work.' She goes out with a rasping chuckle.

Monday 19 December
BOSCHENDAL WINE ESTATE Cecil Rhodes started these fruit farms about an hour's drive away from Cape Town. Now they're a beauty spot with shops and a restaurant.

'Feel the air,' Mum says and we all put our hands out of the car to weigh the thick heat in our palms. The light is blinding, then you walk under a tree and suddenly it's black and cool. The smell of newly mown grass being watered. Pink hydrangeas in wooden tubs. The landscape ringing gently with insects and birds.

In the restaurant the black waiters are dressed in white with pink sashes and caps to match the tablecloths. So humble, so eager to please. In England, diners are terrorised by the waiters, here vice versa.

One of them is asked to take a photo of another table. We all watch nervously in case he doesn't know how to do it. Then, as the shutter clicks, Yvette turns to me and says, 'Easy to teach monkeys to press buttons.' Smiling, she dares me. I smile back.

Driving home in a slow circle round Lion's Head. I suddenly realised why it is so compulsive – the brute force, the thickness. My acting is often

Lion's Head — view from city centre

described as ratty or rodenty. Richard must be a thicker, heavier animal if there is to be a tragic dimension.

Tuesday 20 December

Ashley has invited me to his firm's Christmas party. He is a champion of workers' rights and of breaking down colour barriers. Thus the party tonight is to be held in one of the Coloured townships and he has said it will be 'an education' for me to come along.

Dad is very amused as he sees me to the car. 'Well, my boy, you can't tell me things aren't changing in this country. There was a time when one wouldn't shake a black by the hand, scared some of the colour might rub off; now one's doing the foxtrot with them. Anyhow, I'm sure you'll have a good time once you get used to the smell.' Yvette giggles, daring me.

The dance hall turns out to be a mixture of Spanish restaurant and Country-and-Western folk club. We walk in past a group of Coloured youths. One says to another 'Lotta white faces here tonight, ol' pallie.' I feel quite nervous. Going into this 'non-white, non-European' place breaks every rule that I was taught. Those taboos tacked round our edges as children, sealing us in.

I am put on a table with Ralph, Ashley's Coloured manager and his girlfriend Patti, so I can 'talk' to them. Bottles of wine and whisky are plonked down.

At first Ralph is rather guarded on the subject of the referendum and apartheid, which fuels my interest. A few whiskies later, I steer him towards these topics again and now it all comes pouring out, but again not what I expected. Perhaps this is the 'education' that Ashley meant. Ralph talks like a white: how you can't change overnight; how if you did he'd be blown away in the crossfire between the races; how lazy, stupid and dishonest the blacks are. Doing a passable impression of Monty I smile wisely and ask him to think why the blacks are like that. 'Look,' he says, 'don't tell me about their backgrounds. I also come from a poor background, I also been thrown out of places that I go to with my white friends. But I don't steal. Maybe if you lived here you'd understand. Things are changing, but slowly. We don't want another Rhodesia. Or look at the rest of black Africa. Or at your own country – what about that bomb the other day in Harrods? Look, I'm selfish. I gotta think of me first, get me sorted out first then I can start worrying about my neighbour. But please don't get me wrong – I am against apartheid.'

The band strikes up. Ashley crosses the room and asks a large black lady for the first dance. A ripple of applause as they glide on to the floor. She looks rather embarrassed.

'Look!' Esther almost shouts, snatching my arm. 'Look – my son is dancing with the tea lady! Will you look at my marvellous, wonderful boy. He could have chosen anyone for the first dance, instead he chooses to dance with the lowest paid member of the firm, will you look!'

I say to Ralph, 'How old are you?'

'Thirty-five.'

'Really? We're the same age. Strange to think that we both grew up in this city in very different ways. Did you ever come out to Sea Point?'

'Oh yah man, Sea Point is where all the action was, still is.'

'Really? Where?'

'You know those tall blocks of flats on the beach front? Well, in the maids' rooms, at the top and at the bottom of those blocks. You know what they say: "Life's full of spice at the top and at the bottom." '

Later, as we leave, I give Ralph and Patti my address in London. He says rather furtively, 'Maybe I'd see things differently over there.'

Driving back we pass the black township Langa. Yvette tells how she worked in a hospital there until the '76 riots. Afterwards, her black assistant rang her to ask when she was coming back. Yvette said never, she wasn't allowed to anymore, and they cried together on the phone.

Wednesday 21 December

Wake inexplicably depressed about Richard III. Why bother playing the part? Olivier's interpretation *is* definitive and so famous that all round the world people can get up and do impersonations of it. At parties in New York, in bars in Naples, on remote Australian farms and forgotten South Sea Islands, people get to their feet, hoist one shoulder up, shrivel an arm and limp across the room declaring, 'Now is the winter', or its relevant linguistic equivalent. Why these thoughts suddenly? It's this fucking mountain I keep circling!

I remember now this feeling in the air. December in Sea Point. Exams just over. Six weeks of summer holidays starting. Long hot days ahead . . .

We've just finished supper when Howard Davies rings. He says their plans have changed again. He's no longer doing the Nicky Wright play, Adrian is. The Peter Barnes play is postponed to the Barbican '85 season. They're bending the rules slightly for the new season at The Other Place (which was to be exclusively brand new plays) and now in Slot Four is a revival of Trevor Griffiths's *The Party* which Howard is directing with David Edgar. I know the play only by reputation. He wants me to play the part originally played by Ronald Pickup. The Olivier part is being offered to McDiarmid, the Frank Finlay part to Mal. I promise to try and find a copy in Cape Town, but it might be banned either by the South Africans or Trevor Griffiths himself. Ask him about the rest of the season's casting. Rees and Branagh are definite, McDiarmid eighty-five per cent but should be one hundred per cent after *The Party* offer. 'We regard you as sixty-five per cent,' says Howard.

We watch an old home movie from 1957. It's been transposed on to video so the quality is appalling, but it's still quite compulsive viewing. If you had to recreate what memory *looks* like it could be this. The amateur cameraman can never settle on anything properly so you have these restless, tantalising glimpses of people and places and days from long ago. You ache for close-ups to be held longer but they never are. Sequences flit by in bleached colours and hazy outlines confirming the popular belief that the past was one long summer's day. Surprising how exhibitionist I am at the age of eight: a smiling little boy always in the foreground trying to hop into shot. At one time I appear in hat and moustache apparently doing a Charlie Chaplin impersonation. Where is the shy, frightened recluse Monty and I have spent so long digging out?

'That came later,' says Mum firmly.

Next to her on the sofa Dad sleeps soundly. For as long as I can remember, as soon as any form of entertainment commences – play, film, television or even a home movie – he falls instantly into a deep and contented slumber. Dad lives for his business, lives in a practical commercial world. Perhaps the world of the imagination really has no appeal whatsoever. When he finds himself in the kind of place where lights will dim in one area so that a fantasy world can begin to glow in another, he chooses the darkness.

Now his head jerks up briefly with a sharp snort from the throat, startling us all except Mum who has learned to ignore these abrupt comings and goings of her husband. On the screen in our home movies, a child looms into close-up with large ears and hair carefully brushed for some ancient birthday party.

'Which one?' he asks, only fractionally awake.

'Joel,' Mum says briskly, without altering her concentration.

'Juhhh . . .' we hear, as his head falls forward again.

He's always had some difficulty recognising one son from another. Often when he addresses me, he starts with a little roll-call: 'Randall . . . tsk! Joel . . . tsk! *Antony!*'

The highlight of the film is a sequence where Mum and Dad are dressed as Twenties flappers for a fancy-dress party. Bathed in this film's eternal sunshine, they dance the Charleston in the back yard of the old house in Marais Road. He has on an enormous false Groucho moustache which, with his own big nose and heavy glasses, makes it look like he's wearing one of those joke-shop faces. We all cry with laughter while he sleeps on soundly.

Thursday 22 December

Find a copy of *The Party*. Difficult to read – so was *Maydays* – but that same sense of potential theatrical vibrancy once you've understood the arguments. But I am worried by Shawcross, the part on offer; Howard said that he's the one through whose eyes the audience see the action, but all this means is that he's the straight man to the fun parts, Tagg and especially Sloman, a wonderful part.

Adrian rings. Puffing deeply on a cigarette between phrases, he reads me the synopsis of Nicky's play set in Cairo in the Second World War. It's based on a true story and sounds fascinating, although the character is too close to Richard III for comfort – trampling over all obstacles to get promotion. I'm not sure how to react to a synopsis. Adrian makes a little speech about how they're all desperate to make next year work out for me, how I must have 'two whopping great leads' and how much he wants to work with me again after *King Lear*.

I make a return speech on how keen I am to make next year work, that I am not playing silly buggers and if they could show me the second part in script form I'd sign on the dotted line tomorrow. But Shawcross isn't it.

Adrian says, 'Yes, but that's not meant to be your big second part. Nicky's play will be that. No, that's just an extra.'

We agree there's nothing further to be said until I've read something. A first draft might be ready by early January. Wishing one another Merry Christmas the call ends.

Juices start to flow for Nicky's army play. Harry Andrews from *The Hill* (and countless childhood improvisations) with ramrod back, lifting his chin to stretch the neck from a perfectly starched collar; an animal scenting prey . . . promotion.

Another restaurant, another family meal. An argument rages about maids and how to treat them. Verne's husband Ronnie is furious because their maid is using so much gas and electricity in her room. He suspects she has boyfriends staying over.

Joel says, 'Well if you want to keep a maid you'll have to put up with her human needs.'

'Not necessarily,' says Ronnie crossly, 'not given her IQ.'

No one will come clean over how much they actually pay these maids, least of all Mum about Katie. Joel says that if Katie earned what she deserved after all these years of service she'd be richer than all of us put together.

I finally get trapped into a furious row about apartheid, the one that Yvette has been spoiling for ever since I arrived. She says that I've no right to come here and criticise as I'm doing nothing to help the situation either here or back in England.

I'm somewhat floored by this. She's absolutely right; here I am having a wonderful holiday and, like most liberal white South Africans, making sure that my conscience doesn't intrude too much on my comforts. This country is so seductive.

Friday 23 December
Drive to Hermanus on the east coast. We've taken a house there for Christmas week. Mum says that Sea Point is unbearable during the festivities: 'An influx of blacks and Coloureds camping all over the beaches, the worst element, drunks and skollies!' She says this deterioration of her beloved Sea Point has converted her from middle-of-the-road liberal views to a stauncher, harsher belief in apartheid.

After a couple of hours we stop at a fruit and vegetable shop in the mountains. Dad gulps down a fruit juice and says, 'What a waste of a good thirst, hey?'

An Afrikaner father and son come into the shop. Both are dressed typically; khaki shirts, khaki shorts, long khaki socks. When Civil War starts here these people won't even have to change into uniform.

A warm, pink African evening. We sit around on the stoep of our holiday bungalow, moths fluttering round the overhead light. Everyone tired after the long drive, all the packing and unpacking. Randall has brought along a record player and a collection of nostalgia records, Bing Crosby, Jimmy Durante, Louis Armstrong. He and Mum start to dance rather beautifully.

Dad dances on his own, dressed in his short summer pyjamas, skinny white legs sticking out.

I do hope my face turns into his as I age. It's a marvellous face for an actor; a cross between Anthony Quinn, José Ferrer and Onassis.

He tells the story he's told a hundred times before and which we never tire of. His mother and aunt sitting on the porch at Marlborough Mansions, both very old, both afflicted – his mother with arthritis, which makes her constantly flick her wrists up and down; his aunt with Parkinson's disease, which makes her head shake from side to side. A hawker arrives selling fruit and vegetables, calls up to them. One appears to be shaking her head, the other beckoning with her hands. The hawker is nonplussed. Dad acts this last bit out and then starts to cry with laughter, tries to carry on speaking but his voice is a helpless falsetto. The more he tries the more we laugh. He takes off his heavy black glasses – his face is softer, gentler – and wipes his eyes with the side of his hand. It is an image of him I will always remember.

Saturday 24 December

Hermanus grew up a resort for the British officials when South Africa was still a colony. Hence it's like Frinton-on-Sea; hence Mum loves it and I hate it. It's hardly like being in South Africa at all. Cute bungalows with trimmed lawns. Little gift shops selling sachets of pot pourri.

Even the weather is English – grey and windy. I sit on the lawn in swimming trunks, clutching a bottle of sun oil, grimly waiting for snatches of sunlight, sulking that we've come here.

Refuge in Peter Hall's Diaries. Why have people been so rude about this book? It seems to me full of honesty and wit. Makes me warm to the man whom I never saw once (never mind met) in my seven months at the National. The portrait of Ralph Richardson is beautiful.

Another entry (5 October 1979) about John Wood's Richard III: 'He's the first actor since 1944 to have challenged Olivier in the part on his own ground. He hasn't unseated him yet, but he might next time.' Wood tells Hall he feels a complete failure and later Hall confides to his tape recorder, 'The trouble with John is that he has a too acutely developed sense of history. He looks forward a hundred years and wants to see his Richard III written there.'

Have to stop reading. Too close for comfort.

In the late afternoon the sun finally comes out and we go for a swim in Fick's Pool. You climb down steeply into a gorge. Descending shelves of rock and sand with cascading plants giving it a Babylonian feel. People stand along the top among trees looking down as if into an arena. At the bottom there is a tidal pool flushed by waves breaking over the sea wall.

Randall, Joel and I swim over to a patch of sunlight on the water – the only part the late afternoon sun can reach. This is one of the happiest times of the holiday. A feeling of warmth and pride in our brotherhood. We must look rather handsome, us three, with dark wet hair, glowing with suntans, gleaming in the water.

Mum and Dad sit high on the steep bank, perched like two old birds looking down on their young – Dad no doubt wondering, 'Which one is that?'

Christmas Day

Car-loads of family arrive from Cape Town. The adults slip effortlessly into their roles and relationships. Dad and Joel are best at making the braai, Randall best at mixing the drinks, Mum best at nagging the men about drinking too much, Verne and Yvette make salads, Ashley sprawls and chats to anyone passing. It's like they've played the scene a million times in a long running comedy. The jokes are delightful, the timing second nature, the rapport effortless, but complacency threatens to settle.

The children don't enjoy it half so much. They lounge around under a tree, bored, limbs just sprawled any old how, like puppets tipped out of a toy box.

In the middle of all this a little old Coloured man arrives. The gardener come to water the plants despite the fact that it rained heavily during the night. Actually, he's come for his Christmas box. He is very drunk, and stands with the hose drooping, watering his shoes. Everyone ignores him; no Christmas box offered, he staggers away.

In the evening we drive into town. In the dark this place loses its Englishness and looks like something out of Mid-West America in the Fifties (I'm thinking of *Last Picture Show*). There is only one shop open, Princess Café, a little oasis of glaring neon on the main street, selling everything from vegetables to videos and doing a roaring trade in computer games as well. Open-roofed cars draw up with blonde teenagers, bottles of pop, a wild night out. They tumble into the shop, reappear a moment later restocked, drive off. A group of drunk Coloureds shout after them from the pavement. A Coloured policeman strolls into the light and stands there, looking very relaxed.

Boxing Day

We're going for a walk after dinner. Gather outside in the garden in the night air. I feel my senses coming back to me after another long noisy meal, eating myself silly, drinking, drinking; the day's suntan burns on my body, making it ache.

There is a fresh sea breeze blowing. We stand looking up at the sky which is bright with stars. Dad says that in the Karroo on a clear summer's night you can drive without headlamps. Someone runs into the house to switch off the lights and the sky is even clearer. Yvette points out Orion's Belt, Scorpio, the Southern Cross. 'How do you know?' I ask her. 'My late Pa taught me,' she says. We stand quietly, almost religiously, in the dark garden, crickets ringing softly around us. It's so magical that when a strange formation flies into view overhead, glowing shapes in a perfect pattern, some of the children gasp. 'They're just birds,' an adult says and everyone giggles with relief. A child says sadly, 'I thought he'd come.' An adult says, 'Tsk, ever since they saw *E.T.* . . . .'

Tuesday 27 December
Awake these mornings increasingly depressed. Only a matter of days
before I have to go back. Mouth a few of Tartuffe's lines as I lie in bed,
and instantly feel nauseous.

A wonderful morning. Baking sunshine. We go to the main beach. White
sand stretching for miles and miles until it disappears into a bluish haze
of heat and sea-spray. Distant transparent mountains. This vast beach
landscape is inappropriately called The Grotto – named by some colonial
official, I would imagine, whose mind was elsewhere at the moment of
christening.

 This morning it is inhabited mainly by holidaying Afrikaners – which
also has an inappropriate ring to it. With their reputation you can imagine
Afrikaners doing everything else but holidaying. Afrikaners. The word
itself conjures up images of ox-wagons climbing up sheer cliff faces;
fearsome bearded men and lantern-jawed women standing back to back,
armed only with one rusty rifle and The Gospel According to Themselves,
holding their own against whatever opposition has come their way: hordes
of Zulu warriors, the full might of Imperial Britain, current world opinion.

 In a different way these people intimidate me as much as those drunk
Coloureds on street corners because, I suppose, I spent nine months in
National Service where the Afrikaner officers regarded me very much as
a third-class citizen: English-speaking *and* Jewish.

 I get pleasantly pissed on a bottle of excellent white wine, put on the
Sony Walkman and listen to that favourite tape of opera choruses. With
the flick of a switch, full orchestras and choruses materialise on this beach
for some exquisite brain-washing. Literally. My brain is washed with
music. How is it that nobody else can hear? All around is my wonderful
noisy family, arguing, wise-cracking, child-battering, parent-bashing, all
in dumb show, carrying on as if everything was normal and the beach
wasn't awash with these tremendous sounds.

 The chorus from *Boris Godunov*. This is my *Richard III* music – instant
delusions of grandeur. Brass and percussion, bells and chimes and Russian
choirs. Unbelievably, I'm soon going back overseas, probably to do a play
called *King Richard III*. Overseas. When I lived here that mythical place
sounded so far away, so difficult to get to. Over seas. How many and how
wide? *I* could never reach there. Now the thought of me going to play
Richard III for the Royal Shakespeare Company seems as improbable.
It's something to be dreamed about, half pissed on a beach.

Wednesday 28 December
A cool, grey day.

Breakfast is accompanied by Randall's record collection of old favourites: 'Yellow Bird', 'Chanson d'Amour', 'Moonlight and Roses', 'Let Me Call You Sweetheart'. People soft-shoe shuffle to the table, sit swaying in their seats, sing along between mouthfuls of steak and eggs.

I feel very energetic and dance around the room, Richard ideas tumbling out. It seems to me his face should look quite monstrous. Build a massive forehead and flat broken nose. To look at him should fill you with pity and horror. Karloff's monster in *Frankenstein*. Is there a way of making his head appear too big for his body? Also, Margaret calls him a 'bottled spider' – a striking image, whatever it means (I'm not bothering to look up the editor's notes yet). The crutches could help to create the spider image.

Long walk with Mum across the cliff tops. Wonderful criss-cross rock formations, stacks and pillars; plateaus so cross-hatched it's like taking a stroll in a Hogarth etching.

We have one of our talks. A familiar pattern. She begins by interrogating me very thoroughly about life in England and in the theatre, savouring every detail. It's so clearly what she would have wanted for herself, had the choices been available. So she listens in wonderment – a curious reversal of roles – like a child hearing of the joys and thrills promised in adult life. But then she'll catch herself and her maternal instincts will return in force. She'll advise and criticise: this could be better, that could be worse. And bombarding me with choice pickings from her varied and sometimes off-beat philosophies – The Power of Positive Thinking, Spiritualism, et al.

We sit on a bench high above the sea, thick pea soup bashing itself senseless on the rocks below. She says nobody believes there is a future for their children in South Africa any more. Her friends and relations are leaving in droves, many going to Israel, which seems like jumping from the frying pan . . .

She talks about Granny and her late father escaping from Russia at the turn of the century. Only two generations later and everyone's on the move again.

The odd thing is that nobody here seems to make any connection between escaping persecution in Russia or Germany and supporting apartheid.

I sketch Richard's head from this morning's thoughts. Interesting how the melting-pot works – the drawing has the bulk of Lion's Head; Klaus Kinski's eye; and a harelip from the Coetzee book I've been reading here, *Michael K.* Of course there's no way I could look like this. It would be very limiting to glue down so many of my features and wear so much prosthesis, for a part that long. But I love the thickness of this face; in a way, going back to the original Laughton image. With Brando's Godfather thrown in.

Herman's Head

Thursday 29 December
Driving back into Sea Point late this afternoon, the scene looks so familiar. The end of a hot day: people trudging up from the beaches in flip-flops, towels draped over their shoulders. The joggers are out everywhere, heads bobbing up and down.

I stroll down to Queen's Beach, trying to store this feeling, this hot sea air, to take back to London. A black man is struggling to take off his shirt but is so drunk he cannot undo the last button. He leans back against the wall, his head thrown back, mouth open, eyes sightless towards the sea, his fingers fumbling with that last button. Again and again he tries. He lets out a terrible moan.

I hurry back to the cool dark safety of the house. Blinds drawn against the strong sunset. The smell of furniture polish. The clink of ice in our drinks.

Friday 30 December
Last day.

I had given Katie twenty rand for Christmas. At breakfast she tells us, 'I bought beautiful shoes, in cream, Lady Di-style. And my hat also I find is one of hers. I thought I couldn't wear those little hats she wears, so I bought this wide-brimmed one. Then I see she wears these also. You do look smart in a hat. After wearing a dockie all week it makes all the difference. Hell, Madam, I did look smart. At church all my friends commented.' She says all this laughing, an infectious bubbling laugh.

I want a photo of her.

Mum insists she takes off her working apron. When I say it isn't necessary Mum says, 'Let her look nice too.'

'That's right,' says Katie, going into a panic but still laughing. 'What's people in London gonna think of me if they see me like this?'

'Put on your other apron,' Mum shouts as Katie disappears into the maid's room, 'the nice one!'

Katie reappears wearing a different apron. When we pose for the photo she becomes very serious and stands to attention. I tickle her and she screams to Mum, 'Ooo Mommy, Ooo Madam help!'

Granny joins us for a farewell lunch. She can't hear too well, which either creates awkward silences when questions aren't answered, or else she doesn't realise a conversation is in progress and will start one herself. Again it strikes me how young and inexperienced Mum and Dad become in her company.

Afterwards I accompany her to the car to say my farewells. Her cheek, as I kiss it, is like very soft tissue paper. She says, 'I wish you much good health and every success.'

I say, 'Hope to see you soon. Maybe next time in London.'

She chuckles and the car pulls out of the driveway.

Now it's Katie's turn. I go into the dining room, the room cool and dark as always. She is bent over the table clearing up. I stand silently behind her, watching her work. At last she turns with the tray full.

'I've come to say my farewells.'

'No. Not already. Really, already?'

We hug and I slip some money into her hand. She has prepared a little speech. 'Master Antony, may God grant you every happiness . . .' but her eyes moisten and she can't finish.

'Thank you for everything . . .' I say and get no further myself.

At the airport the family farewells are more festive and chaotic, the kids all taking photographs, the hugs and kisses posed for the cameras.

In Johannesburg, it's pouring with rain, preparing me for England. But it's a warm rain, and the thunder and lightning are unmistakably African, reaching away into vast empty spaces.

The white police in the airport are armed, the black ones not. Presumably in an emergency the latter would be required to hurl themselves bodily at hijackers.

On the plane it's a relief to hear British accents again. Waiting for take-off I suddenly remember Richard's line, 'Sent before my time into this breathing world scarce half made up'. Maybe that's the solution to his appearance – foetus-like. Smooth, almost slimy baldness. Unformed features. What has made me suddenly think of this? Yesterday at Fick's Pool there was a mentally-retarded boy with no eyebrows. Also Yvette was talking about their youngest daughter being born three months premature, the nurse saying, 'Go on Mrs Sher, hold her, she won't break.'

The plane lifts off into the storm, bravely plunging into dangerously dark-blue clouds, forked lightning in the distance. You think you're through it, the clouds lighten and soften and then it's like your head has been plunged underwater again – it's dark and murky and the plane rocks. Below there are glimpses of the outskirts of Jo'burg, suburban homes with large lawns and swimming pools; now farmlands, the fields a blackish green in the stormy light. We break out of the clouds but a higher bank towers above us for what looks like hundreds of miles. You fear for your safety – we must be so tiny against this colossal wall. One of the wings keeps brushing the edge of the cloud and disappearing. Now we're engulfed again, thick grey-blue darkness, then light suffocating whiteness, and then suddenly we lift up out of it and we're climbing into a perfect evening in the heavens. Below us are the familiar calm fields of clouds, above space as high as we dare go.

3. Acton Hilton, Canary Wharf and Grayshott Hall 1984

New Year's Day, 1984

A day in groggy limbo. Wake in the early afternoon after last night's New Year's Eve party at Dickie's. What with coming from South Africa to England, summer to winter, 1983 to 1984, and then waking up with jet lag and a hangover to find it already getting dark, my grasp on reality is not all it could be.

Evening. Caryl Churchill's party. Another party?!

Spend most of the evening with the actress Julie Walters and the designer Bob Crowley. Julie's just back from a promotion tour round the States for the film of *Educating Rita* and is in exhilarating form; being with her is like riding a spinning top. Bob tells me he's designing *Henry V* and *Love's Labour's* at Stratford and that Bill Dudley will design *Richard III*. When I tell him that I haven't decided to do it yet, he says, 'Oh, but you must. It's like the Paul Simon song, "Something so right".' Bob's mouth always twitching towards a smile; his cheeks look as if he stores goodies in them, like a hamster does.

He points to Julie's handbag. It's a miniature violin case in plastic. Rather like the one he designed for me in *King Lear*.

Nicky Wright arrives and I make a bee-line for him. He says there'll be nothing to read till late January.

That settles it. The decision will have to be made on Richard alone.

Monday 2 January

Phone Bill. His manner is slightly impatient. 'You must realise, Tony, that I'm the only one at the directors' meetings who keeps reminding them that you haven't yet agreed to Richard. Everyone else believes you will do it, that you must do it at this stage in your career. The character actor's Hamlet.'

Drive into the country with Dickie. Wind and rain. Low dark skies. The countryside looks like it's been dipped in blue ink. Callas singing the magnificent aria from *La Wally*.

We discuss the situation and agree that I'm just playing games, and they're not even proving effective as negotiating tactics. I'm obviously going to do *Richard III*. I'm totally obsessed by it, like being in love – this one person dominating your every thought. All day, every day, since it was first mentioned, I've been on the prowl for bits of Richard. Everything feeds the obsession – Lion's Head in Sea Point, disabled people Christmas shopping in Oxford Street. And alone in the privacy of my own home with curtains well drawn and doors securely locked, I try saying aloud, 'Now is the winter . . .'

Dickie suggests I reconsider playing Shawcross in *The Party*, thinks it would be good for me to play a less flashy part.

Evening. Joyce Nettles, the RSC casting director, rings. Says she doesn't want to put any pressure on me, but the first Stratford leaflet has to go to print tomorrow. I am about to tell her I'm on board but get side-tracked into a discussion about *The Party*.

She asks, 'Is there any other part you'd consider?'

'Well yes, but it's spoken for.'

'Sloman?'

'Yes.'

She urges me to tell Howard Davies. 'He ought at least to know,' she says. I tell her I couldn't oust Mal in that way. She says he hasn't been offered it yet, and volunteers to talk to Howard for me. I make her promise not to. But the temptation has unsettled me. Go to bed very edgy. It's almost as if the holiday never happened. Winter howling at the window.

Tuesday 3 January

MONTY SESSION He's very taken with my description of the house in Sea Point looking like a shrine to me.

I outline the situation at the RSC. Like Dickie, he urges me to play Shawcross. 'You know I never give you specific directives, but I'm breaking the rule. Play this part. It's important that you do.'

'But why? It's perverse and masochistic.'

'Bullshit! Playing all these showy parts is what's masochistic. You'll burn yourself out. Play this part, it'll be much harder.'

'It won't be hard. I can do it standing on my head. The only hard part will be seeing everybody else have all the fun.'

'Precisely. You still want to come home from school with prizes and say, "Look, Mommy, I'm best". You saw the shrine. Now bury all that.'

I promise to read the play again.

ACTON HILTON BBC TV rehearsal-rooms in Acton, where we'll adapt our stage production of *Tartuffe* for the telly. The building is so high it's like being airborne again. Way below are the factories, suburbs, railway lines and cemeteries of Acton and Willesden.

Steph Fayerman says, 'Isn't it nice to get into a lift and go *up* for a change?' After months and months underground at the Barbican, at last a rehearsal room with windows.

Tartuffe read-through for the TV crew, RKO money-men, and our producer Cedric Messina, a one-man Roman epic in name and size. Not a single laugh from this assembled group. Reminiscent of those depressing early rehearsals at the Barbican. But we know better now. Chris Hampton sits at the end of the table grinning and corpsing.

Chris Hampton

Lunch with Bill in the canteen. I find myself saying, 'Look, Bill, this is unofficial but I am going to do Richard, it's definitely on.' This comes as no surprise to either of us, but the relief of having said it is enormous. We're free to talk at last with all the enthusiasm that's been bottled up since November. He says that, while Richard might be a psychopath, he prefers to think of him as a product of his time: civil war has raged throughout his lifetime, the Crown constantly up for grabs, everyone somehow crippled by it all, guilty and neurotic about who killed who, why and when. I ask to meet up with Bill Dudley as soon as possible to devise the deformity.

Bill agrees: 'Richard has lived with his shape all his life, so has everyone else at court. It is an unremarkable factor in their lives. So it would be good if we could have it for rehearsals and everyone can get used to it. Then we can forget about it and concentrate on his character, instead of whether this arm is shorter than that one, or the hump two inches higher or lower.'

Agony when lunch ends. We could go on talking for hours.

Stand on the platform, waiting for the tube; it's a bitterly cold day but I hardly feel it. I'm glowing with excitement and relief. Can't sit still on the tube, can't concentrate on my newspaper.

Ring Sally to tell her I've decided. She makes rather a good suggestion about *The Party*: bring it all out into the open, talk to Mal, get him to read the play and give him first choice of the two parts.

Thursday 5 January
Anxiety about not getting to the gym enough. I mustn't let it slip now: for Richard, I'll need to be stronger and fitter than ever before in my life.

ACTON HILTON The rehearsal-room is laid out with a forest of vertical poles to denote doorways and walls. Without my glasses I keep crashing into these on fast exits, suddenly finding one between the eyes like I've stepped on a garden rake.

Excellent rehearsal of the first Tartuffe/Elmire scene. Bill is tactfully scaling down my performance for the camera, keeping the good gags, helping me cut out the hops, winks and eyebrow dances – my survival tactics. He urges me to consider the brilliance of the arguments, points out how Tartuffe's proposition – 'Love without scandal, pleasure without fear' – is a definitive statement on hypocrisy. 'Tartuffe's brochure, right? If he were to print one to circulate round the ladies of Paris, what would the cover say? "We offer love without scandal, pleasure without fear." '

Bill directing TV Tartuffe

His imagery is very inspiring today. Talking about how much Tartuffe is getting off on the religious kick, he says, 'He'd love to screw stark naked except for the giant rosary entwined around their bodies like a snake.'

We try the scene again without all the business. I can feel the power of the words doing the work. Must trust language more.

Read *The Party* again – the second version which the National toured. The play gets better with each reading, but the part gets worse.

Friday 6 January

NATIONAL THEATRE With Susie [Susie Figgis, film casting director] to see Fugard's *Master Harold and the Boys*. Over drinks at the bar I tell her I've decided to do Richard. She is visibly unenthusiastic. Tells me that she's casting a film at the moment and was talking to the director about me. They had both agreed it was time I left the RSC. 'He won't,' the director had said, 'they're bound to offer him Richard the Third,' making it sound such a boring, predictable idea. Poor Susie: she just happens to be the last in a long line of friends who have not rejoiced in my decision, and it's the final straw: 'I hate this inverted snobbery about the RSC!' I cry. 'It only happens to be the greatest English-speaking company in the world!' Realising I'm in a bar at the National, I lower my voice and hiss through gritted teeth, 'And I'm terribly, terribly happy there!'

The play is disappointing; maybe I was looking forward to it too much. It seems rather fey and cute compared to the South Africa I've just seen. Still, the last half hour is very moving. Susie has bought me a copy of Fugard's Notebooks which I start reading avidly. Beautiful sketches of South Africa.

Saturday 7 January

A beautiful day, a day of laying ghosts. Drive to Stratford to find a home for the season. A bright, English winter day; Elgar playing on the car stereo, the air so cold and clear you can see for miles.

Coming into Stratford I feel a little wobble. The last time I saw this place, a year ago, I was making a hurried exit in a taxi to London for the operation on my Achilles tendon. A few belongings packed, a canvas I had started crammed into the back seat, it was drizzling, the future rather bleak.

But today the town is welcoming, it smiles. You can't drive over that bridge, see that stretch of river, see that great ugly building floating on it, flying the RSC flag, and not feel your heart leap.

The welcome at the theatre is wonderful in a totally matter-of-fact way. Round every corner there is a familiar face that looks up and says, 'Oh, hello Tony, what are you doing here?' When I tell them I'm coming back they say, 'Oh good', and seem to mean it. Eileen knitting at the stage door, Traude buzzing around the canteen, Vic from the props staff and . . . Black Mac.

Mac was my dresser on *King Lear*. A fearsome army sergeant from the camp nearby who, improbably, dresses at the theatre in his spare time. Short, squat, glasses, no teeth and an impenetrable Newcastle accent. His only softening feature is a floppy fringe of grey hair. When I first joined the company, he terrified me so much I almost asked to be moved to another dressing-room. His army slang is crude beyond belief and brought back gruesome memories of my National Service. He seems to re-invent male chauvinism every time he opens his mouth. Women are known as 'split-arses'; his own wife is known as 'the Vampire'.

He divided actors into ranks: stars are known as Mark-Ones, supporting actors are Boffins, and play-as-cast actors are Peasants and treated accordingly. He'll gleefully tell how in one company the Peasants finally revolted, stuck a coat hanger down his back and hung him on the back of a door for several hours.

Needless to say, all of this macho aggro is superficial. Mac has a heart of gold, is a gentle vulnerable man, brilliant at his job and eventually we got on famously. I was nicknamed Animal (or 'Animil', as he spelt it on a card) because of my wild curly hair. He used to ring me up in London after the accident. 'How's the fokkin paw then, Animil? Cushy, skiving get-out innit? I'd've kep you working on it if you were under me down the camp.'

We are delighted to see one another, stand there patting stomachs, commenting on weight gained.

'What you gonna do here then, Animil?'

'Richard the Third.'

'Oh yeah? We haven't done him for a while. You'll be a fokkin Mark-One then.'

'And I want you to dress me.'

'Righto. Well, you have a word with the split-arse upstairs.'

The theatre manager, Graham Sawyer, takes me to view various RSC properties. Finding a decent place to live is almost as important as the parts you play. I've decided to live outside Stratford this time. Instantly fall in love with a cottage in Chipping Campden where the actor Dan

Massey is living this season. He's pottering around with a mug of coffee, classical music playing. Magnificent banked garden; I run across it, hail plopping down, to peer into a glasshouse at the far end. Perfect to paint or write in. Upstairs the bedrooms have low sloping ceilings, thick beams, little windows in strange places. Dan says, 'I know you're going to come and live here, I know it.'

He's right. The others I look at don't compare. I tell Graham to book it for me.

Sunday 8 January
Murderers and Monsters.

Sketching Ronnie Kray's face. It's a more feasible version of the head I drew in Hermanus. It has the thickness, the strange heavy brow, the eyebrows joining over the nose, a puffiness round the eyes (from boxing). A bruised sadness in the expression.

BBC 2's 'Horizon' – an episode called 'Prisoner or Patient'. Using the Dennis Nilsen case to consider the whole question of psychopaths, a term which divides the medical profession. A psychiatrist defines it as 'a term used to describe people who've behaved anti-socially from a very early age. The core of their personality seems to be an extreme egocentricity, a complete disregard for the feelings of others, and as a result they tend to leave a trail of chaos behind them, in human terms.'

(Richard's mother, Duchess of York:
'Tetchy and wayward was thy infancy;
Thy school-days frightful, desp'rate, wild, and furious;
Thy prime of manhood daring, bold, and venturous;
Thy age confirm'd, proud, subtle, sly, and bloody:
More mild, but yet more harmful, kind in hatred.')

Another psychiatrist (who gave evidence for the prosecution at Nilsen's trial) refutes the use of the term completely since it implies there can be a cure, which apparently is not the case. Nilsen was sent to prison rather than to a mental home because his condition was considered to be untreatable, incurable: thus evil rather than mad.

Some mental patients are interviewed, filmed in ghoulish silhouette, made more sinister by their voices thick with drugs. In talking about his psychiatrist, one commits a spectacular Freudian slip: 'He washed his hands with me.'

'The World About Us' on the Great White Shark. Interview with Peter

Ronnie Kray

Benchley who wrote *Jaws*. Asked why this shark has suddenly become such an international superstar, he suggests that in appearance it is 'a nightmare creature' which touches a primal nerve in our subconscious. This is made worse by the fact that it can cross over from our nightmares to real life and commit the ultimate horror – it can eat us.

I like the phrase 'nightmare creature'. It's an image I've got to find for Richard.

Monday 9 January
BARBICAN Meeting with Howard Davies about *The Party*. I tell him that I believe Shawcross is underwritten and needs a personality actor (someone naturally watchable) on whose shoulders the whole play could gently rest.

Howard: 'That kind of actor will make it boring.'

'No, I'd make it boring. I need a character to play.'

I have made up my mind not to bring up the subject of Sloman unless he does. He does. I tell him I wouldn't consider playing it now unless Mal has first choice of the two parts *without* knowing that I'm after one of them. Mal is so selfless he'd do anything to keep everyone happy.

Howard says he isn't sure himself if he can see the casting the other way round, but agrees to get Mal to read the play, looking at both parts.

CITY GYM In the changing-room I'm lamenting the fading of my South African tan when I notice a middle-aged man limp in. Using the mirror I discreetly watch him change. One leg is stick-thin. He limps off to the shower, using his crippled leg only for balance; it has no strength, has to be hoisted along by a hip movement, thrown forward to the next step.

Could be useful. But didn't somebody tell me that is how Alan Howard played Richard? Lifting his bad leg with a chain and hoisting it along?

Tuesday 10 January
MONTY SESSION As it's drawing to a close, I mention the 'Horizon' programme and ask his opinion on psychopaths. He agrees with the psychiatrist who refused to use the term, and says, 'It's just a convenient way for Medicine to sweep certain people under the carpet.' But he doesn't accept that anyone is incurable.

I ask, 'How do you explain Richard the Third then?'

'Well, how did you feel when you were on crutches last year?'

'I hated people staring at me.'

'What did you want to say to them?'

'Fuck off! What are you staring at?'

'Precisely. Anger.'

He says Richard is revenging himself on the world, destroying a world he sees as hating him.

I mention the angelic-cripple syndrome of Quasimodo, Smike and the rest. Monty says that's where Drama falsifies the world, romanticises it. Like whores with hearts of gold.

'We treat the disabled appallingly,' he says, 'they come up against dreadful prejudice. For example, people in wheelchairs are automatically assumed to have no sex-drive because the lower halves of their bodies *appear* to be out of use. The disabled person experiences all this frustration and given the chance, will lash out.'

'So are you saying Richard's behaviour is normal?'

'In the circumstances, absolutely normal.'

I suggest we set aside one of our sessions to discuss Richard's problems instead of mine. Monty roars with laughter and says he'd rather do it over dinner, after-hours.

Friday 13 January

The first Friday the Thirteenth in the year 1984, and the weather is bizarre. A powerful wind. Driving through Regents Park, the car is suddenly surrounded by thousands of brown leaves. Then the wind, growing stronger by the minute, rocks the car along Westway, rips at the door when I try to get out, wrestles with me rudely as I walk towards the Acton Hilton, clutching at my specs. On the seventh floor a very uneasy feeling. The windows seem to be taking a lot of strain. The sky is weird, lit from underneath, it might boil over.

Evening. Watch a video of the South Bank Show Arts Review of 1983. I recorded a speech from *Maydays* for them. Not a pleasant sight. For the first time I understand why friends like Dickie warn me against staying too long with the RSC. The speech has flair but is quite, quite empty. It can happen so easily at the RSC given that we play to a relatively uncritical audience who come along *expecting* to see brilliance. Also, you easily develop a swagger from having to prowl those vast stages in Stratford and the Barbican. Taken to the extreme (who shall be nameless), RSC acting can cease to bear any relation to recognisable human behaviour.

Saturday 14 January

News report – yesterday's wind reached hurricane strength. Several people were killed, a concrete tower collapsed and, amazingly, a gargoyle was torn off the side of York Minster and flew through the air.

Last run-through of *Tartuffe* for the technical crew. An army of cameramen, sound men and other technicians follow the action around the rehearsal room, their noses buried in large fold-out studio plans. Discussion with Cherry Alston, the make-up supervisor, about my bum. The problem is that my legs are still very tanned from South Africa, my bum very white. Bill giggles and says he rather likes the idea that Tartuffe has been sunbathing on Orgon's patio. Cherry professionally jots down, 'body make-up for Tony'.

Ali Steadman

Nigel Hawthorne

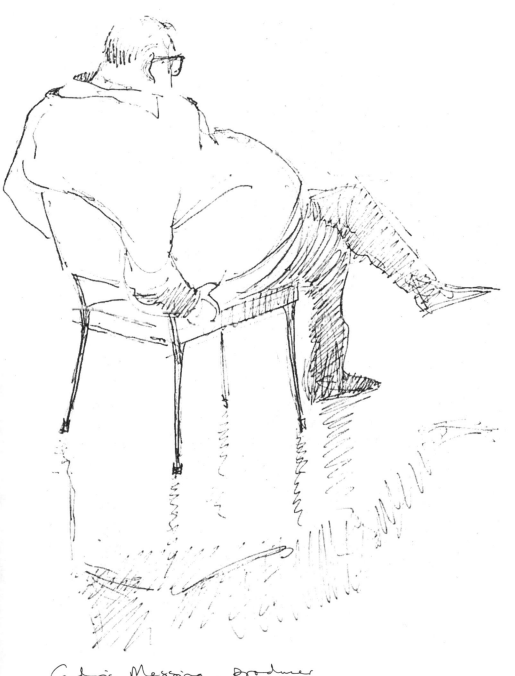

Cedric Messina, producer

Sunday 15 January
Fellini's *Satyricon*. Must be about the tenth time I've watched this inspired, inspiring film. You want to hold on to image after image, treasuring each one like a painting. The two men collapsing in a ploughed field with a smoky dawn rising. A human carcass on a crucifix with a vulture flapping on it. A giant stone head being trundled through the streets. His re-creation of another age is totally convincing, in an impressionistic way. People *behave* differently: kiss by pecking, chew food with an unfamiliar rhythm, stare at you through heavily made-up, stoned eyes. A sense of decadence in the colours he uses: the colours of illness, milky blues and yellows, watery greens and purples, the colour of runny eggs, of mould.

Everything we want for *Tartuffe* and *Richard III* is here in this grotesque world. Fellini uses real freaks and cripples with no moral qualms at all, so there's lots of useful material for me. A cripple – the sequence where they kidnap the hermaphrodite – is a bundle of clothes on crutches, knees bending the wrong way round, like a bird's. No single bit of the body seems connected to any other bit, a looseness, so that if you undid the ragged clothes the whole thing would tumble apart.

The ferryman, in the sequence where the hero screws the Earth Mother. Like my foetus idea: half formed features, damp strands of hair, no eyebrows, lazy eyes. A bit like Brando. He kills someone and does it almost gently, without anger or emotion, but like an animal holding on until the prey stops struggling.

Tuesday 17 January
Urgent message to ring Harold Pinter. I have to steady myself. With him, I tend to go hurtling backwards over the years, deflating like a balloon, until I'm a sixteen-year-old schoolboy taking those blue Methuen Playscripts to Esther's Elocution classes. The photos of Pinter on the back always seem slightly blurred (as if he was hurrying past the camera), adding to his mystique.

I dial. It rings. Is answered.

'Harold?' A terrifying silence. (If I was tasteless, I would write 'a menacing pause'.) I lean into the phone nervously: 'Harold?'

'Yes?' Stern, guarded. Clearly no one he knows addresses him as Harold.

'Hello . . .' My voice growing thinner and squeakier by the moment, 'yes, uhm, it's Tony Sher, I have a message –'

Instant warmth. 'Tony, hello, how good of you to ring back, how are you?'

He's directing a new Simon Gray play and wants me to do it. 'I've spoken to your agents but there seems to be some uncertainty. *Are* you staying with the RSC?'

'Well, yes, I think I am, I think I'm going to do Richard the Third, I mean, I am, yes, I am. Definitely.'

'Richard the Third? Isn't that funny, I was just saying to Simon Gray this morning that he's bound to be going back to Stratford to do a Richard the Third.'

'I know, it's terribly predictable.'

He laughs. 'What a pity. The part in Simon's play is wonderful.'

'Oh dear. Don't tell me.'

'Still, so is Richard the Third I suppose.'

He wishes me well, says he'll come up and see it and makes me promise not to stay with the RSC forever.

Put down the phone and it rings again immediately. Howard Davies. He says Mal has read *The Party* and is willing to play either part, but that he (Howard) can't really see it the other way round. Also he doesn't see why Mal should always lose out in casting because of his generosity. I heartily agree, thank him for his honesty and wish him good luck with the production.

So it's still just *Richard III*. Slight temptation to read the Simon Gray play . . .

Wednesday 18 – Saturday 21 January
BBC STUDIOS, WHITE CITY Recording *Tartuffe*.

I'm not needed on the first day, but pop in for a make-up test. Find they're moving so fast they might get to me by the evening. The make-up stays on, my costume is hurriedly found, and before I know it I'm on the studio floor doing my first scene. Rather like someone popping into hospital to have a corn removed and finding themselves undergoing major heart surgery.

The atmosphere in the studio is tense and rushed, everyone working against the clock – television's disease. First takes are being accepted far too easily. At the end of the day Bill looks like a ghost. It was his first time ever in a studio. Says it was one of the scariest days of his life, and rather like those disaster movies where the stewardess finds herself flying the plane.

But Bill and Tom Kingdon, the technical director, find their feet quickly over the next few days and it all becomes much better paced.

'Top of the Pops' being recorded in the next studio. I go out into the assembly area where the groups are lounging about. I am dressed in full Tartuffe gear, long black wig, black smock, stockings, but don't look at all incongruous. I could be the lead guitarist from any one of these bands.

Complete chaos on Friday. Nigel Hawthorne is suddenly summoned to accept an award for 'Yes Minister' from Mary Whitehouse's Viewers Association. It's to be presented by Margaret Thatcher, who has written a sketch(?!) which she is going to perform (?!!) with Nigel and Paul Eddington. So, Nigel heads off to help launch Thatcher's new career while, back in the studio, schedules are frantically re-arranged. I end up working non-stop from 10.00 a.m. to 10.00 p.m. with lunch and tea breaks being used for make-up changes. Spend all day in a state of suppressed fury that this has been caused by a publicity stunt for Mary Whitehouse, who ranks high on my list of major irritants, alongside queuing in banks and can-openers not working.

Nigel returns and we do our main scene in two takes, both excellent, both very different and inventive, trusting where the other leads.

In the evening much merriment over the bum scene (which might cause Nigel's next meeting with Mary Whitehouse to be in the Number One Court at the Old Bailey when she digs up some ancient law – Aiding and Abetting the Airing of an Arsehole?). In the make-up room all the actors are sitting in their chairs being made up, while I have to kneel on mine pointing in the other direction. In the studio it gets quite embarrassing. Whereas in the theatre the whole scene just flits by (trousers down, trousers up, before you know it), in the studio they keep calling a halt and I'm left stranded on the table, exposed bum in the air, while technicians stroll around whistling, adjusting lights and camera angles. The make-up girl dashes in to touch-up the false tan on my nether cheeks. As she's bent over her task, I happen to burp violently.

'Oh, that's very nice,' she says.

'You're lucky it didn't come out the other end.'

'I dunno. I've always wanted a parting in my hair.'

I glimpse one of the scenes being played back on a monitor. I'm no longer sure I have successfully scaled down my performance. I thought I was going from the theatrical to the televisual, but might have taken a wrong turning and ended up with the operatic.

On the last evening we finish with time to spare so they decide to do re-takes on the much over-exposed bum scene. Back to kneeling in the make-up room and then on to the table in the studio. During the take Nigel starts corpsing and the scene grinds to a halt. He says, 'This isn't like me at all. I'll be all right now.' Again we try and again he corpses. Ali and I take a sadistic delight in this, having disgraced ourselves so often in the theatre. Eventually they have to compromise on a different angle and actually remove Nigel from the studio. He is led away, still protesting, 'But it isn't like me at all, I promise you.'

Wednesday 25 January

BARBICAN Press conference. In this morning's *Guardian*, Nicholas de Jongh has somehow got hold of all the information about next season and leaks it, making today's conference somewhat pointless.

Waiting to go in, I meet Ken Branagh for the first time. We share a common problem – living in the shadow of Olivier's films, *Henry V* and *Richard III*. Because they're on *film*, they have entered this century's consciousness in a way that is quite daunting for any actor or director approaching the plays. However much people might glory in the memory of Gielgud's or Warner's Hamlet they are not there to be hired from the local video shop. Branagh says when he was at school he used to do an impersonation of Olivier's Richard without even knowing what it was. He says, 'Olivier's performances are there, indelibly. We might as well put them to one side and just get on with the job.' Which makes me feel much better.

De Jongh has the gall to show up for the press conference. So Terry begins, 'For those of you who haven't read this morning's *Guardian*, let me outline our plans . . .' He says this glancing in de Jongh's direction and smiling politely. Quite deadly. Also throws a few well chosen barbs in the direction of Michael Ratcliffe who has just taken over as the *Observer* critic and has been RSC-bashing in his first columns. Much turning of heads over in the thespian corner to identify this new critic. It's difficult getting to know what they look like since their natural habitat is nocturnal – the dark of the auditorium.

Terry is a magnificent speaker – a gift for fluency without referring to notes, never drying or stumbling. It's rumoured that politics was his second choice of career.

When it comes to question time, there's an embarrassed silence from the assembled journalists. Terry encourages them to ask the actors questions.

Nothing. Over in our corner, the director John Caird whispers, 'Mister Sher, will you be playing the part in a hump?' and Roger Rees adds, 'And will it be a hump from stock or a spanking new one?'

Things are grinding to a halt. Terry politely requests that they all lay off jokes about how difficult the Barbican is to find, it's been done to death and now is a good time to stop. This topic seems to animate the journalists more than anything else.

One says supportively, 'In a recent survey it was proved that eighty-four per cent now find it easy to find.'

'Eighty-four per cent of what?' asks the playwright David Edgar.

'Of people who find it.'

'How can they ask the people who don't find it?'

'They don't. The other sixteen per cent do eventually find it, but found it difficult to find.'

A moment later a very harassed Steve Grant (from *Time Out*) bursts in clutching briefcase and coat. Takes his place looking puffed and bewildered, and begins leafing through the publicity handout.

'Clearly one of the sixteen per cent,' whispers David Edgar.

Thursday 26 January
My day always starts with scanning the TV listings and setting the video recorder. If you have long enough you can research any part without moving from your living-room.

'The World About Us' on matadors. When I go to Spain, I find the bullfight compulsive viewing. Dangerous theatre. Watching the fighting bulls today, I realise they have many of the qualities that I've been thinking about for Richard. Sketching them is a similar sensation to sketching Lion's Head; the folds are silky smooth but inside there is a rock-hard power. Like sharks, they have the appearance of a 'nightmare creature' – something to do with their blackness even in bright sunshine; you can hardly make out their eyes or mouth; the head is a black stump; the white horns always defined against the black. Look at the head closely and it has a primeval, reptilian quality; heavily wrinkled, a stupid brutal face, slightly sad. Ronnie Kray.

When they first burst into the ring there is great agility, they spring, change direction, like they're dancing. The massive hump – this, of course, is most relevant to me – is full and hard, a pack of muscle. Later, pierced like a pin-cushion, it deflates. The blood is a crude orange splash bubbling down their flanks, like someone's thrown paint at them. When they charge,

their muscles seem to dilate, their size doubles, their weight doubles –
the nightmare creature thunders forwards.

The moment of dying. Kneeling. The struggle to get back on to its
feet. Everything would still be all right if it could only stand up again. But
its legs are turning to air. (Brando does this after he's shot in *Last
Tango*.)

Dragged out at the end, so flat, so soft, that great body half its size, like
a sack of water slipping along the sand, rippling, changing shape but
nothing really there.

The Visit. Documentary about P C Olds, shot trying to arrest a criminal;
spine severed, crippled from the waist down. Dead eyes in a handsome
face. Athletic body going to seed in a wheelchair, which he calls 'the pram'
or 'the prison'.

Interviewer: 'Is it worse than death?'

Olds: 'Oh yes. Oh, take it from me. Don't take it from people who've
made some sort of life out of it, you know, who say that life in a wheelchair
makes no difference to them and that they found themselves and they
found God and they found all sorts of things. I found nothing. I've lost
everything.' (His bitterness comes out as a tiredness, a dullness. A sneering
dullness.)

Interviewer: 'Will you ever come to terms with it?'

Olds: 'No.'

Interviewer: 'Shouldn't you try, for your own sake?'

Olds: 'I've tried. It won't work.'

Interviewer: 'Why not?'

Olds: 'They didn't kill me did they? I was robbed.'

Interviewer: 'Robbed of what?'

Olds: (little smile, daring) 'Death.'

Because he's a man only recently disabled (in his own words, 'I was
a motorcycle-riding, fornicating, criminal-catching cross between Telly
Savalas and Dennis Waterman'), he has no defence mechanism in operation. You can see his pain clearly; he is a man turned inside out, every
breeze hurts.

This is what Monty was talking about: the opposite of the angelic
cripple.

Round and round I go, mountains and sharks and bulls and P C Olds and
Ronnie Kray. It starts to confuse. Must remember that it felt the same
finding Lear's Fool. Different ingredients cooking together.

Gave up smoking today.

Saturday 28 January
Custom of the Country at The Pit. Very excited by Nicky Wright's writing. Terrific wit and surrealism. Towards the end he manages to get a fascinating collection of people on stage at the same time: two ghosts, a live man bound head to foot in bandages, and two Afrikaners playing host to an African chief.

Started smoking again.

Tuesday 31 January
MONTY Last session.

I confess I've been feeling not only rather bitter, now that all the theatre awards have been announced and the Fool didn't win anything, but also angry with myself for caring. An old record playing: be the best, bring home the prizes. He says I'm confusing issues. It's not the old record; an award for the Fool was a valid expectation, one that other people might have shared. 'You've been right to feel cheated, angry. Now let it go.'

'But awards are stupid. I know that.'

'Agreed. But it is nice to receive them. Nice. No more than that. Nice to be validated in your profession.'

'The work should be enough.'

'Of course. It is. It makes me very happy when I cure a patient. But I get a very special pleasure if I hear a third party say, "God, that person has really changed." '

'But that's like reviews. Needing the pat on the back. I've been so liberated this past year by not reading reviews.'

'No. You'll be truly liberated when you can read reviews and not care what they say. When you are confident enough in your own work you'll be able to read a review, accept praise or criticism when it's deserved, reject the rest.'

'Impossible.'

He smiles. We've been here before.

But it's worked. I feel the bitterness of this last week, a small constant irritation, washed away. Invisible mending.

As we come to the end of the session I say, 'Well, what do we do next?' half hoping he'll suggest booking a few more sessions.

He says, 'I want you to go away now. You might come back occasionally, to deal with a specific problem: But there's a danger in this work that every single particle gets opened up and dissected. You've made a lot of progress. And you've learned a skill. The old records will still play. But you can recognise them now and turn away. And occasionally you won't. But through choice, not compulsion.'

The end of a long – a year-long – journey we've travelled together. I feel the beginning of tears. How ironic it would be if the one thing I've never been able to do in these sessions – cry – should happen now. The actor in me notes how appropriate that would be, and with that thought the feeling goes.

The RSC have sent the Peter Barnes play. It might still be done at the end of this year in Stratford or next year at the Barbican. Directed by Adrian or Terry or both together. Called *Red Noses, Black Death*, it's about a little monk called Flote forming a troupe of clowns to cheer up people as they die from the Plague in thirteenth-century France. Astonishing, original piece of writing! He fashions a new language, so over-ripe and wonderfully rancid that it reeks, it glows with colours you've never dreamed of. A stew of Fellini and Mervyn Peake. As a part Flote isn't as exciting as the whole piece, but that's a safer way round, and it will be a pleasure to play someone *good* for a change.

I'm sitting back, stunned from the experience of reading it, when the phone rings. Snoo Wilson. Another writer in touch with parts of the brain not yet known to science. 'Novel number two gently easing its way out of the sphincter. A brightly coloured turd to drop on the populace.' He says that almost all the finance for his *Shadey* film has now been found, and that Otto Plaschkes thinks it might be possible to postpone the shooting until after *Richard* has opened and then work round my Stratford schedule.

At last 1984 is shaping up. At least one of these projects or the Nicky Wright play is bound to work out.

Sketch the bottled spider. Very pleased with this.

After *Molière*, a late-night drinking session with Mal. As I was leaving South Africa, Joel slipped me some of their illegal firewater – their equivalent to poteen. He put it in a brandy bottle so I could get it through customs.

As you take your first mouthful you find yourself re-enacting a scene from those Westerns where the baddie forces Jimmy Stewart to drink alcohol for the first time: your hand clutches the glass; fearing you'll break it, you slam it down; at the same time a cat has landed on the inside wall of your throat, claws out; then the cat begins to descend. Your mouth is

The Bottled Spider

straining open, your eyes are watering; at last you give out a kind of inverted gasp, a sound somewhere between 'ahhh', 'no' and 'help'. You smile foolishly at your drinking companion, wipe away the tears and try to say 'Wow!'

The drink has none of these effects on Mal. But then he's about ten-foot tall, built like a mountain, and can trace his ancestry back to the Vikings.

He takes his first sip. 'Mmm. Very nice. Tastes a bit like gun oil.'

'I think I'll dilute mine with a bit of water. Would you like some?'

'No thanks, I'll stick with it neat.'

'Righto.'

We go over the events of the last few months and compare notes. Everyone seems to have behaved honourably. Events happened exactly as they were reported back to each of us.

Buckingham and Sloman now officially on offer to Mal, but he's not sure whether to accept. Various reasons. He's up for a film. Also he's missing his wife and kids terribly. Their home is near Stratford and signing on for another two-year cycle will mean another long stint in London away from them. I point out that if he doesn't do the RSC season he'll get some other job which will inevitably entail London. Or he'll be unemployed. He says he'd be perfectly happy working on a farm so long as he was near his family.

I tell him how much I want him to play Buckingham. Our friendship goes back to Richard Eyre's 1976 Company at the Nottingham Playhouse. The rapport we'd bring to the Richard/Buckingham double-act would be invaluable. Mal says, 'The same could be said for the Shawcross/Sloman relationship in *The Party*. It would be great for me to make that first entrance out of the pile of cushions and find you there. I'll make a deal – you play Shawcross, I'll play Buckingham.'

I gulp. Then hear myself saying, 'All right.'

'You realise this could be the gun oil talking.'

'It isn't.'

'You'd do that?'

'Yup. If Shawcross is still available, that is.'

'Let's phone Howard now.'

'It's quarter past two.'

'He won't mind being woken with this news.'

We decide it might be better to leave it until the morning. Mal gets up to leave. He is in a state of strange euphoria – a mixture of the drink and our pact. He keeps on saying, 'You'd do that? You are sure it isn't the gun oil talking?' Mal on his feet is a formidable height. I stand with my neck craned back, saying, 'Yes I would. No it isn't.'

He says, 'I'll phone you in the morning before I tell Howard, just to check.'

'Wassamatter? You don't trust me?'

He hugs me. I disappear momentarily inside his vast anorak. He goes out in to the night saying, 'You'd do that?'

I go to bed wondering how the day has taken such an unexpected turn. It seemed so perfectly sorted out this afternoon. Slipping in the Snoo Wilson film between *Richard III* and the Wright/Barnes slot.

Wonder what I'll feel like in the morning.

Wednesday 1 February

I wake. Someone is kneeling very gently on my forehead. From the inside. I sit up. I lie down again. Stay very still. A distant memory trudging through the slushy grey paddy-fields. Suddenly something much worse than the hangover. Sit bolt upright. What have I done? Struggle downstairs, head lolling, feet flopping.

Phone Mal nervously: 'Mal?'

'Tony!'

'How are you this morning?'

'Fine. You?'

'Oh, a little shaky. Listen uhm . . .'

Long pause. I can hear him smiling. He says, 'Yes?'

'Uhm . . . I think it *was* the gun oil talking.'

He takes it very well, says, 'We're back to square one, then. I've got to do some serious thinking over the next few days.'

Thursday 2 February

GARRICK CLUB A literary lunch. I've been approached by Antony Harwood of Chatto & Windus to write and illustrate a book on the next part I play. I've told him about *Richard III* and he thinks this might be ideal. Also present at lunch is Giles Gordon, who is to be my literary agent.

I agree to the book in principle, but say I won't go ahead with it unless the production is a success. They agree to wait until after it opens. A man comes into the dining-room to tell us that the head of Chatto is by chance lunching here today as well, and would like to say hello. Carmen Callil.

Her name is spoken with fear and respect in the literary world. Australian, feminist, friend to Germaine Greer. In the Garrick, women are still barred from some of the rooms at lunchtime, including this dining-room. I am warned she could therefore be at her most fearsome today. We hurry to her call.

She turns out to be small, dark, attractive, not much older than me, not at all frightening-looking. But nevertheless Giles and Antony both stand with their hands behind their backs like schoolboys. This makes me nervous, so I stand to attention.

They discuss a possible schedule for the book: Giles wants it brought out within two months of delivery to catch some of the Stratford trade. This does make Carmen quite aggressive. 'Two months! You know perfectly well that's impossible, Giles. I wouldn't insult the author by rushing it through like that. D'you think any of the others would? Faber, Methuen?'

'Here is Methuen,' said Giles, 'let's ask him.'

We all turn round to find a man with a large beard sitting behind us reading. He looks up and smiles as if to say, 'It's all right, I wasn't listening.'

Friday 3 February
Jim brings me back an RSC leaflet from *Merchant* rehearsals. Strange to see *Richard III* in print and to see my life mapped out until September. The first preview is on my birthday, 14 June, which must be a good sign.

Sunday 5 February
'The World at War' on telly; an episode called 'Inside the Third Reich'. A lot of footage I hadn't seen before. Goebbels seen doing some spectacular rabble-rousing. He is crippled and would have been a good model for Richard III if I was going for a rodent. Wish I'd kept a closer watch on this series. I've missed the one on Mussolini, who's a better, bull-like model. Hitler himself seems too obvious, but there are interesting shots of him looking old and tired towards the end. A secretary describes him after the defeat in Russia – sitting still, staring at the floor. This could be useful for the last movement of the play. I've been wondering what new note I could hit as Richard starts to lose his grip. The answer could be a stillness, a manic-depressive slump. Could pay off well for the final oration to the soldiers. He begins slowly, quietly, halting. It looks like he's forgotten his words, he's not going to make it. Then gradually we see the

"Inside the Third Reich"

old power and charisma flooding back and the speech becomes awesome – Hitlerian.

From *Mein Kampf*: 'If we cannot conquer we will drag the world into destruction.'

From *Richard III*: 'March on! Join bravely. Let us to it pell-mell – If not to Heaven, then hand in hand to hell!'

After the failed assassination attempt they filmed the executions of the conspirators (particularly gruesome – they were hung with piano wire from meat hooks) for Hitler to watch on his own. Richard must do something equally kinky with Hastings' head.

Also footage of the mentally ill whom the Reich tried to eliminate as part of their programme to purify the race. Richard's appearance should make you gasp like these faces. Perhaps ears are the answer to the make-up. Can make the face look very odd and lopsided, and would hardly interfere with the acting.

Mal rings to say he's decided to do the season. Great relief.

Monday 6 February
Charlotte has arranged two research trips for the next two days: today to a spastics' work centre, tomorrow to a disabled games group.

Driving to pick her up in Chiswick, a strange coincidence: I round the corner to see a badly disabled man struggling along the pavement, his walk a weaving dance. I screech to a halt, whip out my sketch pad and, from my rear-view mirror, begin drawing furiously. A woman standing at

a bus stop bends down and peers into my car suspiciously. I fumble for my *A–Z* and disguise my sketch within it, while pretending to be lost. The disabled man passes. I sketch him from behind as he struggles on. Looks rather like the crippled man in *Satyricon*. The effort of walking is so extreme that it's as if the body is all disconnected. He has to sit on a low wall to rest. An attractive blonde woman passes him. He says something and reaches for her. She breaks into a little run.

Lady Anne?

CENTRAL MIDDLESEX WORKS CENTRE A small pre-fab building on a rather bleak hill near Pinner. It's run by Barrie Knight. He is very impressive to meet. Caring, patient, listens carefully. He tells us his own story: no medical training, was an engineer, only got interested in the subject when his own son was born spastic. Eventually led to running this place where his engineering skills are used in adapting machines for the spastics to operate. They come here daily and are paid wages.

He explains what the term 'spastic' means: damage to the brain before it is fully developed, causing physical and/or mental disability. The muscles don't behave in their normal way; the voice is often but not always affected. The initial damage is caused either by a lack of oxygen at birth or by the baby falling or being dropped at an early age. He mentions that spastics' hands are very distinctive, they develop extreme flexibility and their grip might be more intense and vice-like than a normal person.

Some of this is feasible for Richard.

Against my better judgement it has been agreed that, if questioned, I shouldn't declare my reason for being here but should say that I'm a friend of Charlotte's, who is a physiotherapist. My natural squeamishness makes me apprehensive as we head for the work area. 'And be careful,' Barrie whispers, 'they're all very good lip-readers.'

Charlotte's medical training enables her to plunge straight in, going round the benches chatting, asking what they're making. I start to follow nervously when a hand shoots out and grabs my arm. 'Good,' whispers Barrie, 'now you'll see what I mean about the grip.' And he leaves me.

It's a baptism by fire. The grip belongs to Michael, one of the most severely handicapped people in the room. Scrunched in his wheelchair, head lolling back, teeth gnashing, mouth grimacing (almost grinning) with the effort to speak, saliva dripping freely on to his jumper. I say, 'Hello. What are you making?' On his bench is a little machine that presses screws through black rubber washers. He gives me a demonstration. With hands shaking and jerking, mouth biting and chewing, he struggles to get the items into place on the machine. Each time he succeeds he accidentally knocks them away again. I could so easily reach down and do the job in two seconds. At last it's done – a black rubber foot with a screw through it rolls out of the press and joins the little pile that is his morning's work. He sits back panting and smiling. His dark eyes are bright.

I move on. It gets easier. A lot of them smile very readily, their grins are infectious, cheeky. One man works a large noisy machine and has to wear a special mask and goggles because of the dust. 'And these?' I shout over the din, pointing at his ear-pieces, 'Are they for the noise?' He lifts his jacket to show a Sony Walkman, and grins.

A man in a wheelchair beckons us over, whispers conspiratorially, 'I've got a walking frame as well, but I'm back in the wheely today, they say I'm getting too independent.'

But one figure is disturbing. He has been silently following us since we came in, watching from behind the pillars.

Trying to keep any panic out of my voice, I ask Barrie about him. He turns out to be titled aristocracy, or more accurately, has just inherited the family title after his father's recent suicide. The father was a high ranking army officer. The only outings he had as a child were to the barracks – hence the upright bearing. The rest of the time he was hidden away by two aunts in a back room of their house. Now they have died as well and he has come here. But Barrie fears that too much isolation has taken its toll.

He is seated at his place now, head occasionally moving from side to side as if repeating 'No' slowly. I glance over his shoulder at the little book which he constantly carries. It's an appointments diary, with no entries. He looks up at me. I risk a smile. Much to my surprise his face lights up briefly, he grins and looks away bashfully.

We get into conversation with a middle-aged man working a much more complicated machine than the others. He is angry: 'I'm not mental. Like a lot of them in here. So there's no one to communicate with. Have to keep to myself.' His speech is badly impaired and his movements convulsive, but there is a constant struggle to control it. When saliva threatens to slip out of his mouth he'll toss his head back and swallow it rather than permit any further degradation. He is proud of his blue jumper with red deers which he knitted himself, and of the fact that at home he has to look after his sister who has a bad heart condition. 'Life is unfair,' he says.

As we are about to move on he says to me, 'I know you. I know your face.'

'Really?' Try to remain relaxed. He probably watches television and has seen me in *The History Man* or something. But I'm hardly ever recognised.

'I can't think where I've seen you,' he says.

'I used to come for treatment at St Vincent's up the road. I had a leg injury a couple of years ago. Perhaps it was round there.'

'Perhaps,' he says, staring hard.

'Anyway, see you, good luck.' I hurry away, wishing I'd insisted on being open about why I'm here.

Run straight into more problems with a lady called Carol. Her job is counting brass plates. 'Count 'em in my sleep,' she says grinning. She has large beautiful eyes and a radiant smile. Her small body is strapped tightly into her wheelchair, where it arches and struggles as if independent of her head.

'Did you have a holiday last year?' she asks.

'Well actually yes, I went to South Africa for Christmas.'

'Are you from there?'

'Yes I am, originally.'

'I knew it!' she cries delightedly, 'I knew you weren't English.'

'Oh?' I say, a bit miffed.

'Have you been to Israel?' (My God, she's on to my Jewish past as well.)

'Yes I have.'

'Did you like it?'

'No, I didn't.'

'I want to live there.'

'Really.'

'What do you do?'

'Well, Charlotte's a visiting physiotherapist and I'm a friend of hers.'

'Is that your profession?'

I laugh nervously. 'No, I'm an artist.'

'Where do you work?'

'I . . . work at home. I'm a freelance artist.'

To prove my alibi I take out my sketch book, go into a corner of the

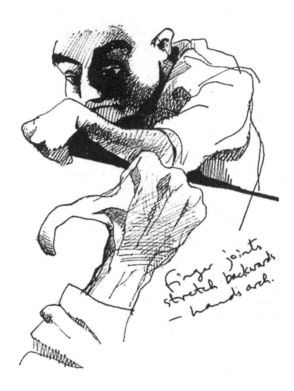

Finger joints stretch backwards – hands arch.

room and start sketching. Barrie had said this would be all right. No one takes any notice, except Carol, who keeps grinning at me, almost flirtatiously.

At 12.30 it's lunch time. They file out, a procession of strange walks that I would not dream of inventing. One walks as if treading water; another with splayed feet, the gait as if drunk; one has a walking stick with a splayed claw at the end – I could use that in the play.

Last out is the man who boasted about his walking frame – he has asked to be allowed to go to lunch on it, specially to show us. He moves past painfully slowly but with great pride. We stand nodding and smiling as if taking a salute. He turns into the corridor and we hear a terrible crash. We rush out to find him lying entangled in his walking frame, struggling. Charlotte is calm and professional: 'Oh dear – still, probably not the first time, how do you get up best?' He grins and puffs and says 'Not to worry', hauling himself up a series of rails along the wall. One of Barrie's assistants comes rushing down the corridor with this man's wheelchair, virtually scoops him into it and drives him off to lunch muttering 'Told you so . . .'

Barrie comes alongside us smiling gently. Points to another man who is wearing a crash helmet. He has fallen over so often his face is cut and bruised like a boxer's – his hands are twisted in such a way that he cannot break his falls.

Barrie says we're welcome to come back whenever we like. There's a Richard III lookalike whom he feels we should see but who isn't here today. We thank him and leave.

Drive back quite dazed.

Tuesday 7 February

Charlotte comes round to the house before this evening's visit to the disabled games group.

'Was yesterday of any use?' she asks.

'Oh yes. But I don't think Richard is a spastic.'

'No.'

'The condition is too convulsive.'

She explains in detail about hunchbacks. Often the condition doesn't arise until adolescence (and most commonly among girls). There are two types: scoliosis, and kyphosis.

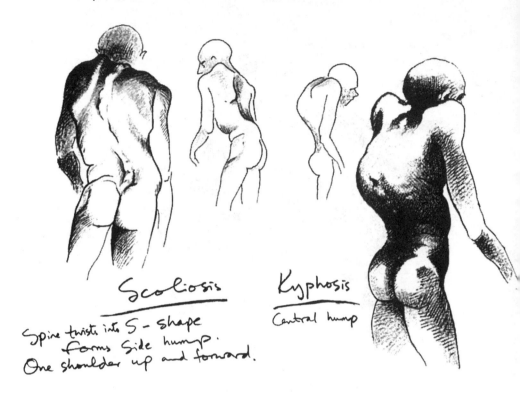

Scoliosis
Spine twists into S - shape
forms Side hump.
One shoulder up and forward.

Kyphosis
Central hump

I instantly decide on the latter. It's what I've been drawing. The bottled spider, the bull. And it's different from Olivier.

'Anyway,' says Charlotte, 'tonight there'll be a much wider range. Every kind of disability, the mentally ill, the blind, everything.'

'Right,' I say, and down a stiff vodka tonic.

KING EDWARD'S SCHOOL, HAMPSTEAD We wander through the large dark grounds until we find a brightly lit hall with a fleet of ambulances parked outside.

The place is buzzing with activity: bowls, table tennis, badminton and various board games. Also a rather ferocious game of hockey – a crowd of people charging around wielding sticks, some on foot, some in wheelchairs. One of the players stops, grins and waves her stick at us: Carol, from the works centre yesterday, who interrogated me so thoroughly.

Charlotte starts to giggle. 'She's going to wonder why we've turned up again.'

I wave back and whisper through a clenched smile, 'Careful. Remember the lip-reading.'

The organiser, a friend of Charlotte's, comes bounding over from the game, sweating heavily. Charlotte introduces him by his nickname, Bones. He's a policeman and does this in his spare time. Tall, well built, rugged good looks of a movie star. His manner is rather brusque: 'We don't do any molly-coddling here, they have to get off their arses and do a bit.' But he's very gentle with them, reassuring, encouraging, very tactile, pretending to bully, but with a Hollywood smile that makes all swoon before him.

Here comes trouble – Carol's helper is wheeling her over. Charlotte smiles and deserts me.

'What are you doing here?' Carol asks.

'Oh, I'm ... well, it's Charlotte, actually. She's a visiting physio –'

'Will you be coming back to the works centre?'

'Yes, I might.'

'Why?'

'Barrie suggested I should.'

'But why?'

'It was Barrie's suggestion.'

'But what are you *doing*?'

'I'm a freelance-artist-friend of Charlotte's. Excuse me.'

As I disengage myself I can't help thinking that this has been a perfect demonstration of Mike Leigh's golden rule for research – always tell the truth about why you're there.

My attention is constantly drawn to a group of three who ignore all the games and remain totally private. In the middle is a man of about fifty. His arms are around a young, frail, dark-haired girl on one side, an older red-haired woman on the other. They move around the hall, heads close together, whispering.

Bones suggests a visit to the archery club in another hall. He dons an anorak, lights a cigarette, tells me how the whole thing started as a small venture and has grown and grown. His endless battles to get money from the council, to organise transport, to find helpers. The ratio has to be one helper to two disabled. I tell him that I couldn't distinguish the disabled from the helpers.

'That's because a lot of them are mentally retarded,' he says, 'and there's no visible disability. When new helpers start, I make it a point not to tell them who's got what wrong. Let the two sides just meet as people.'

At the archery club they sit in a line of wheelchairs. The skill is surprising. One young man is blind in one eye and severely spastic. He battles to fit the arrow in place and then, as he aims, it weaves around

dangerously. I try not to flinch as it strays over his shoulder towards me. But when at last he fires, it is with superb accuracy. Another young man with frail bony features sits in a strange state: he lifts his bow slowly, fits an arrow, considers it carefully, unfits it, lowers his bow, never fires.

Back at the main hall, there are several newcomers. One of the new helpers is a policeman in uniform, a tubby cheerful man who laughs a lot. He twists his cap back to front, does Goon voices, 'Hulloooo, I'm Neddy Seagooooon', mimes karate chops at a thalidomide lady passing in a wheelchair. Another new face is a boy called Gordon with a thin ginger moustache and puffy eyes with scars round them. There is a sense of suppressed violence about him. Someone bumps into him and he says in a quiet, clenched voice, 'I'm very calm. I'm very calm.' The laughing policeman aims a karate chop at him. I hold my breath. But Gordon just says 'Yeah', and moves away.

The threesome sit huddled on a bench in a corner. They share a cigarette, passing it around like a joint. I ask Bones about them. The young girl is the sister of the boy who never fired his arrow. She is partially blind. The man in the middle is completely blind and partially deaf. The red-haired woman is mentally retarded. They each come from different institutions and live for these Tuesday nights. 'We get a lot of love affairs starting here,' says Bones, 'and why not?'

I can start sketching. Enough time has passed, I've blended in. Clamber up on to an exercise horse, an ideal place because no one can peer over my shoulder. Constantly looking over towards me, smiling, curious, flirting, Carol is the only one who takes any notice of me.

Home time. The red-haired lady from the threesome fetches their coats. They rise and almost as one, weave into the arms, hoods, scarves. It looks like they're climbing into one huge garment that will bind them even closer together. But now comes the time for them to be separated into different ambulances.

I have seen enough. I thank Charlotte and Bones, and leave.

Reading the play in bed, the first scene now seems very familiar. A disabled man sitting in the sun, grumbling to the audience about his lot (the man yesterday who said, 'Life is unfair'). Powerless to stop his brother being taken to prison, he makes a few jokes to cheer him up. Passes the time of day with Hastings: 'What news abroad?'

I remember now that my first thought of yesterday was: are these people smiling, or are they in pain, or are they bearing their teeth like animals do when threatened? All these expressions are similar. Grinning or grimacing.

I had set out to look for a physical shape, but maybe what I found is something about *being* disabled.

Thursday 9 February

I *am* going to have to give up smoking and get fitter than ever. And then keep it up for two years. God.

Jim says I should treat it like an athlete's training for the Olympics, says it's important enough for me to give up alcohol and go on to special foods.

In the meantime, Bill comes to dinner, we drink a lot of wine, smoke a lot of cigarettes, and he prepares to tell me what the *Richard III* set is going to be. 'I'm still a bit nervous about the idea,' he says, 'so forgive me if I have difficulty putting it into words.' And indeed he goes into a very long preamble about religion in the Middle Ages while I sit on the edge of my seat stopping myself from screaming 'Yes, but what's it going to be?' His eyes are gleaming with excitement and tension. I do know how he feels: it's the moment when you have to speak aloud an idea that you've been nurturing alone and you know the other person's face is instantly going to tell you whether they think it's a very good idea or a very bad one. The two are often separated by a hair's breadth.

At last: the play is going to be set in a cathedral, with tombs of dead kings and high stained glass windows. Obviously it will be a perfect setting for the religious scenes, but he also wants to use it non-realistically, as if the play is being done as a medieval morality play, so that the battle at Bosworth can take place among the tombs – the final duel, St George and the Dragon.

The concept is stunning, it grips my imagination. As we discovered late in *Tartuffe* rehearsals, the other side of religion is a grotesque world of gargoyles and demons. Perfect for *Richard III*. For much of the early part of the play he feigns piety; the wretched cripple who is forced out of the sensual world into the spiritual one, a holy fool.

Now it's my turn. I show Bill three sketches: the bottled spider, the head I drew in Hermanus, and Ronnie Kray. I try the crutches idea on him again and find myself describing a concept which is clearly in the spider drawing, but which I hadn't actually realised until now: 'We play him as a four-legged creature.' In the text there are many animal references – boar, hog, toad, spider, hedgehog, and best of all (given the cathedral setting), 'Hell-hound'.

Bill says quietly, 'This is terribly exciting.' He reckons that playing Richard as monstrous as this solves in one stroke the biggest problem in the play – *why* is he so evil? Also he points out that Richard's deformity is only ever mentioned by the others in moments of impassioned cursing, as if it's so extreme that it's normally unmentionable. So when Margaret really lets rip in Act 1, Scene iii, the others can shield their eyes and think, 'Oh shit, she hasn't gone and mentioned *that*.'

Without prompting, Bill uses a description I wrote ages ago in Hermanus: 'His appearance should provoke both pity and terror.' This keeps happening in our collaboration – thinking as one.

He stares at my sketch of the bottled spider and wonders whether we could actually create this image, throw a giant shadow on the wall.

I say, 'I'm afraid we used it in *King Lear* – the front-cloth scene.'

'Ah yes. Adrian Noble has already done it. True of so many things these days.' He looks up and grins. It's a source of mild inconvenience, not bitter envy. Bill is not an ambitious man.

He leaves, but the excitement we have generated remains. His reaction to the spider drawing was so positive. Maybe I have found my nightmare creature. And now there is a setting for him – this spooky church.

Monday 13 February

Spend all day doing line run-throughs of *Maydays*. It's been nine weeks since we last did it. An awful lot has happened to us all since then – *Peter Pan*, *Tempest*, *Much Ado*, *Molière*, *Tartuffe* video, and so on.

KING'S HEAD PUB, BARBICAN Before the show, first meeting with our designer, Bill Dudley. An unexpected personality, but then all designers are the least theatrical, the least neurotic members of the profession. Or at any rate, their suffering is conducted in the privacy of their workrooms or the dark of the auditorium. Bill has an East End accent, a passion for playing his piano accordion in a band that tours pubs, and the hugest eyebrows I've ever seen. He says he thought so too until he met Denis Healey at a party. As they leant forward in discussion it was like two stags about to lock antlers.

He's extremely well read and points me towards two accounts of the real Richard III: Robert Louis Stevenson's *The Black Arrow* and Josephine Tey's *The Daughter of Time*. He tells me that next year is the 500th anniversary of Richard's death. He loves words. 'Plantagenet,' he says, savouring it, 'innit great he's called Plantagenet? It's a French flower and yet he's this deformed grotesque.'

He is very taken with the bottled-spider sketch and says he could take it further by designing long hanging sleeves which would make the creature six legged. He doesn't like the thick, club feet in the drawing though, says they could be twisted but must remain quite delicate. 'You should have a sense of him being able to move very nimbly at great speed, straight up the side of a wall if he wanted to.' I don't want the image to become too exclusively spider-like. There must be something of the bull as well. Bill A. points out that bulls have quite slender, delicate legs.

I say, 'At the moment I see him moving quite slowly, heavily.'

Bill A. looks worried: 'But with agility.'

'Well no. Cripples aren't agile. We went through all of this with the Fool. Decided to make him crippled, yet he had to be very speedy with it. It becomes an enormous strain and isn't strictly feasible. I spent a lot of last week among the disabled and didn't see many of them whizzing about. What is it you fear if Richard was quite static?'

'He'd lose the power to surprise.'

This matter is left unresolved as we pass on to the drawings of the head. Bill Dudley is less keen on these, particularly dislikes the heavy forehead on the Hermanus head – 'Looks like Marlon Brando on a bad day.' And pointing to the Ronnie Kray drawing, 'If you look like this, would it suggest a fine and brilliant mind?'

'But isn't that a good thing?' I say. 'He's got this battered boxer's face, this warrior's face. He shouldn't *look* cunning.'

'You're making your job very hard.' He is keen to keep my face long and sharp, to emphasise it with a long wig. This is also left unresolved.

Bill A. asks whether the hump could be made well enough to be shown naked. He's keen to use the church setting to stage the coronation, and in researching has found that Richard and Anne were stripped naked for the anointing ceremony. This is a very exciting image: Richard's back twisted and mountainous, Anne's perfect and beautiful. Beauty and the Beast.

The nerves backstage for *Maydays* are almost worse than for the first performance. It's the closest real-life version of the nightmare all actors have: you're going on stage and the show is only vaguely familiar. But an enthusiastic audience sweeps us along and most of the lines are remembered.

I used herbal cigarettes in the show tonight and will do so from now on. *Maydays* will no longer be able to pass as my excuse for remaining a smoker.

Tuesday 14 February

In Bernard Levin's interview with Ralph Richardson on his eightieth birthday, the great actor said: 'A play always reminds me of an enormous

roller at the top of some hill. Someone takes the blocks away and it begins
to roll inevitably down to its end. Maybe its end is destruction or maybe
it's brought to a halt by a beautiful finish, but it never stops moving and
you're on it all the time . . . Playing with time, which is the most precious
yet the most mysterious element we know. Dear friendly water we know
a great deal about. It's so simple and domestic. But time . . . we don't
know where it begins or where it ends. And to play with it is very thrilling.
When that curtain goes up, time starts for you, you're moving with that
roller and you cannot get off it . . .'

Tonight in *Maydays* the roller is stopped. During the second interval a
power box explodes and the trucks, which carry the sets on and off, freeze
in their tracks. The audience are sent back to the bars and plied with free
drinks, while the stage staff desperately work to restore life to the machinery. People rushing around with torches trying to find the blown fuse. It
goes on for over half an hour, the audience reassemble in the auditorium,
but backstage they have to admit defeat. They can't find the right fuse.

It's the job of the front-of-house manager to break the news to the
audience, but he gets stage fright and refuses to go out and face them.
Then I am asked, but the thought of stepping out there as *myself* is
unthinkable. Finally the stage-manager volunteers to do the deed. The
audience is understandably furious. They have seen three quarters of the
play but will have to come back another night to find out what happens.

They have their money refunded. The cast flock to the pub. An odd
feeling – a cross between the joy of truancy and the frustration of coitus
interruptus.

Struggling into the car-park with the two pairs of crutches that Charlotte
has sent me, when Alison Steadman drives out. She stops in horror.

'Richard III,' I offer as an explanation.

She nods wisely. 'Mike Leigh will be proud of you.'

Back at home I nervously experiment, fearing that they might instantly
prove impractical. The elbow crutches are much better than the armpit
variety, because you can let go and use your hands while they hang from
your forearms. Swinging along on them, stretching like an animal on four
legs, pawing the ground, rearing up on hind legs, I find they have a
marvellous range of possibilities.

Friday 17 February
We're re-rehearsing *Tartuffe* – yet again.

Chris Benjamin is taking over as Orgon and is going to be wonderful, a big baby, a bear ready to chase its shadow. As Dorine says in the play, 'Tartuffe is a man who can spot a victim.' Chris is a natural victim, Nigel never was – his inherent sophistication and wit got in the way. He was a hilarious Orgon, but it was always difficult to believe he could be so thoroughly duped – at any rate, by my version of Tartuffe. People want Tartuffe to be a subtle creature despite all the evidence in the text. The blatancy of his villainy offends modern tastes. And we have actually extended it – he's not just a villain but a demon.

During the chase scene I pull a muscle in my neck. After last year's accident even the slightest injury fills me with terror. I try to ignore it and head off for the gym. Exercising makes it feel a little better.

RIVERSIDE STUDIOS *The Biko Trial.* Strange to see this South African atrocity performed by a group of English stars, lead by Albert Finney. Rather like those Hollywood epics where you're constantly distracted from the storyline by some superstar popping in to do their cameo. However the story does come through and it's terribly, horribly, gruesomely funny. A black man in the front row doesn't see the funny side at all; he winces and glances round each time the audience bellows.

Back at home, a video treat – two episodes of David Attenborough's *The Living Planet.* You can find any character by watching animals.

Insects rubbing their front legs together – could do that with the crutches. Spiders move in a nimble dance, their legs going like fingers on a keyboard, they rotate on the spot. Too lightweight for Richard, I think.

Weekend 18–19 February
Beautiful winter days. Cold clear sunlight. Immobilised by my neck, I stay indoors and watch the three parts of *Henry VI* made for the BBC Shakespeare series. (Couldn't face reading them all; the boring homework side of acting.) Am expecting to fast-forward through most of it and just concentrate on the young Richard, but get hooked early on and end up watching all nine hours of it. Bernard Hill's performance is brilliant as York, Richard's father, glowing with anger, a formidable soldier whom the young Richard worships. Fascinating having my character's background fleshed out like this.

Depressing to see how much dashing around battlefields Richard has to do; unlikely on crutches and no evidence that he's always relied on a-horse-a-horse. But I suppose his condition could have got worse in later life. Crutches suggest war veteran as well.

Monday 20 February
A heavy week ahead – five *Tartuffe*'s, three *Maydays*, rehearsing the telly *Molière* at the Beeb during the days, and my neck getting worse.

BARBICAN Meet Derek Jacobi in the lift. Tonight is his first Cyrano in twelve weeks and he's rather frightened. Says it doesn't help having won all those awards, there will be an added expectancy from the audience. 'I feel like lining up all the statuettes on the front of the stage and letting them get on with it.'

Lunch with Bill. Discuss the crutches in the light of what the young Richard has to do in *Henry VI*. Is the problem relevant? Does an actor playing Antony in *Antony and Cleopatra* have to cross-check his performance against the same character in *Julius Caesar*? But even if we justify it ourselves, is an audience going to sit there worrying? Bill is not a lot of help; his current worry is that he and the RSC musical director, Guy Woolfenden, are having to change all their ideas for the music because *Merchant* is using organ music and *Henry V* is using Gregorian chants. Very annoying when our set is calling out for that kind of music. Still, these constraints can sometimes lead to inventive solutions.

Even more annoying is the news that the Gobbos in *Merchant* are being played as hunchbacks!

TARTUFFE Chris's first performance. He does wonders. What a joy to do this show in the theatre again. The audience are completely hysterical and inevitably the laughter seduces me away from any subtleties I discovered for the telly version. It's back to tail-wagging acting.

Anyway, as Cocteau said: 'What others criticise you for, cultivate. It is *you*.'

Tuesday 21 February
Wake hardly able to move my neck at all. Ring Charlotte and make an appointment. A sense of defeat, having to admit I've injured myself again.

ACTON HILTON *Molière*'s first day in the studio. Bill talks about the play as 'a fairy tale going sour', taking the starting point from Bulgakov's description of 'the spectral fairy tale Paris of the seventeenth century'. The new sets will evoke this – long corridors with false perspectives, the dressing-rooms with rows and rows of masks like a constant audience. Alice in Kafkaland.

CANTEEN I'm having my lunch when I hear a familiar hoarse shout, 'Oy

– Tony!' I whip round, damaging my neck further, to see Michael Gambon
in the lunch queue . . .

Alan Howard (a previous Richard III at the RSC) is standing in front
of him, puzzled as to *who* is being sent up.

Wonderful seeing Gambon again. He and Howard have been rehearsing
a play here. They've just heard it's been cancelled because of the scene-
shifters' strike. Everyone assures us that it will be over by the time we go
into studio in four weeks.

Gambon tells me the story of Olivier auditioning him at the Old Vic in
1962. His audition speech was from *Richard III*. 'See Tone, I was thick
as two short planks then and I didn't know he'd had a rather notable
success in the part. I was just shitting myself about meeting the Great
Man. He sussed how green I was and started farting around.'

As reported by Gambon, their conversation went like this:

Olivier: 'What are you going to do for me?'

Gambon: 'Richard the Third.'

Olivier: 'Is that so. Which part?'

Gambon: 'Richard the Third.'

Olivier: 'Yes, but which part?'

Gambon: 'Richard the Third.'

Olivier: 'Yes, I understand that, but which part?'

Gambon: 'Richard the Third.'

Olivier: 'But which *character*? Catesby? Ratcliffe? Buckingham's a good part . . .'

Gambon: 'Oh I see, beg your pardon, no, Richard the Third '

Olivier: 'What, the King? Richard?'

Gambon: '– the Third, yeah.'

Olivier: 'You've got a fucking cheek, haven't you?'

Gambon: 'Beg your pardon?'

Olivier: 'Never mind, which part are you going to do?'

Gambon: 'Richard the Third.'

Olivier: 'Don't start that again. Which *speech*?'

Gambon: 'Oh I see, beg your pardon, "Was ever woman in this humour woo'd." '

Olivier: 'Right. Whenever you're ready.'

Gambon: ' "Was ever woman in this humour woo'd –" '

Olivier: 'Wait. Stop. You're too close. Go further away. I need to see the whole shape, get the full perspective.'

Gambon: 'Oh I see, beg your pardon . . .' Gambon continues, 'So I go over to the far end of the room, Tone, thinking that I've already made an almighty tit of myself, so how do I save the day? Well I see this pillar and I decide to swing round it and start the speech with a sort of dramatic punch. But as I do this my ring catches on a screw and half my sodding hand gets left behind. I think to myself, "Now I mustn't let this throw me since he's already got me down as a bit of an arsehole", so I plough on . . . "Was ever woman in this humour woo'd –" '

Olivier: 'Wait. Stop. What's the blood?'

Gambon: 'Nothing, nothing, just a little gash, I do beg your pardon . . .'

A nurse had to be called and he suffered the indignity of being given first aid with the greatest actor in the world passing the bandages. At last it was done.

Gambon: 'Shall I start again?'

Olivier: 'No. I think I've got a fair idea how you're going to do it. You'd better get along now. We'll let you know.'

Gambon went back to the engineering factory in Islington where he was working. At four that afternoon he was bent over his lathe, working as best as he could with a heavily bandaged hand, when he was called to the phone. It was the Old Vic.

'It's not easy talking on the phone, Tone. One, there's the noise of the machinery. Two, I have to keep my voice down 'cause I'm cockney at work and posh with theatre people. But they offer me a job, spear-carrying, starting immediately. I go back to my work-bench, heart beating in my chest, pack my tool-case, start to go. The foreman comes up, says, "Oy, where you off to?" "I've had bad news," I say, "I've got to go." He says, "Why are you taking your tool box?" I say, "I can't tell you, it's very bad news, might need it." And I never went back there, Tone. Home on the bus, heart still thumping away. A whole new world ahead. We tend to forget what it felt like in the beginning.'

78 HARLEY STREET I haven't been back here since my accident. The entrance hall with marble staircase. The old woman in a white coat sitting at the reception desk, who looks up and asks, 'Mister –?' The grand waiting-room, freezing cold. One or two Arabs asleep, dreaming of warmer places. False books on the shelves. The same old copies of *Country Life*, Sotheby's Previews, South African *Panorama*.

Completely different atmosphere in the Remedial Dance Clinic itself. Cups of coffee (sometimes champagne) and gossip from the dance world. The physios are attractive blonde girls in jeans or track suits, the patients are proud and beautiful dancers – their injuries seem to make them even haughtier.

Charlotte diagnoses a sprained neck ligament. She explains: 'You know when you eat oxtail stew, well those little horns that stick out the side . . .' I warn her that if she carries on I will pass out and I'm feeling inadequate enough surrounded by these beautiful people. I have a good old moan about being injured again. Charlotte suggests I should take it in my stride like dancers or sportsmen. They accept injury and repair as part of their jobs. Actors only think to train their voices properly.

'But what's the point of all these months at the gym,' I winge, 'if I'm still getting injured?'

'If you hadn't been going to the gym, the injuries would be more frequent and far worse. This is the first since the tendon. Given that your performances are so physical, that's not bad going.'

She attaches suction cups from the interferential machine and sets the various currents in motion ('This will be a gentle throbbing, this pins and needles, this like champagne bubbles . . .'). I lie there being gently electrocuted, jerking and jumping, while she expounds her latest Richard III theory – polio. She does a very impressive impersonation on crutches. Her calves and feet soft and floppy, each step achieved by throwing the leg forward from the hip. It looks like Douglas Bader and could be misread as false legs. But an advantage is that the movement is quite variable and would avoid specific repetitive strain. A problem would be creating an illusion of the muscle wastage which, she says, characterises the disease.

Friday 24 February
Bill A. says he's been talking to Bill D. and they're both worried about my drawings for Richard's head. 'The trouble is there's no relation to your own features. It's just another whole head plonked on yours.' Suggests I think about a boar's head, perhaps with a beard high on the cheekbones and a spiky wig. I seem to remember that Norman Rodway's image was boar-like in Terry's 1970 production.

I think what's happened is that both Bills have taken the Hermanus head too literally.

I try sketching another head alongside a self-portrait, giving it the minimum of prosthesis, and using my own hair, sleeked back. This is feasible.

Broken nose,
bags under eyes,
cauliflower ears,
harelip

Thursday 1 March
Dickie back for good from filming *Passage to India*. Lovely stories about
Lean, Ashcroft, Guinness. I try out some Richard ideas on him. The
usual reaction: 'Would he be able to go into battle on crutches?' I trust
Dickie's opinion so much this unnerves me. Am I trying to be too clever?

Saturday 3 March
Two *Tartuffe*'s. Overhear that in *Henry V* Harold Innocent is playing
Burgundy on two sticks. *Henry* using religious music and featuring a man
on sticks, *Merchant* having a religious setting, organ music and featuring
two hunchbacks . . . all this plunges me into a terrible gloom.

Hurry home to watch Lon Chaney's *Hunchback of Notre Dame*, hoping
there might be something to steal. But it's appalling. Why is it that silent
comedies have survived so well when silent drama has aged so pitifully?
Our sense of humour more constant than our sense of tragedy?

Monday 5 March
Increasingly difficult to play *Molière* in the theatre because we're rehearsing
the television version during the day. Tonight I found myself reaching for
props that weren't there and heading for a doorway that didn't exist. But
the audience was our best yet, effortlessly able to switch from the comedy
to the tragic melodrama, the laughter huge (like *Tartuffe* at times), the
silences crystal clear. At the end cheers, and we were called back for an
extra bow.

Molière has always been the runt in my litter – people unsure about
the play, my performance not really commented on – and hence my
favourite.

Nice to have him cheered tonight.

Tuesday 6 March
ACTON HILTON Mild grey weather. The Irish doorman says, 'Isn't it a
lovely soft day?' and Mal says, 'You can just taste spring on the air.'

Shows falling like flies because of the strike. *Terra Nova* cancelled last
week, *Titus Andronicus* this. The pattern is becoming familiar. Each cast
gets increasingly depressed as their studio dates approach; they are
discovered spending more and more time in the canteen, muttering 'Nuff
to make you vote Tory.' Then comes the day when they're finally cancelled
– at 11.30 in the morning they head off for the pub to get very pissed,
drowning the memory of all the wasted work.

With our own studio-dates ten days away, we're feeling rather apprehensive now.

Exhaustion of the last few weeks catching up with me. And it could all be for nothing, this frantic commuting along Westway, rehearsing, performing, squeezing in visits to the gym.

Thursday 8 March
KOTO JAPANESE RESTAURANT My dinner with Monty. We put Richard on the psychiatrist's couch and analyse him in depth.

I say, 'Tell me how you'd begin if he came to you as a patient.'

'Oi vey! All right, I suppose I would have to start with that mother.' He points out that there isn't a single moment in the play when the Duchess of York talks of Richard without contempt and hatred. She shows no maternal instincts whatever.

'What is it like to be hated by your mother?'

'Very similar to being loved too much. In both cases the mother prevents the child from developing an accurate sense of self. She distorts his view of himself.'

When Richard is in turmoil at the end of the play, in the speech after the ghosts, he keeps asking 'Who am I?' Monty explains that, as Richard hasn't received love as a child, he won't be able to show any himself; hence his contempt for human life. 'What would it feel like to be a mass-murderer?' I ask

'They *feel* very little. Each murder is an attempt to feel, if you like, an attempt to release anger, an attempt at catharsis, and each time it is unrelieved. It's like promiscuous sex, sex without love, without feeling. Each climax is less and less fulfilling so the appetite grows until it's insatiable.' Monty says that, reading the play again, there is less pain and anger in the character than he had originally thought.

I ask, 'Is that because Shakespeare has given him too pronounced a sense of humour? Does that make him ghoulish, inhuman?'

'On the contrary. It makes him very human. He can make us laugh, yet commits terrible crimes. We don't like that. We want killers to be monstrous, inexplicable, inhuman. But how you go about making an audience cry for him as well as rejoicing in his humour, that I don't know.'

'I don't either. But I think it's something to do with disturbing them. By not making his humour too comfortable.'

'Good. I like the sound of that.'

Interesting to compare Monty's view of Richard with that of Stopford A. Brooke in his collection of essays, *On Ten Plays of Shakespeare*, published in 1905. He describes very precisely the worst way (in my opinion) one could play Richard's humour: 'a chuckling pleasure in his cunning'. Yet, strangely enough, he and Monty end up with a similar conclusion. Brooke: 'He who has no love has no true sense of right and wrong, and the absence of conscience in Richard is rooted to absence of love in him. The source of all his crime is the unmodified presence of self-alone.'

An absence of love. Caused by a hating mother. This is what I will base my performance on. But I will have to be quite secretive about it, because it sounds so corny – his mother didn't love him.

Saturday 10 March
Unusual encounter. A stranger wrote, asking to meet. He's an actor playing the little tomboy Cathy, the part I played, in *Cloud Nine*. I assume he will want to discuss the original Joint Stock workshop we did before Caryl Churchill wrote the play, and agree to meet him between shows today.

It quickly becomes apparent he has something else on his mind. He just needs to talk to someone and for some reason has chosen me. He tells me that he is a transsexual (I have to confess to him I'm not sure what that is; he explains it's wanting actually to change sex) and is finding the experience of doing the play traumatic. He's a man who wants to be a woman playing a little girl who wants to be a little boy. The current situation is only part of the problem. A change of sex is of course feasible, but would probably entail having to change professions as well. I'm very struck by his manner. Something beyond despair. He smiles calmly as he describes the hopelessness of the situation, his gaze is very trusting, open.

Monty was quite wrong: I haven't learnt any of his skills. I feel unable to make any useful suggestions, except therapy which he's already done – apparently the therapist was more embarrassed than him and had to look away for much of the time.

I was moved by the experience, inspired by his courage and grateful to have met him. If the *Shadey* film ever gets made and I play the part (which is a transsexual), this meeting will prove invaluable. As I write this it sounds vaguely exploitative, but I really don't believe it is. His openness was a revelation to me.

Monday 12 March

I'm reading one of the books which Bill Dudley suggested, *The Daughter of Time* by Josephine Tey. Although written as fiction it has become the bible of the Richard III Society (which is pledged to restoring his reputation in history). It would appear that the real Richard was a good king, a gentle soul, not at all deformed, and didn't kill the princes in the Tower. Richmond (later Henry VII) might have done it.

Shakespeare's source was Holinshed whose source was Thomas More's *History of King Richard the Third.* But More was only five when Richard succeeded to the throne and and eight when he was killed at Bosworth. His source was Morton, Bishop of Ely (he appears as a character in the play) who in real life hated Richard. Also, More was writing for the Tudors who wanted their claim to the throne made kosher, Richmond being the first Tudor.

An interesting read but useless for my purposes. Except that in the book a doctor studying the famous portrait of Richard diagnoses polio.

Tuesday 13 March

Last *Maydays*. I arrive at the stage door to find our author David Edgar and his wife there. David is so tall his head brushes most ceilings. He is chain-smoking as usual and wears a long grey scarf which itself looks like a giant curl of smoke from floor to ceiling. A joy to fall into the banter again.

David says, 'Ah, Sher. Why aren't you preparing for the performance? Doing aerobics or mirror-exercises with Alison Steadman or something. Shouldn't you be thinking your way into character?'

'I find with your writing it is advisable to leave that to the last possible moment.'

'Have you met my wife, my little wife? Darling, have you met this actor, this little actor? I am surrounded by all these little people. Oh, may I use your dressing-room? Make some adjustments to my person – not before time some would say.'

The show is efficient, workmanlike. Faintly disappointing like all last nights. We want it to be a definitive performance of the play, the same thing that we strive for on first nights. But no performance is ever definitive – the phenomenon doesn't exist.

I feel a sense of relief that it's over. I was proud to be in it and loved the rehearsals and early performances. But in these last few, hectically busy weeks it felt like climbing a mountain.

At the party, David Edgar thanks me and says, 'Although you were thirtieth or fortieth choice for Martin I want you to know that on several occasions when I saw it, you were quite, quite adequate.'

Wednesday 14 March
ACTON HILTON Technical run-through of *Molière*. A depressing, token affair because of the continuing strike. Everyone's heart out of it now. Only a third of the technicians turn up. They know and we know that it's not going to happen on Sunday. Have just to go through the motions until we're officially cancelled. Wig fittings next door; the hours spent stitching each hair into those things. Camera scripts arrive; the hours spent drawing up these. The infuriating, evil, sad waste of it all. Contingency plans discussed half-heartedly. Postponing is impossible. Many of the cast are off to Europe with *Much Ado* and Bond's *Lear*, Mal and Brian Parr off to Stratford to open in *Henry V* and *Merchant*, and then of course Bill and I start rehearsals for *Richard* next month.

Friday 16 March
ACTON HILTON Bill calls us into a circle. Cedric Messina stands up and announces that the strike has 'delivered the mortal blow' to the show and we're cancelled. Apparently there is a faint hope of doing it at an independent studio, as the production company is RKO and not the BBC. We vote to try for this even though it's fraught with problems. I've bad flu to add to my misery.

Saturday 17 March
Incredibly, they've made it work! In twenty-four hours Cedric and the RKO people have found an independent studio and the unions have agreed to allow us to use the sets – although built outside, they were designed by the BBC and, had they wanted to be difficult, the unions could have stopped us – as long as not a single member of the BBC staff is involved. Sadly, this means losing a lot of people who've worked devotedly on *Tartuffe* and this project: Tom Kingdon, Harbi Virdi, Peter Kondal, Cherry Alston and others. A new crew is being assembled and we start tomorrow as scheduled. *Molière* may be jinxed, but it's a survivor.

All day at the theatre, people congratulate us as if we had worked this miracle ourselves. Thumbs are held high across the Green Room, actors whoop and rush into one another's arms.

It's so beautifully American what's happened, so un-English: a refusal to be philosophical about defeat.

Sunday 18 March

LIMEHOUSE STUDIOS, CANARY WHARF, DOCKLANDS The day
spent doing run-throughs for the new technical team, which includes one
of the top lighting men in the country, John Treays. He's only agreed to
do it on condition that he gets next Saturday off for his wedding anniversary, so a helicopter is being supplied to fly him between here and his
country home.

The studio is a converted warehouse in the docklands. The canteen is
on a barge which, as everyone who works here will immediately tell you,
used to be a floating brothel.

Monday – Monday, 19 – 26 March

TELEVISING MOLIÈRE A strict discipline, no booze, no cigarettes. I
need all my energy for a schedule that starts with a make-up call at 7.00
a.m., then televising all day and evening, or else a performance at the
theatre.

It's so sad that the BBC set designer, Cecilia Bereton, won't even be
allowed a credit for these astonishing sets. She's understood the play
perfectly. And Treays lights them like an Old Master.

The new production team do wonders (they have learned the show in
twenty-four hours), but are forced to resort to television's worst habit –
every take is followed by the chorus 'Absolutely marvellous!' Praise tossed
at us like an anaesthetic; it creates a vacuum, makes one lose all sense of
perspective. Once again the clock is uppermost in everyone's mind. The
acting is snatched at and first takes are almost always accepted. I fear for
my performance.

Another problem is the make-up. Elaborate tests, which had been set
up at the Beeb, got cancelled with the show. So the make-up team are
working blind, not knowing the characters, style of the piece, anything.
My first big make-up change into the old, dying Molière (half his face
paralysed from a stroke) happens mid-afternoon on the second day. While
the studio waits with growing impatience, my poor make-up girl, Hilary,
has to improvise her way through this complicated transformation. Envoys
are sent, beads of sweat on their foreheads, teeth gritted into horribly
calm smiles: 'Can we say fifteen minutes?'

'Say what you like,' says Hils, 'we'll be down when we're ready.'

I'm not happy with the end result – the wrinkles lie one-dimensionally
on the skin rather than the face bunching and denting like it does in old
age. This is becoming an increasing problem for me. I cannot perform
with a face less good than I myself have sketched.

We have a little pow-wow on the studio floor. Bill is frank with me ('We're running out of time, Tony'), others are more patronising: 'Everyone in the control box thinks it looks *absolutely marvellous*. Would they let you go on if it wasn't *absolutely marvellous?*' Of course they would, anything to beat the clock. I say, 'Look, never mind, let's just do it' – angry, disappointed, hating the idea that people are whispering, 'Queeeeny Actorrr.'

They are rushing so much now that they forget to tell us that we're doing a take and not a rehearsal. It's thirty seconds before we realise we're doing it for real. I'm so emotional by now that I act the scene rather well, cry for real, and for once am rather pleased when the take is glibly accepted and we charge on to the next scene. I just have to keep reminding myself that it's better doing it like this than not at all.

So these are frantic, unhappy days. In the middle of all this, the Barbican season draws to a close. The last two stage *Molière*'s flit by, then the last three *Tartuffe*'s. It's Saturday night, the last night of the season, and for many of us the end of the two-year cycle that started in 1982 in Stratford. It has been a magnificent company built on absolute trust and love. The chemistry has been unbeatable. And talent-wise, in one company to have had Gambon, Jacobi, Mirren, Kestleman, Steadman, Hawthorne, Godfrey, Postlethwaite, Storry, Cusack, Peck, Armstrong, Rylance, Bradley, Coleridge, Talbot, Troughton, Waller, Shrapnel, Bowe, Benjamin, Carlisle, Hyde, et cetera . . . the list is astonishing and endless.

There is a farewell party, but I have a make-up call at the crack of dawn (and the clocks go forward tonight as well) so can't stay. Try to find the *Tartuffe* cast to say goodbye, but they've all gone into the wings of the main stage to watch *Cyrano*'s last curtain call. It has become legendary – one and a half thousand people rising to their feet as one. R S C veterans say, '*Nickleby* was like that.'

The calmest, best bits of these mad days have been the drives to and from the studios on Canary Wharf. The docklands are a little known area of London: miles and miles of wharfs, wide channels of still water; warehouses, cranes, white luxury yachts in their moorings; and a smell of the sea. In the early morning no one is about, just seagulls circling. Once a man went by on skis. These drives have been accompanied by Mozart's Third and Fifth Violin Concertos played by Itzhak Perlman – so beautiful it almost hurts.

Now it is Monday and the television recording finishes as well. Utter exhaustion and post-natal depression as these months of frantic work come to a pounding full stop.

Richard has not entered my thoughts for two weeks now, but did in a dream one night. Olivier's face in extreme close-up. Viewing it in a slow circle, closer and closer, till I realise it's not on a cinema screen as I thought, nor carved on the side of a mountain as it next appears, but it's actually *there*. Circling the giant. Closer and closer it comes . . .

Wednesday 28 March

Feeling much better after a good night's sleep on two mogodons. Lots of energy. Pop into the gym for the first time in two weeks. Doing the first exercise I hear something snap in my lower back. Try to pretend it didn't happen.

Drive to Stratford with Bev Williams for the first night of *Henry V.* Ex-wardrobe mistress at The Other Place, Bev is a Stratford legend. Liverpudlian, her figure a diminutive roller-coaster of vivacious curves and circles from her hips to the round specs under a Rasta fringe. 'I call myself the little darkie so that some other stupid bugger doesn't say it first and hurt me.' She has also been described as 'the sepia sex sensation of Stratford on Avon' (attributed to the actor George Raistrick), but that is hard to believe as she sits next to me in the car, sucking her thumb, wearing bib-overalls and looking all of ten years old. However, when we get to 'Stratters' she disappears into a loo and then emerges in a stunning black trouser-suit, high heels, deep red lips. We go into The Dirty Duck pub, centre of R S C life. Everywhere she has ex-lovers to greet – they all seem delighted, no embarrassment or guilt, as she goes from one deep hug to another. Earth Mother and Baby Doll in one. Or Sally Bowles. I remember her room in the Ferryhouse with its window seat hanging over the Avon, stacked with cocktail mixes, scented orange candles, records of Piaf and Sam Cook.

Last year, after six seasons working in the wardrobe, Bev finally summoned up her courage, changed her name to Beverly Hills and became an actress.

We are sitting on the patio at The Duck. It's a clear grey evening, the Avon drifting calmly by – it's seen it all a hundred times before, this first night tension electrifying the atmosphere. Even outsiders like us tend to sit rather stiffly, grinning and nodding a lot.

'Tony Sher, there you are! Come here for a hug.'

I disappear into the ample arms and voluminous first-night frock of Pam Harris, The Duck's famous proprietress and Mistress Quickly lookalike. When the company impersonate her voice they sound like Frankie Howerd, but it's so much richer than that – marinaded in brandy and smoked in Piccadilly's untipped.

She is furious with me. 'Why are you living out in Chipping Campden? I know – to try and be good this year! They all try that. Give 'em a couple of months and they're in here till closing time, cars have to find their own way home, yessss. Are you eating after the show, shall I put some champagne to chill? Got all the critics coming in as well, don't know whether to put them in the back, you lot in the front, or vice versa, always such a problem keeping you all apart.'

Henry V. Adrian has done a melancholy, anti-war production of the play. I find myself thinking heretical thoughts – longing for the heroic thrills of the Olivier film. No doubt I will pay for such hypocrisy. The production's concept works splendidly in McDiarmid's sinister Chorus. Branagh is remarkably calm, strolling around that famous stage as if born on it. As for Burgundy's sticks, I don't think they're going to pre-empt the crutches.

Much later, leaving The Duck, I happen to pass the table where a pride of critics sit at their supper.

Billington says, 'Oh dear, you chaps always have to run the gauntlet through us chaps writing about you.'

I say, 'Yes, Pam was wondering earlier whether she should put all of you in the back tonight.'

Coveney: 'But then we'd have to run the gauntlet through you lot.'

Tinker: 'No we wouldn't. We'd leave last.'

Thursday 29 March
Wake hardly able to move my back at all because of yesterday's gym injury. Phone Charlotte and make an appointment. Cancel tickets for *Midsummer Night's Dream* tonight and leave Stratford hurriedly. I don't want the RSC to know that I've injured myself again – I was off for six months after the accident and cost them an awful lot of money.

Charlotte diagnoses a torn ligament in my lower back.

'You have been working very hard,' she says as I prepare to winge.

A corset and home to rest.

Friday 30 March
Wearing this absurd corset, I make my way to Marylebone Medical Library to research. As I get out of the car I hear something give in my neck. This is getting silly now.

With stomach strapped in so tight that I have to breathe in short gasps, and neck at a strange angle (as if trying to look under tables), I introduce myself to the librarian.

'Hello. Charlotte Arnold phoned you from the Remedial Dance Clinic.'

'Ah yes.' She looks faintly surprised. She was expecting a researcher not a patient.

'I'm an actor about to play Richard the Third –' she needs no convincing – 'do you have any books on deformities and so on?'

She smiles politely, reaches under the table and straightens her skirt, which I appear to be trying to look up while panting, and says, 'Please follow me.'

I'm immobilised further with a ton of books and settle at a table. The library is a small basement room; outside the window you can see just a square of sunny pavement. Perfect for long hours of research, reading and sketching. My own pains are quickly forgotten as I encounter every variation of human malformation, many beyond belief. Often the photos are of babies, who look at you with wide serious eyes; the older children look rather dazed, propped up naked in front of the camera, like Auschwitz experiments.

Many useful photos of kyphotic spines.

It might be possible to create the optical illusion of muscle wastage by enlarging the bone joints. This is distinctive in many cases.

The librarian brings me some medical essays on what might have been wrong with Richard, as he appears in Shakespeare's play. How extraordinary that her filing system should extend to this.

Working from clues in the *Richard* and *Henry VI* texts, the theories are varied and some rather fanciful. One suggests his kyphosis was caused by the breech delivery ('I came into the world with my legs forward'), another that breech deliveries can cause cerebral palsy. The oddest suggests he was suffering from a rather unpleasant bowel problem called coeliac disease, which explains why he's so often referred to as 'foul' and 'indigested'.

Play him smelly?

Sunday 1 April
The weather plays April Fool all day – bright sunshine, then snow, hail, sun again.

Dinner with Dickie. The Play For Today he directed, *Under the Hammer*, has been on this week and has been a big success. I think it's his best work yet.

Still battling out Richard ideas with him. He questions me carefully. 'If he has crutches, why does no one mention them in the text?'

'They do. They keep referring to him as various four-legged creatures.'

'Hmmm.' He talks again about how my work is straying away from the kind of acting that he respects (stillness, truth, openness) towards tricksy swagger. He urges me to see Richard as crippled inside, to minimalise the deformity. 'You don't *have* to think of yourself as just a physical actor, you know. You do have other qualities.'

'But in the text, in Richard's first speech, he says that he is "Deformed, unfinished, sent before my time into this breathing world scarce half made up." He's not talking about flat feet, he's talking about something massive. Why should it be such a hang-up otherwise?'

'Because our faults always seem exaggerated to ourselves.'

'Then why do others see it? Why does Lady Anne call him a "lump of foul deformity"?'

'Because she's not that keen on him.'

'So everyone just invents these descriptions, but actually he looks like Robert Redford?'

'Look, all I'm trying to say is don't let it take over. If you're going to use those bloody crutches they must become part of Richard's body in a way, so that the audience can just forget about them after the first five minutes.'

This raises a new problem. How am I going to rehearse? How am I going to hold the script and practise on the crutches at the same time? The only solution would seem to be learning the lines before rehearsals start. This goes against everything Diokic believes in as a director: 'That's terribly unfair to your fellow actors. Come sailing in with your lines learned. The cast are already going to be in awe of you as the leading actor. That way you're really going to distance yourself from them and give them no chance of catching up. Anyway, how can you possibly learn the lines before you know the first thing about your character, his relationship to the other characters, the situations of each scene? It's unthinkable!'

Good to be put through this, although somewhat alarming.

Monday 2 April

MANOR HOUSE HOSPITAL, HAMPSTEAD In pursuit of her polio theory, Charlotte has arranged for me to meet Tom Wadsworth, an orthopaedic surgeon. I am met by a bustling, cheerful nurse with a thick German accent. She seems very excited by my visit. 'So you are an actor. Which king is it you are to play?'

'Richard the Third.'

'Ach no! You are too young and healthy. Go away, you must not do it!'

Luckily Wadsworth comes in before I can be thrown out. He is a short, round, middle aged Yorkshireman with small eyes hidden behind half glasses. At first his manner seems wearily professional but it soon becomes apparent that the man is a raging and delightful eccentric. When he talks you miss every other phrase, the Northern sounds buzzing quickly and elusively round the sunny room.

'So you're to play a scoliotic . . . this book . . . illustrated by . . . best medical illustrator in . . . borrow it if . . . back to me sometime.'

This throws me somewhat, since I have definitely decided against the S-shaped scoliotic back with side hump. I say, 'Actually, I'm thinking more along the lines of kyphosis.' I'm hoping he'll be impressed by my knowledge of the jargon, but he doesn't seem to have heard at all.

'Scoliosis . . . now what happens is, y'see . . . twists round . . . respiratory difficulties, of course . . . this comes up . . . this over here . . . there you have it.' He sits back, puffing from his impersonation of a scoliotic.

I am phased, but determined. 'I see. What would happen if it were *kyphosis?*'

At this point the door opens and the German nurse bustles in with his morning mail. She says something about a complaint which jolts him into life.

He says, 'Can you fetch Mister uhh . . . some tea?'

'Perhaps he would prefer coffee.'

'I would, yes please.'

'It's only Manor House coffee, I'm afraid,' she chuckles, 'not Maxwell House.'

'Poison,' mutters Wadsworth tearing at his letters, 'Complaints! . . . What's she talking about? . . . strange sense of humour, stranger than mine . . . mustn't be churlish . . . Out-patients! Disgraceful! Naked people lying in corridors . . . right, that's that.' He tosses the papers aside. 'Where were we? Respiratory problems . . . scoliosis.'

Clearly I'm not going to get him on to the subject of kyphosis, so I try a different tack. 'Actually, it's terribly useful what you told me, but I was hoping to ask you about polio.'

'Poliomyelitis?' he asks, and continues to correct me each time I use the abbreviation, to check we're talking about the same thing. I have difficulty pronouncing new words and eventually make a brave stab at it, but it comes out as 'poliomuhhhs'. But this won't wash with him. 'Poliomyelitis?' he asks. Firmly, as if to break down a stubborn intern.

What he tells me about polio*myelitis* is both encouraging and unhelpful. It is a virus leading to muscular paralysis which can affect any of the limbs to various degrees. It is therefore difficult for him to generalise about the symptoms and most of my questions are met with the answer, 'Depends on the extent of the paralysis.' But he does confirm the floppy, outward-turning feet that Charlotte demonstrated, and talks about a shapelessness of the limbs, a lack of curvature in the muscles.

The inconsistency of the disease allows me a wide range of possibilities.

Wadsworth says, 'Yes, give him a scoliotic back . . . some poliomyelitis in a leg . . . bit in the arm . . . should do the trick.'

'Uhm, probably be *kyphosis*, but anyway, good, yes, thank you. Are there any other side-effects to the disease?'

'Respiratory difficulties,' he replies briskly

'No, I mean to polio.'

'Poliomyelitis?'

'Yes.'

'Can't think of any.'

'Eating problems?'

'Nope.'

'Sleeping?'

'Nope.'

'Sexually?'

'Nope. Doesn't affect the groin area or the libido. Though . . . depending on the extent of the paralysis . . . your chap might have difficulty with positions.'

'Positions?'

'Positions.'

And on this thought-provoking note he wraps up the interview.

The cheerful German nurse ushers me out. 'And where is it you are to play this terrible king?'

'Stratford-on-Avon.'

Her eyes go misty. 'Ahh. One of the first places I visited when I came to this country long time ago. And a more beautiful place on God's earth you could not ask for.' Then, looking at me, she shakes her head and says, 'Too young, too healthy, don't do it.'

Tuesday 3 April
STRATFORD Hump-fitting with the Bills A. and D.

The Technical of *Merchant* is in progress on stage. We stand watching the television monitor in the Green Room. I still find it annoying that the Gobbos are hunchbacks.

'We can hardly be accused of plagiarism,' says Bill A., 'giving Richard the Third a hump!'

We go over the road to the wardrobe building and find that Frances Roe, head of wardrobe, has laid out a grisly exhibition in the fitting-room. 'This is Ian Holm's foot, this Ian Richardson's and here's Alan Howard's.' They are boots built up to look like club feet. Howard's is the most spectacular with studs and the chain used to drag the foot along. 'Now over here,' she says, leading us across the room as if in a department store, 'I dug out some of the humps we've used. Just to give you an idea of what you might want. This is Alan Howard's again, and here is Anton Lesser's.' These are vests with the humps built into them. 'They're both side humps but we've also done two lovely big central humps for the Gobbos this season.'

Frances hands me one of the hump-vests to try. I shrink away. The idea of building my deformity on top of another actor's seems wrong. Worse than that, it seems somehow unclean. Not the garment itself which is spotless (scene in Stratford's Sketchleys: 'Just two jerkins, one doublet and the hump then?'), but the notion.

'Isn't there some other way of doing this?' I ask.

Bill D. to the rescue. He finds a body stocking and says, 'Climb into that and we'll shove in bits of padding.'

It's a form of body sculpture. For a couple of hours I stand there while they force armfuls of padding into the stocking. An enormous wide back, huge shoulders bulging up into the hump which rises to join almost at the top of the head. Bill D. says he's been looking at a book on the making of the film *Alien* and has been inspired by the shape of the creature. 'Like there's no neck, just this massive energy coming up the back and going straight into the cranium.'

By padding the hips, knees and ankle joints we twist the body. This is a crucial experiment. My theory is that it must be possible to *build* the deformity and not have to *hold* it. It's clearly going to work. The optical illusion is that both legs are permanently twisted in one direction.

The image is complete and we look at it on the crutches. The massive top-heavy bulk and especially the thickened arms make the legs look very thin. And the enlarged joints make the muscles look wasted. The whole thing makes perfect sense – a man who has had to work hard at building up the strength in his upper body because of a weakness in the legs. Like those disabled athletes in wheelchairs. The bulk looks so heavy it seems to throw the body forward, and appears unsupportable without the crutches.

'Now, what colour is he in?' Bill D. asks. 'It's gotta be black, hasn't it? Gotta be black. Dusty black to start with, inky black later on.'

'Is this a good moment to discuss the head?' asks Bill A. slightly cautiously. This is already a bone of contention. I offer a deal: I'll drop all ideas of facial prosthesis except for a broken nose and cauliflower ears, in exchange for not having to wear a wig. They seem pleasantly surprised. Bill D. counter-offers: no wig, but a hair-piece at the back to fill in the gap where the hump meets my head. 'That way we see your own forehead going into your own hairline going into the hump. The join is thus totally invisible.'

Now he takes polaroids to work from, pretending to be David Bailey at Richard III's wedding: 'Look this way Your Highness, smile if you can; Lady Anne in a bit, down a bit, that's it luv, try and stoop down to your husband's level . . .'

We yell with laughter, a lot of it relief. Bill D.'s invention is endless: 'The Mighty Hunchback. Sounds like a new hamburger chain. Or the new VW.'

I drive back to London feeling very high. But later I have another look at the polaroid I bought back. The misshapen white body stocking and NHS crutches make me look like I've just returned from a disastrous ski-ing holiday. It's difficult to tell whether this is a good idea, or one as daft as this photograph looks.

Thursday 5 April
Bullied by Charlotte back to classes at the Body Control Studio – so much part of my recuperation after the accident. Alan Herdman's Pilates Exercises are based on the principle of all support coming from the stomach. You stretch and strain on various racks while Alan stands above you and prods steely fingers into your middle, saying 'Stom-*ache*!' – instantly giving you just that. My favourite bit is at the end, when you put on moonboots and hang upside down for ten minutes. The spine relaxes, all the organs re-arrange themselves and you come away feeling beautifully stretched.

Video of last night's *QED* programme on a travelling medical team in India's remote northern villages. A lot of footage of polio victims. Some cases are so extreme that they're reduced to moving around in various squatting positions, little wooden platforms in each hand. Would it be possible to play Richard scrunched up like this, as an alternative to the crutches? I try it. It's agony.

Maybe Bill A. is right about extreme agility. Maybe it would be possible to develop such speed and flexibility with the crutches that they become a positive asset. It's a red herring to think of disability in terms of speed. It's more to do with a different rhythm. That's what you see when you look at someone who is disabled: they have a different *rhythm*.

Saturday 7 April
My last cigarette. Ever. I hope.

Sunday 8 – Saturday 14 April
GRAYSHOTT HALL HEALTH FARM, HINDHEAD, SURREY Charlotte said it sounded like something out of a James Bond movie. Not at all. A large, sedate Victorian house in vast grounds. Quiet pink corridors. People drifting along them in dressing-gowns, smiling at you in a euphoria of well-being or in the last stages of acute starvation.

On arrival you have a consultation with one of the medical staff. My man utters 'My, my's and 'Dear oh dear's as he scans the list of injuries Charlotte has drawn up. 'Well Mister Sher, you are clearly reaching an age when you're going to have to start taking things a bit easier.'

Next, there is an introductory talk by the resident director. All the newcomers gather nervously in the drawing room. The director is a very short, very old and, no doubt, very healthy little man. His manner is that of a bank manager. Toothbrush moustache, and spectacles which magnify his eyes alarmingly.

The men among us, we are told, are here because of the stress of business – 'either earning too little or too much' – the women because 'running the home isn't as enjoyable as it was before the war'.

He now launches into his main lecture on the Body and Health. His metaphor is the automobile: we wouldn't dream of abusing our motor cars in the way that we abuse our bodies. He expands this argument under the headings of Overloading, Servicing and so on.

A group of Israelis in front of me, who speak very little English but have managed to catch these constant references to motor cars, begin to exchange worried glances.

Our little director concludes by listing the various medical services available and mentions that there is an army psychiatrist who swims in the pool every morning. How we are to avail ourselves of his services is left unsaid. Presumably just by plunging in and swimming alongside: 'Ah, morning Captain, I have this problem with foreplay . . .'

THE JACKET POTATO The medical consultant and I had agreed that I should 'eat normally' while I'm here as I haven't come to lose weight. I'm ravenous by dinner time, after fifty lengths in the pool (no paddling psychiatrists in evidence), and greedily order roast turkey while all around me pale lips pick at lettuce leaves and sip at lemon juice. My smugness turns to horror when the meal arrives. At first the plate appears to be empty and I assume the meat will arrive on a separate dish. But the next that arrives contains only a minute portion of carrots and sprouts. Puzzled, I re-examine the first dish and discover that the soft pastel design on the bottom is in fact a wafer-thin slice of turkey. This would appear to be their idea of 'eating normally'

I go to bed depressed. A week ahead of virtual starvation and no cigarettes or booze.

Breakfast is coffee and a slice of toast with honey.

By lunchtime, after a morning's jogging and swimming, I have lost all sense of humour on the subject. I will now kill for food. Luckily, lunch is a salad buffet and you can help yourself. I notice that the experienced inmates have learned how to pile their plates so high it looks like they're carrying top hats. This skill is quickly acquired. You layer your plate with a foundation of solids (boiled eggs, tomatoes, tuna), then build on top with the runny, squashier salads (coleslaw, cottage cheese, vegetable mixes) which you can compress to make more space, and finally you lay the light flyaway stuff (lettuce, grated carrots) on top. I leave the dining-room bloated and ill.

But by dinner, after hours of jogging, swimming, the gym, a real hunger has set in again, a meat-eater's hunger which no amount of salads will ever relieve. Glancing up from the pitiful smudge on my plate which they call roast beef, I notice that jacket potatoes are being carried to certain tables; the Israelis are having lots. Am I hallucinating? Is it possible in this place – *jacket potatoes*? I suffer from acute shyness in public places, especially hotels, but a suicidal courage takes over now and I find myself leaning over to the next table and asking one of the potato eaters whom they have bribed and how. Apparently the potatoes are freely available if authorised by your medical consultant. Which means waiting until tomorrow.

I return to my room to face another night of hunger. A terrible battle with myself ensues, a battle of Faustian proportions for my soul: should I or should I not drive into Hindhead and get some fish and *chips*? Self-control prevails. I stay in my room counting the hours until morning.

As soon as the front desk is open I rush over and, trying to keep the quaver out of my voice, say, 'I'd like to have a jacket potato in the evenings . . . please.'

'Are you on a diet, Sir?' the receptionist asks.

'No,' I answer weakly.

'Are you sure?' I stare at her with incredulity. 'It's just that we do have people trying it on sometimes.'

'Well . . . can't you check?'

'Oh don't you worry Sir, we'll check all right.' She is smiling almost dangerously.

I stand there with a growing feeling of guilt as she phones the sister-in-charge to check my file. She listens intently, nods, thanks the sister and puts down the phone. 'Yes, that seems to be all right Sir, we'll put you down for a potato this evening.'

The day is easier to get through after this. And sure enough, at dinner, it arrives at my table, big and steaming. There is even *butter* with it.

The days are happier from now on.

I'm reading three books: Simon Callow's *Being an Actor*, which is delightful and makes me laugh aloud and often, in recognition of an actor's life; *Gestalt Is*, essays and lectures by Fritz Perls and others (note for Richard – 'Killing is always a sign of impotence'); and *The Illustrated True History of the Elephant Man*, which doesn't illustrate at all what it must have *felt* like to be Merrick. What comes closest is his own two page autobiography. It's childlike, servile, no sense of self – a deformed view of himself and the world.

You get a daily sauna and massage as part of the tariff. In the sauna cabin one longs for silence as the men chatter endlessly about the heat, or how much weight they're losing, or golf.

On the second day, I'm in the middle of a shower when the head attendant rushes up to me, says, 'Forgive me Mr Sher, I didn't realise who you were', and starts pummelling my hand as I stand there naked and embarrassed. It turns out he's a theatre buff and from then on he follows me everywhere, talking and questioning, into the rest-room, plunge pool, sometimes in the sauna cabin itself.

An announcement is put up on the notice board: 'Cocktails will be served in the drawing-room before dinner.' The inmates flock to this event, hoping against hope that the management has gone crazy and ordered crates of rum and mixers.

We are given Slimline Bitter Lemon with bits of mint floating in it.

'Yuk,' says a fat woman in a loud dressing-gown, 'thank God for the bottle in the room.'

So she's the one. There is one room which always has an empty champagne or vodka bottle provocatively left outside the door.

Dickie arrives for the last few days of my stay to suffer the agonies and share the joys of this place. I brief him, laying particular stress on the importance of getting a jacket potato written into the deal at your first consultation.

On Wednesday morning I read Wardle's shocking review of *Merchant* in *The Times*. Sends chills down my spine. It's not a pleasant experience reading someone else's bad review. Of course there's also a feeling of relief – it wasn't *me*.

Ring Jim (who plays Salerio) and he says the opening went well. He hasn't seen any reviews and I have to tell him how bad *The Times* is. But I refuse to read any of it out to him.

Jogging alone across the common, an unusually ugly stretch of National Trust land. As someone said in the sauna, it looks like the kind of ground the army uses for practice manoeuvres. Low mean bushes and sandy paths. But plodding along, in my new track suit and joggers, is an excellent feeling – the cold air, the noise of my panting, my eyes blurring from the exertion – a feeling that at last I'm doing what Jim suggested ages ago: I'm in training for an Olympic event. The sun comes out and I rest in the hollow of a tree. There is an eiderdown of thick soft moss to sit in. Spring sunlight, the green of distant fields. It makes me realise how little I have been able to relax this holiday – Richard III is constantly ticking away inside.

ISLINGTON Arriving home there is a pile of mail and a package – clearly a script. Puzzled, I open it: *The Desert Air* by Nicholas Wright. There's a special excitement just holding a new script you've been offered.

It's a hot day so I take it outside to read. The garden, still grey from the winter, is just about to fold open like a fan and dazzle.

The play is a puzzle. Begins with a wonderful piece of surrealism (General Montgomery viewing the latest secret weapon, an invisible tank) but then goes into long expositions about the war in Yugoslavia. Unclear what Nicky is saying or *how* he is saying it. The character Hippo is excellent though. He would obviously be fun to play, but would be more attractive if he wasn't going to have to be alongside Richard, and following a string of other aggressively ruthless characters: Tartuffe, Martin in *Maydays*.

Physically, am I right for it? Could I ever be nicknamed Hippo? Anyway, unless I get to like the play more I won't do it. That has to come first.

The dry week brought to an end with an excellent bottle of '76 Montrachet. No desire for a cigarette yet.

Sunday 15 April

Jim back in London for the weekend. He's much less affected by the *Merchant* reviews than I am. I suppose part of my reaction is selfish – I'm worried what this will do to company morale and how it will affect *Richard III*. He says he's still so thrilled just to be on that great and famous stage. Recalls his first visit there with his twin brother, in a school party from Bilston, to see *Henry IV – Part One*. 'We were unable to speak on the coach going back, just sat staring out of the windows, programmes on our laps. We didn't know what had happened to us, but it was monumental.'

Re-read *Desert Air*. It's getting better, but still a feeling of dissatisfaction and confusion.

A new factor is this terror that's been put into the air by the *Merchant* reviews. It's absurd for me to put all my eggs in one basket and do just *Richard III*. I must do a second play. Yet this mustn't fog my judgement of *Desert Air*.

Tonight Tommy Cooper collapsed on stage at Her Majesty's Theatre and died. When he fell, going on to his haunches, reports say that the audience thought it was part of the act and howled with laughter. He had a natural comic's face so the look of stunned surprise must have been hilarious. Precisely what I wanted for Molière's death and never quite achieved. As he is dying on stage, Molière cries, 'Don't laugh, don't laugh.'

Wednesday 18 April

Jim, Dickie and my agent, Sally, have all read *Desert Air* and are not complimentary. The only way I could do it now is if Adrian Noble feels similarly dissatisfied and will encourage fairly drastic rewrites.

KING'S HEAD PUB, BARBICAN It's my first proper talk with Adrian since *King Lear*. Brings back the exhilaration of working with him. Reams of ideas tumble out, his talent almost made visible, along with the twitches, spasms of eye-rubbing, the tuggings at his collar as if he can't breathe. A man possessed. Almost as if there is an excess of talent and he's having to get rid of the overflow. When he communicates ideas they are so lucid – *the* gift of a good director.

We talk about *Richard III* and I mention my worry about the humour in the play – I'm finding it increasingly funny each time I read it – in terms of it being a tragedy. Adrian doesn't see this as a problem, in fact the reverse, points to what we did in *King Lear*, but says, 'Richard can only have a tragic dimension if you can find the potential for good in him.'

At last he says, 'Well, what did you think of Nicky's play?' I tell him about my reservations. When I say that I find the style of the play confusing and inconsistent I touch on a tender spot for Adrian. He says, 'I don't understand this worry people always have about style. What's great about theatre is that you can do anything.' Of course, Adrian's signature as a director is freedom of style.

He doesn't share my doubts about the play, says, 'I got a buzz out of reading it, I can see it clearly.' But he promises to talk to Nicky about my reservations and hopes things will still work out. I get a feeling I haven't really communicated to him my thoughts on the play. It's terribly difficult communicating bad news to Adrian because his own energy is so positive. So, as we're parting I emphasise, 'I don't think I'll be doing it unless it changes quite drastically.' He grins and nods cheerfully.

I could still end up stranded in Stratford for a year playing only one part a couple of times a week. Nothing else they've offered has really excited. How absurd to be under-employed like this. How absurd that I should have agreed to it. Richard III has a lot to answer for.

Thursday 19 April
Horizon – two-part documentary on American mass-murderer Kenneth Bianchi ('The Hillside Strangler') who killed ten girls around L A. He is strikingly handsome, tall, well built, sexy, charming. Outwardly a lot going for him. A far cry from the Nilsens, Christies and Bradys of this world. Must re-think what Dickie has said about finding Richard's inner ugliness, inner deformity.

Again psychiatrists struggle to define the term 'psychopath': 'A history of lifelong, almost pointlessly lying . . . habitual lying . . . easier to lie than tell the truth. Lying is usually done to persuade a person or simply to make the psychopath feel better.'

Another says, 'Science doesn't really know. There may be genetic and environmental influences intermingling . . . we don't really know for sure. He may simply be evil.'

Outside In, Stephen Dwoskin's autobiographical film. Very useful for Richard. Dwoskin has severe polio in both legs and has to wear complete calipers, so the legs can't bend at all. He walks with crutches and even then has enormous difficulty throwing each leg forward. I must use this – the hip throw. Sexual area. Thrusting. In pain and pleasure.

Dwoskin records his fantasies: beautiful women cleaning his room, dancing at a party, or stripping at the top of a difficult flight of stairs – out of reach. A naked woman puts on his calipers and tries out his crutches.

The tone is light and frivolous – Dwoskin frequently falls over, like a cartoon man – but it doesn't take much to twist these images into something more perverse, more Richardian.

Extraordinary sequence with a semi-naked woman lying on a black bed. She's bathed in a cool white light, her skin like porcelain against the black of her hair, bra, knickers. He comes alongside her, a dark silhouette, carefully props himself up on his crutches and stretches out a hand – it turns from black to white as it enters the light – to touch her. Again and again without ever making contact. The cripple reaching for a beautiful *whole* body.

Another sequence of him limping slowly out of the darkness into a square of light.

A way of starting the play? The stage in darkness except for a pool of light. Empty. You hear 'Now is the winter' coming from the darkness, then he starts to limp into the light . . .

THE PIT, BARBICAN *Volpone*. A joy. Richard Griffiths and Miles Anderson are an inspired double act. A lot to learn from Anderson's portrayal of evil. He sits back in Mosca's immorality. It's as natural as breathing. And he's not afraid to shut off the charm and frighten the audience. But then the face is magnificent, it can change from beauty to ugliness. John Dicks (Corvino) understands the style so well; I will long remember the moment someone makes the sign of the cross in front of him and he frantically tries to claw it out of the air. Bill's production is brilliant but . . . he plays it uncut. Four hours! Who wants to sit in a

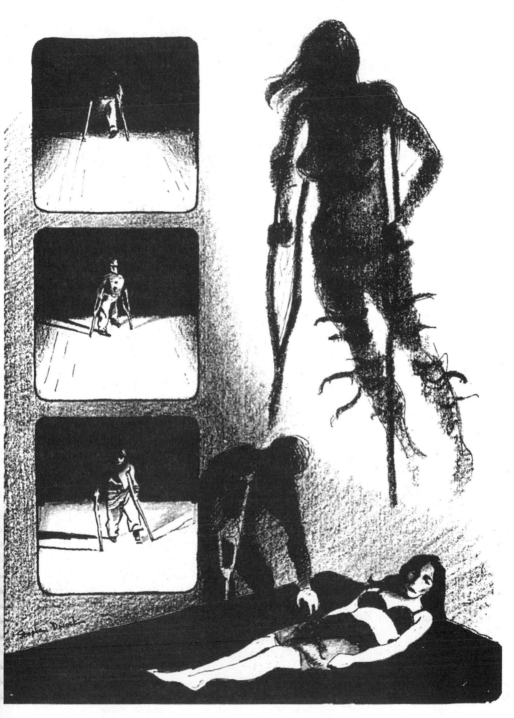

Dwoskin film

theatre for four hours? It almost alienates this devoted fan. Particularly since I know he will try it on with *Richard* and I will have to fight him to the death.

Good Friday
Last night I dreamed I was running. All the training, all the exercise had finally paid off. I was running without panting, without hurting, without fear of injury. My legs were stretching into long powerful strides. The lawns were passing beneath me like carpets unrolling. A familiar distance effortlessly covered.

I woke with a terrific feeling of hope.

Dickie and I go into the West End to see *Scarface*, the new Al Pacino film. The cinema is next to St James's Square where the Libyan Embassy siege continues. We round the corner into Waterloo Place and there's that huge sheet of blue tarpaulin which has been on the TV news all week. It looks like an avant-garde theatre curtain, and indeed a crowd of holidaymakers stand across the street behind barriers, waiting for the show to start. The mood is festive, hot dogs and ice cream, buskers with performing budgies and dogs.

Suddenly a group of high-ranking police officers arrive, jumping dramatically out of their cars before they've stopped. They hurry across the road clutching briefcases and raincoats, and disappear through the blue curtain. The crowd stirs. Will the show start now that the leading actors have arrived?

We go into the Plaza and watch a relentless, three-hour succession of slayings, maimings and coke-sniffings. Emerge grumpily on to the street at the end, Dickie remarking that it would have been more fun watching the blue curtain.

Saturday 21 April
Growing excitement now. Tomorrow I move to Chipping Campden. Dashing around all day, settling bills, last minute shopping, writing letters. The day is hot like summer.

Try out bits of *Richard* now and then – a line, a hip thrust – keeping him near.

RIVERSIDE STUDIOS With Dickie to *Poppie Nongena*. It's not awfully good. Like most political theatre it's over-intense and faintly embarrassing. And yet I sit in a state of tearfulness all evening, partly because of the show's anti-apartheid sentiments, but mostly because I identify with these South African actors here in London. It must be tremendously exciting for them. At the end, the big black Mama leads them in a circle round the acting area and the audience rise to their feet and cheer.

The most remarkable feature of the show is the singing. They have no instruments to give them the note. They just stop speaking, put back their heads and open their mouths. A sound comes up out of the earth, strokes your spine and goes straight to heaven. The audience holds its breath.

Back home for the late-night film, a favourite, *Everything You Always Wanted To Know About Sex But Were Afraid To Ask*. In the Haunted House sequence Woody Allen whispers to the hunchback, 'Posture, posture!'

And so farewells. Dickie has bought a bottle of champagne. We raise glasses.

'To Richard the Third.'

4. Stratford-upon-Avon 1984

ROYAL SHAKESPEARE THEATRE First day of rehearsals. Solus call. After waiting almost six months for today I manage to arrive late, having misjudged the drive from Chipping Campden. Charge into the Conference Hall, hurling apologies down to the other end of the room where a little group sit waiting: Bill A., Alison Sutcliffe who is to be the assistant director, and Charles Evans the deputy stage-manager.

I'm delighted to see that Charles is on the show; he did *Tartuffe* and *Maydays*. Charles has the looks of a disgraced cherub, blond curls over red shiny cheeks which seem permanently in a state of excitement. He greets me by sticking his tongue out like a gargoyle and flattening it on his chin.

I say, 'Oh God, *Charles*! You're not doing Richard are you?'

He laughs, a cross between a squawk and a shriek. Exceptionally loud, it is achieved by opening the throat very wide and sucking the breath inwards with alarming force.

Bill has been on holiday in Spain and looks brown and well fed. To my relief he explains that we won't be able to do a company read-through till next week because *Romeo* is still to open, and *Merchant* yet to have its understudy run; they get priority. So we'll work on bits and pieces till then.

The Conference Hall has large Gothic doors opening out on to gardens, and the river – you can even see The Duck. Now Charles closes these, shutting out the daylight. Home for the next seven weeks.

Bill says, 'Right – cuts.'

'Ah,' say I, 'a pleasant surprise. I was expecting a fight.'

'Well, I've done some. Not a lot. Not as many as you'll want. But some.'

Before I can say anything he launches into an attack on 'lazy cutting, careless butchery'. He says the play is not just a comic melodrama; it might be the work of a young writer but it has considerable maturity; we mustn't keep the action going at the expense of the texture and careful structure of the play. He quotes the example of the Queen Elizabeth scene which is often cut in its entirety, but is a marvellous replay of the Lady Anne scene.

'Agreed,' I say, 'we mustn't lose it. But it is too long.'

'We'll discuss that when Frances Tomelty is here. I'll just give your cuts for now, all right?'

'Fine. We certainly mustn't fight on the first day. And not in front of Charles.'

Charles shrieks, causing papers to fly off the table.

Bill says he'd like to use the New Penguin edition to rehearse with, and the Arden for notes – these are much better and wittier, but so profuse there are only about two lines of the play itself per page. Alison will cross-check both versions and when there are discrepancies we'll choose whichever is more useful for our purposes.

The moment has come to start reading.

Nervously trying to delay, I suggest that we might think about the first two lines of the play as a potential cut, and thus avoid the most frightening part of playing Richard III. 'Instead, it could begin, "And all the clouds that lour'd upon our House . . ." no?'

'Just read it,' says Bill grinning.

' "Now is the winter of our discontent . . ." '

I read badly, rather monotonously or else I over-stress. Mercifully Bill stops me after about ten lines and starts to pick at words and discuss meanings.

We have begun.

Bill D. shows me the designs for Richard's three costumes.

The drawing of 'Richard/Basic' is magnificent – a cross between a pirate and a slug, all in slimy black, wearing an ear-ring, hair spiked punkishly (modelled on Ian Dury who has polio), the crutches twisted and gnarled. The nightmare creature is there.

In the second drawing (after 'a score or two of tailors to study fashions to adorn my body') he has Richard in bottle-green, toad-like, and with a heavily brocaded, multi-layered hat like the ornate heads of some reptiles. Somehow the green seems wrong. Black, although traditional, is so powerful. He agrees to change it and stick to black throughout.

The final drawing in black armour is another strong image – a fighting machine hurtling through battle.

Afternoon session with Mal, looking at the Richard/Buckingham relationship. Much easier reading, now there are two of us. Bill wants there to be a tension between them throughout, for their rapport to be dangerous and competitive.

Interesting discovery: one assumes Richard to have an instinctive respect for Buckingham, but early on he describes him as a 'simple gull'. Buckingham hasn't got a genuinely criminal mind, however ambitious and ruthless he might be. He is astounded when Richard gives him the chop because he hasn't seen the inevitability of it: everyone surrounding Richard has eventually to be disposed of, on the principle that anyone Richard can trust must be untrustworthy.

Food for thought here – the loneliness of dictatorship.

A gym has opened in Stratford just in time for me. I enrol immediately. It's at the Grosvenor Hotel and is called Grosvenor Bodily Health (the initials are thus GBH).

Driving home, I fantasise the *Richard III* reviews. From the good ('The Best since Burbage') to the bad ('Haven't scoffed so much since O'Toole's Macbeth. After Richard on crutches can we look forward to Hamlet on a stick and Lear's iron-lung?').

Dinner with Jim at Lambs, Moreton-in-Marsh, an old haunt from *History Man* days, when I lived in Stretton-on-Fosse. The management have changed and the new man is a scoliotic. Interesting that he wears a thin shirt and yet you don't notice his back at first. Then, when you do, you wonder how you could have missed it. Must be a trick in the way he's learned to hold himself and move.

I am eager to talk to him about it, but am dissuaded by Jim saying that, if I do, he'll walk out of the restaurant. However, after the meal the man offers us a brandy on the house and asks where we work, and then inevitably, 'What plays are you doing?'

'Richard the Third,' I answer, watching closely for his reaction; but there is not a flicker of recognition. 'And Jim is doing *The Merchant of Venice*.'

He asks, 'Is *The Merchant of Venice* lighter than *Richard the Third*?'

I think for a moment. 'Yes, I suppose it is' (said the Jew to the Crookback).

Thursday 26 April

Wake early and lie thinking about this business of whether Richard has to be sexy. The other day Adrian was talking about the Rustavelli production and mentioned how sexy Chkhivadze was. 'But then Richard's *got* to be sexy hasn't he? For the Lady Anne scene.'

And yesterday Eileen at the stage door whispered to me, 'We've heard you're going to play him on crutches. You're not, are you? He's got to be sexy. You can't be sexy on crutches.'

And then there was Bev saying, 'Richard the Third is the sexiest of them all.'

Why this obsession with him being sexy? How many severely deformed people are regarded as sex symbols?

Leafing through the Arden Introduction, I find that the ever-surprising editor Antony Hammond has included an anecdote from the original production concerning stage door groupies, which would seem to indicate that Burbage didn't stint on the sexuality either. It's from John Manningham's diary and also happens to be one of the earliest anecdotes about Shakespeare himself.

'Upon a time when Burbage played Richard III there was a citizen grew so far in liking him, that before she went from the play she appointed him to come that night unto her by the name of Richard III. Shakespeare, overhearing their conclusion, went before, was entertained and at his game ere Burbage came. The message being brought that Richard III was at the door, Shakespeare caused return to be made that William the Conqueror was before Richard III.'

Making Richard sexy seems to me the same as making him funny; it avoids the issue, avoids the pain.

CONFERENCE HALL Our rehearsal room used to be hired out for conferences to the citizens of Stratford. One wall belonged to the original Memorial Theatre and survived the Great Fire in 1926. It is a beautiful room full of old things from old productions: a goblet, a sceptre, a throne. Theatre props age faster than their real counterparts. The cardboard shows, the plaster shows, they look crude and childish, reminding you of school productions.

There's an old wind machine on the shelf above the door, there's a sword rack, there's a horse you strap round your middle and jog into battle with. It's full of ghosts – one of them sits on an upper level looking down, a white polystyrene figure from some long-forgotten show, sitting intently forward, elbows on knees, keeping a watchful eye on this latest production. The Ghost of RSC Past.

It is the perfect rehearsal space, miles high, full of light and air. On the ceiling giant circular skylights; one sends a shaft of sun on to our table as individual members of the cast come in one by one to read their scenes. The light is soft but clear; it illuminates these new faces.

Roger Allam (Clarence) in beret and granny sunglasses, looking like a jazz musician.

Brian Blessed (Hastings) a small mountain, teeth he could hang from a trapeze with, a chuckling squeeze-box voice: 'Such an exciting project, so thrilled, Tony how d'you do, so pleased to meet you, Michael Gambon tells me you're hell to work with . . . Charles! Are you stage-managing? Charles is a sweetie, lousy in bed but what a cook!'

Penny Downie (Lady Anne), Australian accent when she isn't reading, striking classical profile, long blonde hair. Instant rapport – we look one another in the eye as we read. Whatever Richard's own sex appeal may or may not be, the sexuality in the scene is undeniable. The in-and-out rhythm of their last exchange.

We assume grief-stricken people to be good purple wronged. Is she? I.2

RICHARD That was in thy rage.
Speak it again, and even with the word
This hand, which for thy love did kill thy love,
Shall for thy love kill a far truer love;
To both their deaths shalt thou be accessory.
ANNE
I would I knew thy heart.
RICHARD
'Tis figured in my tongue.
ANNE
I fear me both are false.
RICHARD
Then never was man true.
ANNE
Well, well, put up your sword.
RICHARD
Say then my peace is made.
ANNE
That shalt thou know hereafter.
RICHARD
But shall I live in hope?
ANNE
All men, I hope, live so.
RICHARD
Vouchsafe to wear this ring.
ANNE
To take is not to give.
She puts on the ring
RICHARD
Look how my ring encompasseth thy finger,
Even so thy breast encloseth my poor heart.
Wear both of them, for both of them are thine;
And if thy poor devoted servant may
But beg one favour at thy gracious hand,

190

200

Penny Downie

Finally Frances Tomelty (Queen Elizabeth), eyes like black coals, a mane of hair, two miniature silver spoons for ear-rings. At one point Bill compares Richard to Macbeth – she instantly crosses herself.

I say, 'I don't think that superstition applies if you're just rehearsing.'

'It's not a superstition to me,' she says, 'I've lived through it.'

Of course – she was Lady Macbeth in the O'Toole production.

The theatre is buzzing with excitement after last night's visit by Prince Charles and Princess Di to *Henry V.* They were Ken Branagh's personal guests and apparently had requested that their visit be unofficial. They said they would just slip in. How the two most famous people in the world thought they could just slip in to a busy public place is a puzzle. Inevitably, by the interval a crowd had gathered in the front of the stalls, staring up at the dress circle where they were sitting. The second half couldn't start for some time because the audience was pointing in the wrong direction. Afterwards, Branagh went to meet them and Prince Charles apologised for upstaging the show.

Friday 27 April
Awake early again. The text for this morning's thought is 'lump of foul deformity'. After only two days' work on the text I've become less interested in the physical shape, and more in Richard's mind, his intelligence and cunning. I now feel encumbered by the monster image. But we are being pressurised to make up our minds – the wardrobe staff can't begin to make my costumes until the exact measurements of the deformity are settled. This seems to be putting the cart before the horse. Ideally, I would like several weeks working just on the text, then a couple of weeks experimenting with shapes and movements, and only *then* should we decide what he's going to look like. Of course that's impossible with the theatre system in this country. For instance Bill D.'s set designs had to be in by February. And however exciting they might look, they closed all other options long before rehearsals – and the real exploration of the play – had even started.

FIRST SCENE Up until now we've been sitting round the table reading and discussing the text. Today we venture out on to the rehearsal floor. Pleased that my early idea about the harmless cripple sitting in the sun seems to work. I position myself over at the proscenium arch, very much on the sidelines, calling out and reaching for Clarence and Hastings as they pass, as if to say, 'Forgive me, it's so much trouble to get up.' Then at the end of the Hastings episode, my line 'Go you before and I will follow you' becomes 'Oh please don't wait for me, I take hours.' Richard exploits his disability to lag behind, to plot and chat to the audience.

Both Roger and Brian seem to be terrible corpsers like me, so rapport is quickly established.

Lots of hump jokes already. Roger goes to pat my shoulder, remembers the hump, and asks, 'Uhm, which side will you be dressing, Sir?'

LADY ANNE SCENE (Act I, Scene ii) Penny has never seen the play or even the film, which is a terrific advantage. Bill says to her, 'We associate grief with goodness. Grieving people get our sympathy, we automatically assume them to be good people wronged. This is not necessarily so.' He wants her cursing in the scene to be 'a perverted form of praying, calling on an avenging God'.

He has a brilliant idea for the beginning of the scene. The procession with the corpse is illegal, not a state funeral as it is often played (Richard has murdered Henry VI after all). So Bill wants the pallbearers and guards to be nervous and edgy, eager to get it over with. Lady Anne, high on grief, does the famous 'Set down' speech as a deliberate piece of street theatre. A little crowd forms – people already in the church either praying or screwing among the tombs. Richard is just one of the crowd. At the given moment he steps forward and so the wooing begins.

Before Penny leaves the rehearsal we show her Bill D.'s designs for Richard. I say, 'Given that you have to be seduced by him, how important is it to you what he looks like?' Penny stares at the drawings open-mouthed – she is the first of the cast to see our idea for Richard's image – and finally she says, 'I'll have to think about it.'

SOLUS I tell Bill how the whole monster/crutches image seems like an imposition now. He seems a little thrown by this, says, 'Well, we must try it. We can't just abandon it.' We agree to set aside a session to experiment, to try it in action. I will have to learn the first speech over the weekend so that I'll have my hands free to use the crutches. And wardrobe will make a rough of the deformity we've discussed, for me to wear.

An excellent session, discussing Richard's soliloquies. Then, we discuss how to start the play. I describe the sequence from the Dwoskin film – starting the speech in darkness, slowly limping into a pool of light. Bill's idea is for the lights to discover Richard already there, but static. '*If we use the crutches –*' Bill prefaces this carefully – 'I want to save the surprise of them for as long as possible.' He asks me to experiment sitting on them like a shooting stick. So the audience would think that was the shape: an armless lump. Then on, 'But I, that am not shap'd for sportive tricks', whip out the crutches from behind and charge down stage. They do work terrifically well for a trundling bull-like charge.

We discuss another idea I've had, about the seeds of Richard's megalomania. Actually the notion comes from what Monty was teaching: learning to like yourself – in Richard's case it becomes a love affair. He begins the play full of self-loathing ('Deformed, unfinished . . . half made up'), then after the wooing of Lady Anne there is a burgeoning narcissism ('I do mistake my person all this while!').

Bill rejects this. He feels that it's too early in the play for such a radical change of character.

THE DIRTY DUCK Bill and I are having supper when Pam dances up to our table, a kind of Hawaiian dance with the little fingers of each hand turned upwards. She tells us, 'There are great expectations for the fruits of your partnership.' She knows more about what's happening in the RSC than anyone who works there. All of company life passes through The Dirty Duck. But her discretion is legendary and she prides herself on it.

She tells us about the pub. It was originally called The Black Swan. She says no one knows when or why it was changed. Some old-timers think it got nicknamed by Australian soldiers during the war, because down-under black swans are known as 'mucky ducks'. At the moment the pub sign outside bears both names, one on either side.

She asks what time *Richard III* will finish; this crucially affects her trade.

'Hopefully before eleven,' says Bill, looking shifty. The touchy question of cuts again. When Pam goes, he says grumpily, 'I didn't realise, along with all the other artistic considerations, drinking time had to be allowed for as well.'

I am still reeling from shock. 'Hopefully before eleven' means *three and a half hours*. He says that he wants cuts to occur naturally as we rehearse scenes, for the cast to volunteer them, not for him to impose them.

I say, 'I'm sorry, that is not a good idea. Nobody other than me is going to volunteer cuts. All the other parts are too compact already. It is always much less painful for a cast to have the cuts from the start. What you never have, you don't miss.'

'I know. Don't lecture me.'

This is said lightly, but startles me. Now that I think about it, I have noticed a new edge in our relationship since Wednesday, probably because we're both tense about the enormous task ahead. Earlier this evening I had been arguing for Richard's throne to be carried. It seems to me that if you are King and happen to be crippled, you don't walk, you get carried. I delivered what, I suppose, was a little 'lecture' on how we have to create the paraphernalia of dictatorship, a display of megalomania. Bill suddenly said, 'Yes, I have grasped that he didn't want to be King for the book-keeping!'

But eventually he did agree to the throne-carrying and actually that led to a happy solution of the horse problem: they've decided against real horses because of the unpredictability of their bowels, and instead are going to create the image with horses' armour. The problem was how to get these monstrous skeletons on and off. Alison Sutcliffe suggested ritualising it even more and carrying the horses like the throne, with poles through the sides, and so continuing that image.

Lie in bed wondering about the opening speech, how to combine charm (which Bill feels is vital to the part) and pain (which I feel is necessary). One solution would be to do it like the MC from *Cabaret*, a vulgar, circus presentation of his deformity: 'Deformed!' . . . drum roll . . . 'Unfinished!' . . . cymbal crash . . . But the idea is too Adrian Noble-ish, and smacks of the Rustavelli version too. Another way would be to do it very Brechtian: come on completely normally and strap on the pieces of deformity as I describe them, so that only by the end of the speech is the image created. Richard as actor. But that's been done too – David Schofield twisting his naked body into the Elephant Man at the start of that play.

Somehow have to find a character whose charm is dangerous and whose humour is cruel.

Tonight I wanted a cigarette for the first time. Resisted it.

Saturday 28 April

Shakespeare Birthday Celebrations. A procession through town with the flags of every nation unfurled along the way. Last night at The Duck, Pam was telling us that the police had been wondering all week what to do about the Libyan flag while the siege in St James's Square continued. A shop next to the Libyan flagpole was asked, rather ominously, if they minded being used as a first-aid station. Luckily the siege came to a peaceful end yesterday, the embassy has been closed down and so the flag has just been removed altogether.

Reporting the deportation of the embassy staff, the *Daily Mirror* carries the headline, 'Good Riddance!' Bill recalls similar examples of the tabloids slang-slinging and rabble-rousing during the Falklands: 'Up Yer Junta!', 'Barging the Argies', 'Gotcha!' (when the Belgrano was sunk). He says it's useful to think about Richard's oration to his soldiers in these terms: 'He should aim for a lofty style, a *Times* editorial, but it should instinctively come out on the lowest possible *News of the World* level.' ('A scum of Bretons . . . these bastard Bretons . . . shall these enjoy our lands? Lie with our wives? Ravish our daughters?') 'Or to put it another way,' says Bill, really warming to his theme now, 'he aims for the inspiring patriotism of a Henry the Fifth, "Once more unto the breach" kind of stuff, but all he can muster is, "Do you want some smelly dago sticking his dick up yer missus?" '

It does help me to think of Richard's verbal style throughout as that of a tabloid journalist, that brand of salivating prurience.

Sunday 29 April
LONDON Haven't seen a newspaper all week, and didn't know *Animal Farm* had opened at the National. Or how it was being done. So reading the *Observer* theatre review, this phrase reaches up off the page to deliver a hammer blow between the eyes: 'Ingenious short crutches in order that they can walk on four legs'.

My imaginary reviews now read, 'Mister Sher takes his starting point for Richard the Third from *Animal Farm* . . .' Something in the air is warning me against the crutches. Jim urges me to be patient, not to ditch them yet.

To the Body Control Studio to distract myself with some physical pain.

Dinner with Max [Max Stafford-Clark, Artistic Director, Royal Court Theatre]. He's full of stories about the battle to stop Rees-Mogg closing down the Royal Court – which, thank God, is finally won.

Every possible avenue was explored. It was discovered that an influential Arts Council personage was landed gentry near Lyme Regis, where the playwright Anne Jellicoe is based these days. Max asked her to go to Lady X on bended knee. Jellicoe replied, 'It's no good *me* asking, darling. I know you all think I'm terribly SDP, but down here I'm thought of as a communist plot.'

Monday 30 April
STRATFORD Bill D. has seen *Animal Farm*. He says the crutches are

much shorter than ours and doubts whether comparisons will be made.

QUEEN MARGARET SCENE (Act 1, Scene iii) Pat Routledge (Queen Margaret) arrives, a small fresh figure in a blue and white cotton dress.

The scene is Queen Elizabeth and her faction, the Woodvilles, arguing with Richard and his faction. Queen Margaret turns up (she's been in exile in France) and curses everyone in sight.

Bill wants to try a different way of playing the scene. Instead of speaking her asides in a corner, he wants to have her wandering around us muttering. As if she hasn't just returned from exile but is always around and we've learnt to put up with it. 'Oh I see,' says Pat, 'it's the mother-in-law that won't go away.'

WARDROBE The buildings are set behind the Waterside cottages. You go up an alleyway, there's a little courtyard and then the wardrobe stretches beyond. The smell of hot irons, washing powders, dyes.

I try on the rehearsal 'rough' – it lives up to its name. Rather balloon-like, pantomimic, a black diving-suit, it does little to convince me that this shape is still a good idea.

Tony, the armourer, is present. He and Bill D. discuss ideas for Richard's armour. Sounds very exciting – layered plates like an armadillo, or the scales on a beetle.

Now Tony steps forward to start measuring me up. 'Hang on,' I say, 'you realise we haven't settled on this shape yet?'

A horrible pause. People take refuge in hierarchy in times like these: the armourer steps back with his measuring tape and looks to the Head of Wardrobe who smiles politely and looks to the Designer who, finding no one left but me to look at, goes 'Uhhh –?'

'I thought you all knew,' I say. 'Bill and I are having a session tonight with this body stocking and the crutches. I've learned a speech and we're going to try it all in action.'

Everyone looks uneasy and displeased.

Afterwards, I ask Bill D. what the panic is about, as we've got six weeks to go. He explains that it's traditional to start with the leading actor's costumes. The prospect of leaving them to last has filled the wardrobe staff with horror.

CONFERENCE HALL Climbing into the diving-suit for the test session, the overriding feeling is one of foolishness. The Bills and Alison chat among themselves, pretending not to watch as I begin my first cautious movements around the room. There is a large mirror at one end in which I can observe as well.

The feeling quickly turns from silliness to excitement. Charging head on, the massive back rolling heavily like a galloping bison. Spreading the crutches sideways, I look like some weird bird or giant insect. The wing-span – Richard's reach – is enormous and threatening. The range of movement is endless: backward dancing movements like a spider, sideways like a crab. And you can cover distances very swiftly with that sweeping, scooping action, almost like rowing, the polio-afflicted legs being carried along underneath.

We try 'Now is the winter'. For the section about his deformity I deliberately, slowly, exhibit it. Bill A. likes this, says, 'It's like a poem of self-hatred. A mannequin parade of the latest deformities.'

At the end of the session everyone is smiling. 'Looks promising,' we all say to one another cautiously, but excited. It certainly does seem to contribute to, not hinder, our early work on the text.

Bill: 'But if we stick with the crutches we're going to have to wring every possible change out of them. And have long periods when he's not on them at all. We must make it clear that he can function without them, although not half as well.'

Drive home to Chipping Campden. It has just gone dark. The sky is still glowing blue, the countryside weird grey cut-outs in the swinging headlamps as the car twists and turns down the narrow lanes. It makes a crazy theatrical effect. I'm trying to contain the excitement, the jubilation. Tchaikovsky's First Piano Concerto is playing. Glorious slush.

Yesterday all was lost. Today it is a triumph. I must steady myself.

Tuesday 1 May
The freak sunny weather is finally over. This morning the fields are in a soft wash of mist.

LADY ANNE SCENE I wear the diving-suit. The first time with another member of the cast. Again I have to muster my courage and again feel immensely silly. Actually it *does* look silly today because I have to wear my specs and am trying to hold the script and crutches at the same time. But Penny is very encouraging, thinks it's going to work.

I like her enormously. Her enthusiasm, her appetite for work, that Australian directness. Bill D. has designed a conventional Lady Anne costume with tall pointed medieval hat. Penny says, 'But the bird's been up all night, carting this stiff around. She's tired, dirty, her hair's wild. It's Cassandra, not Mary Poppins.'

After lunch, another procession of newcomers to read their scenes.

Harold Innocent (King Edward) with that magnificent Hogarth head, beetroot coloured, and clear blue eyes; the aspect of a furious newborn infant thinking, 'Call that a delivery?'

And said, 'Dear brother, live, and be a king'?
Who told me, when we both lay in the field
Frozen almost to death, how he did lap me
Even in his garments, and did give himself,
All thin and naked, to the numb-cold night?
All this from my remembrance brutish wrath
Sinfully plucked, and not a man of you
Had so much grace to put it in my mind.
But when your carters or your waiting vassals
Have done a drunken slaughter and defaced
The precious image of our dear Redeemer,
You straight are on your knees for pardon, pardon;
And I, unjustly too, must grant it you.
    Derby rises
But for my brother not a man would speak,
Nor I, ungracious, speak unto myself
For him, poor soul! The proudest of you all　　130
Have been beholding to him in his life;
Yet none of you would once beg for his life.
O God! I fear thy justice will take hold
On me and you, and mine and yours, for this.
Come, Hastings, help me to my closet. Ah, poor
    Clarence!　　*Exeunt some with King and Queen*
RICHARD
  This is the fruits of rashness! Marked you not
  How that the guilty kindred of the Queen
  Looked pale when they did hear of Clarence' death?
  O, they did urge it still unto the King!
  God will revenge it. Come, lords, will you go　　140
  To comfort Edward with our company?
BUCKINGHAM
  We wait upon your grace.　　*Exeunt*

Now Yvonne Coulette. She is playing the Duchess of York, Richard's mother (Monty's main culprit). I look up as she comes in and my heart misses a beat. She is the spitting image of my own mother – the same grey bubble curls, strong cheekbones, small deep-set eyes. I try not to keep staring at her, but it's difficult to concentrate.

At the party to celebrate the tenth anniversary of The Other Place, Trevor Nunn comes over to Bill and me and talks about *Richard III*. He feels there is a problem in the middle section of the play. 'Don't play it uncut like your Volpone,' he says to Bill.

Next Terry comes over and also advises Bill to wield the knife freely.

'Tell him, tell him!' I urge from the sidelines, hopping up and down. Bill's face grows heavy as he wonders whether it's too late to recast.

Bill A.

Terry says to me, 'You are wrong about Nicky Wright's play, you know. We must talk about it sometime.'

Now David Edgar, unrecognisably aggressive, in defence of Nicky's play: 'What *is* the matter with you? The play's fine!'

'Let's talk about it,' I say. 'This isn't like you.'

'I can't play the nice guy all the time,' he says and strides off.

I'm rather shaken by this. Clearly Adrian has reported our conversation and it has not made me popular.

Wednesday 2 May

It's the full company read-through today. Driving in, I am so nervous I have to stop the car to write this down: 'There must be no further hesitation or doubt. There must be no further *fear*. Richard must be played by a confident actor. Manufacture it. Like with *The History Man*.'

THE READ-THROUGH The cast gather in the Conference Hall in a huge horse-shoe shape, about thirty-five strong. Bill A. takes the centre.

He talks about how Shakespeare wrote the play drawing from two traditions – Greek tragedy (the choric mourning scenes) and medieval morality plays (Richard is drawn from the figure of Vice). The death of the real Richard III in 1485 marked the end of the medieval world and the beginning of the Tudors and Modern English History. Up until then there had been an unshakable belief in the control of God; now was the beginning of Humanism, of doubt, curiosity.

He says we can see Richard either as an Antichrist figure or, in Jung's words, as 'modern man in search of a soul'.

Now comes the moment of revealing the set (or 'wedding cake' as he calls it). The model has been covered with a cloth until now. He whips this off to reveal the cathedral – gasps of approval from the cast. Some creep into the centre to see better and crouch there like a tribe of hunchbacks. Bill says, 'As you can see, we resisted the worst idea we came up with – setting the play in Orwell's 1984 with high grey walls and giant portraits of Tony Sher everywhere.'

Bill D. takes over, grinning like a magician at a children's party. He says the set is an almost exact replica of Worcester Cathedral but suggests we should also think of it as a city in miniature, a political anthill. He has been inspired by Queen Elizabeth's line, 'Pitchers have ears'. The tents on either side of the stage for the camps of Richard and Richmond will be like the mouths of Heaven and Hell in morality plays.

The dreaded moment has come: Bill says, 'Right, let's read it. Tony, "Now is the winter" please . . .'
' "Now is the winter of our discontent
Made glorious summer by this son of York . . ." '
I charge at it and swiftly stumble and fall. Despite my resolutions in the car this morning, I am shaking so much I have to hold the book with both hands. I read badly in that I *act* it far too much, shouting and demonstrating. Not surprisingly there is no laughter, but an uneasy tension. Luckily Blessed lightens the atmosphere by getting up out of his seat and being deliberately bad and reppy. He does bits of the blocking we have worked out, whistles, burps and farts.

Richard is such a huge part. You climb up and up. You do 'Now is the winter', you do the first Clarence and Hasting scenes, you do the whole of the Lady Anne wooing, you do 'Was ever woman', you do that long Queen Margaret scene, and you're still only in Act One – with four more to go.

Am pleased that my voice holds out well (another perk from not smoking), but I must devise a way of saving some really big guns for the final oration.

In the last section of the reading everyone gets very giggly. When the two armies are camped at Bosworth, Ratcliffe's line finally does it –
'Thomas the Earl of Surrey and himself,
Much about cockshut time, from troop to troop
Went through the army cheering up the soldiers.'
– an image that conjures up both a rather naff ENSA concert party, and a gay porno movie: *Boys at Bosworth?*

WARDROBE Chris Tucker arrives. He is the country's top expert in movie prosthetics (his masterpiece was John Hurt's Elephant Man) and has been hired to build the deformity so that we can reveal it naked at the coronation. He has a sculptured mane of silver-grey hair. Stands looking down at me in the silly diving-suit. One gets the impression that working for the RSC is his idea of slumming it.

He says, 'You've got it all wrong. Humps are not central, they go over to one side.'

'Oh, but we're not going for scoliosis,' I say, 'we're going for kyphosis,' hoping to dazzle him with the little science that I possess.

He simply ignores me and looks to Bill D. for an explanation, expert to expert. Bill employs charm: 'The sight of the back, of the vertebrae, should make the audience arch in their seats and feel it down their own spines. Like when the radio announcer has a frog in his throat, the whole nation clears theirs.'

Building the deformity is fraught with problems. How to design something that won't take three hours to glue on? Where to join it to me if it's going to be revealed naked? How to make it strong enough to withstand the Princes being carried piggyback?

Chris Tucker eventually says, 'This is all getting frightfully theoretical. I think we should stop talking, take a cast of his back and try some experiments.'

It will all have to be built of latex. He looks with distaste at the huge dimensions of our rehearsal 'rough' and says, 'I'll have to get a cement mixer in.'

Dinner with Harold Innocent. He says, 'I like my Richards funny. The audacity. He keeps on saying to the audience, "Oo aren't I awful? But I won't say sorry." '

Thursday 3 May
I've discovered I have something in common with Richard; neither of us can afford to indulge in self-doubt or fear. But in the dead of night, when we're unconscious, these horrors creep into our beds. This morning I wake terribly afraid again. No hope of getting back to sleep. Get up and try and learn lines. Something's wrong: they're not sticking. Perhaps it's still too soon. They're just words, there's nothing to hang them on yet. The associations I will use to remember them by – the moves, the gear changes in the scenes – they're not there yet.

Drive in feeling rather edgy. Yesterday I heard the Bills had decided that the tombs on our set won't ever need to be climbed on. Apparently a lot of money will be saved on the budget if they're built much lighter. This seems crazy to me. How do we know yet that we won't want to climb on to them? Again, it's shutting off options before we've started. With them dominating the set like they do, surely they're crying out to be used somewhere? It's not my business though. Do I just let the matter rest? Or do I risk giving Bill A. another 'lecture'?

I find him hopping around the rehearsal room on the crutches. We each try out different walks, the other watching.

Then, just before the others come in, I tentatively bring up the subject of the tombs.

He says, 'Where are you thinking of using them?'

'I don't know. But I guarantee there'll be somewhere.'

'You're right. We must keep the option open. I'll talk to Bill Dudley.'

QUEEN MARGARET SCENE It's increasingly difficult forcing the text to fit Bill's idea. Richard and Elizabeth are having a row. Margaret keeps wandering around muttering. If we can hear and see her, what do we do while she speaks? How do we sustain the momentum of a row? And if we're that used to having her around cursing and swearing, why do we bother to confront her this time?

Pat is doing very interesting things though. Her walk is very upright, very barmy. She keeps directly behind my back a lot of the time, deftly moving when I turn so I can never face her.

Rich discovery: once she confronts us all, we use mockery and jeering as a defence, banging the tables (I clang the crutches together – another use for them), drowning her out. And I play the court jester, doing mock bows, or sticking my bum in her face. It feels tribal, un-English. Bill says, 'Remember that what is thought of as English behaviour is only one hundred years old – people walking in straight lines from their front door to Tesco's, not looking, not speaking.'

Mal has gone very quiet. I ask him what he thinks of the morning's work. He says, 'It's all wrong. It undermines Margaret's power.'

I'm rehearsing on the crutches today. For many of the cast it's their first viewing. No one comments until after the rehearsal when Peter Miles (Lord Stanley) comes up to me. 'Are those crutches part of the production or are you just getting into character?'

'No, we're thinking of using them.'

'Attack me, then.'

'Sorry?'

'Attack me. Say we're in battle. Attack me.'

'Well, I'd rather not, but I assure you they're formidable weapons.'

He looks unconvinced and goes.

Bill has witnessed this, and puts a comforting hand on my shoulder. 'Tony, it's a problem any production of *Richard the Third* has to face. Shakespeare has written this severely disabled man who is supposed to be a great warrior. The crutches only emphasise this contradiction.'

LADY ANNE SCENE Penny has learned the lines and is starting to take off. I can't keep up; although I learned these lines this morning I keep stumbling over them now. Get increasingly angry with myself. What unnerves me is that it's so untypical of me. Usually lines come easily. I keep telling myself this is a good thing – stops me acting too much too soon.

When Lady Anne spits at Richard it's a crucial moment. Bill suggests I savour her saliva on my cheeks, my lips. But I think it has to shock Richard more. It has to touch the centre of his being, the part of him that first realised that he was *different*. He could kill her at that point. It releases a charge into the atmosphere. Now he plays for broke. The crying that follows ('Those eyes of thine from mine have drawn salt tears') comes effortlessly. I don't mean he is genuinely moved, but the actor in him is performing brilliantly and can produce real tears. It's not difficult for him to bring off the impossible now.

Low and tired after the morning's work. It all stems back to the *fear* and doubt that crept into my bed during the night. Go for a run round the sports fields, across the river, relaxing in the exertion. A fresh, cold day. The wet grass unrolling beneath me like in the dream I had. Feel much better.

PRINCES SCENE (Act III, Scene i) For scenes involving children, the RSC always has two alternating sets of child actors, and a chaperone in attendance at all times. Vera has been the chaperone for twenty-four years so the children give her no trouble whatsoever. Mind you, apart from the evidence of school uniforms, there is nothing remotely childish about these boys at all. They don't fidget or pick their noses, whisper or slouch. They sit upright and alert and have already learned their lines perfectly.

The idea of Richard playing with the Princes is obviously going to work well. The boy actors abandon their stiff professional reserve and gleefully respond to the chance of punching and kicking me. Then at the point of the famous insult ('. . . little like an ape . . . bear me on your shoulders!') Bill wants the young York to leap on to Richard, who gives him a dangerous piggyback ride. Is it still a game or is he going to throw the child?

The problem remains – will the hump contraption be strong enough to take this? Secretly, I'll not be too sad if it isn't. I have the Brando/gorilla impersonation up my sleeve as an alternative. And Bill did say the other day, 'It would be good if somewhere in the play Richard parodies his own deformity.'

As Hastings leads the Princes off to the Tower, I hear Blessed mutter to them, 'Come on lads, lots of fun in the Tower, video games and everything . . .'

QUEEN ELIZABETH SCENE (Act IV, Scene iv) Richard is persuading Queen Elizabeth to let her daughter marry him, despite the fact that he's murdered most of their nearest and dearest.

When we're working on Richard's big speech to Elizabeth, the section 'Day, yield me not thy light, nor night thy rest!' comes out sounding like King Lear summoning up the elements. Gambon haunts this rehearsal room for me. I didn't realise at the time how much I was learning from him. You plant your feet on the ground, you reach up or down, and you drag the elements towards you.

At several points in the scene Richard refers to Elizabeth as 'mother'. This follows the cursing by his own mother – there is something crucial here, linked to Monty's theory.

Friday 4 May
The RSC employs two local taxi drivers, Larry Adler and Bill Kerr. Larry is German and Bill Kerr was in the RAF during the war. A fierce rivalry exists between them, partly because of their work, but also because Bill Kerr is convinced Larry was actually in the Bunker. Nothing could be further from the truth. This morning it is Larry, with his quiet Continental manners, who drives me down to Chris Tucker's home in Berkshire to have the cast taken of my back. I use the journey to learn lines. On the back seat the diving-suit is crammed into a cardboard box like a great pet slug asleep in its basket.

As we drive south, the fields of rape are startling on the landscape. One of the most breathtaking sights of the year. Unearthly yellow against the surrounding green fields and the slate grey of the sky. You round a corner, see it, and your mouth falls open at nature's chutzpah.

CHRIS TUCKER'S His home/workshop is a magnificent sixteenth-century manor house in several acres of land near Newbury. He is much friendlier on his own territory. His study is filled with awards, video tapes, scrap-books, and his masterwork – Hurt's head from *Elephant Man*. It stands on a little plinth in gruesome three-dimensional technicolour. Convincing even to the touch. The bony bits are hard, the pendulous sponges of skin soft and clammy. Next to it, equally whole and real, stands Gregory Peck's head from *Boys from Brazil*, with dog bites in the neck. 'Looked much better when it was bleeding, of course,' says Chris.

Into the workshop where a bespectacled lady sits patiently sewing chest hairs on to a limbless torso. The shelves are lined with face casts of famous actors – it's difficult recognising these white masks without hair or distinctive colouring. For instance, a beautiful young girl's face turns out to be Peter Firth. 'People as they really are,' says Chris.

There are several of Olivier. 'That's Sir about ten years ago, that one's more recent. He wasn't at all well when we took it.' He removes this one from the shelf, and I instinctively reach out for it. Rather reluctantly he hands it over, as if it's a priceless antique. Strange to hold this face in my hands. The expression rather grim as the plaster was applied. You can't help thinking of a death mask.

'Is that Charles Laughton up there?' I ask Chris.

'Alas no, I haven't got a Laughton. A friend in New York has one. But there aren't a lot about.'

The Plaster Room. I strip to the waist, wrap a plastic skirt round my middle and lean forward on the crutches. Chris glues a rubber cap over my hair and with two assistants, applies the algernate – a thick orange jelly used by dentists to take tooth casts. It's icy cold and doesn't warm with the body heat. That's the first shock. This iciness settling round your neck, shoulders, back. Gallons of it are slapped on, heavy streams coursing round my neck, globs plopping on to the newspaper on the floor. Stalactites forming from my nose, chin, ears.

'Mister Sher doing his Oscar-winning performance as a candle,' says Chris merrily. And the constant instruction: 'Please try not to move *at all*.'

Now dusty white strips of plaster are dipped in water and layered on top. He has to work fast now, forming sections with ribbed breaking points. As the plaster sets a warmth mercifully permeates the alginate at last. But it also gets heavier and heavier. I struggle to keep still as the weight increases. My arms and hands on the crutches are taking the worst of it. They start very slowly to go dead. You feel it happening and can't do anything to relieve it. I go into a numb daze. Watching all that's happening in a large mirror above the work bench: three people working round my body with the silent, concentrated urgency of a heart transplant.

A noise like ice cracking. I have almost been asleep. They are levering off the hardened sections and laying them upside down on the table. A huge white beetle trapped on its back. Next the algernate is carefully peeled off and laid into it. The cast itself will be taken from this floppy mould which contains details of every pore, hair and mole.

'You can move now,' says Chris. I look at the clock. I have been standing here for one and a half hours. My forearm has swollen where the crutches were digging in.

Salmon and pâté sandwiches, apples from the orchard and coffee are supplied to revive this torture victim.

Chris measures the diving-suit using a pair of pincers as if he can hardly bear to touch so amateur a creation.

'Now are you sure you don't want a hump to one side like Sir had?'

'Quite sure.'

Driving back, dozing against the window, ticking, tapping, in its frame. In and out of consciousness. The fields of rape luminous even on a cloudy landscape. Astonishing. As if chunks of the sun have fallen to earth.

HASTINGS' HEAD SCENE (Act III, Scene v) Shakespeare doesn't specify where this scene – Richard and Buckingham plotting their next moves after the execution of Hastings – is taking place. Bill wants to set it on the forestage. I argue for using the whole set.

I must confess to an ulterior motive. I'm keen to fly somewhere in the play and this seems to be the scene. In the text, when the Mayor enters, Richard and Buckingham intimidate him with lots of Errol Flynn acting ('Look to the drawbridge there!' . . . 'Hark, a drum!'). I see Richard flying through the air on a rope, crutches dangling, the spider image complete. I've been going round for days suggesting it to whoever will listen – the Bills, Jim, Mal, Eileen at the stage door. All greet the idea with blank faces. One or two shake their heads gently. Bill A. uttered a disapproving sigh. I've taken to sulking and muttering, 'Adrian Noble would've let me fly.'

Today, when I suggest it again, someone reminds me that there's a memorable moment in the film when Olivier slides down a bell rope. I drop the idea like a hot brick and will never bring it up again.

When we get to the bit where Hastings' head arrives I am irresistibly drawn to suggesting business nicked from the Liverpool Everyman production: dropping the head into the Mayor's hands, passing it around like a rugby ball. We must be careful though. This kind of Ortonesque excess is tempting. You could do the whole production like this. (We *did* do the whole Liverpool production like this.)

I think it's important for the head to be better made than stage heads normally are; the one we're using in rehearsals is a featherweight papier mâché thing with a perfect lacquered smoothness to the neck wound. Hastings's head is fresh so it would have a certain floppiness – Richard could put his finger in the cheek or mouth if he felt so inclined – and the windpipe and neck muscles would be sagging through the hole. Also the human head is one of the heaviest parts of the body.

I argue that if it's made well enough we could do anything with it and it will still be horrific. Bill dispatches a shrieking Charles to go and weigh his head (by lying on his stomach, propping his chin on the bathroom scales and squinting at the gauge) and to see if the budget will stretch to another Tucker commission.

I want Richard to have a moment alone with the head at the end of the scene. Not sure what for yet. I offer Bill an image of Richard laying the head on the floor and lifting both crutches high to smash down on it – blackout!

'I don't understand what that means,' Bill says, 'Richard wanted Hastings dead. That's all.'

'I think he's kinkier than that.' (Dennis Nilsen; Hitler watching film of the executions.)

I hold the head wondering what else I could do with it and immediately Bill cries, 'That's it! That's disturbing. Just looking at it and thinking, "This was a person." ' A chorus of 'Mmmmmm's from the others watching.

Perhaps sniffing it, scenting it like an animal finding another dead? A parody of Hamlet holding Yorick's skull?

SOLUS Who is Richard actually talking to in his early soliloquies? Bill's idea is rather brilliant: 'He talks as if to an equal. Or perhaps just slightly down – he does have to explain things a bit, recap now and then. Think of the audience as a convention of trainee Richard the Thirds. An EST session.'

ARDEN HOTEL BAR Jo Scanlon, our historical researcher, is bringing in reams about the coronation ceremonies of the time. She has also done historical biographies of all the characters to distribute to the cast. But Shakespeare's play departs so drastically from history that these will be of curiosity value rather than of any real use.

Bill and I discuss how to end the coronation (and the first half). He suggests ending with Richard and Lady Anne's naked backs to the audience; Richard reaches for her face and kisses her. I suggest adding to that, the throne arriving down the aisle, Richard kisses Anne, crawls towards the throne, clambers into it and, leaving her far behind, is hoisted into the air.

Bill wants to have a grotesque dancing figure on one of the tombs during the coronation ceremony, 'a dwarf or a jester or something. A gargoyle come to life.' I suggest this person could then become Richard's Fool. Another hunchback perhaps? Now that one of them is King they'll all be flocking out of the closets. Dive into the text. 'Look!' I yell, 'In the nightmare speech at Bosworth, Richard says, "Fool, of thyself speak well. Fool, do not flatter." '

Bill winces and shuts the book. 'The whole point of that speech is that he's alone.'

'Yes, but the Fool is a kind of mirror-image –'

'Shut up and go and buy us a round.'

A long day ends with the other RSC driver, Bill Kerr, taking me home. Larry, this morning, drove silently; his car smelt of after-shave. Bill Kerr smokes a lot, is loquacious and tonight is in a ghoulish mood. As we pass a dark humped shape on our left he asks, 'Anyone told you about Meon Hill?' There was an infamous murder there some thirty years ago, thought to be a ritual black magic killing. A quiet Stratford street sweeper was found on the hill with a pitchfork through him ('Quite dead of course,' remarks Bill Kerr) and his constant companion, a mongrel dog, was hanging from a nearby tree, its throat slit.

A fox suddenly appears in our headlights. This prompts Bill Kerr to relate the story of how his neighbour had all his chickens massacred by a fox. Apparently they don't eat them, just kill them for sport and pleasure. The next morning there were only three survivors among the carnage. These three had not been touched, yet sat on their roosts stock-still staring without blinking. They had gone mad with shock. Nothing could be done to revive them – eventually their necks had to be wrung so they could join their murdered brood.

Saturday 5 May

I dream a clear image of one of the crutches catching between paving stones and myself crashing forward on to my face. Blood and smashed bones. Hurry into rehearsals to find out what the stage floor is like. Stage-managers are dispatched to fetch samples. The simulated paving stones prove to have almost no gaps between them. And so, alert over, the day can begin.

BAYNARD'S CASTLE SCENE (Act III, Scene vii) Whenever we come to this difficult scene we usually just stand and stare at the text dumbly. But today this yields results. In Shakespeare's stage directions it says, 'Enter the Mayor, Aldermen and Citizens'. And Catesby asks why 'such troops of citizens' have been assembled. Clearly they've got a large audience; Richard and Buckingham are performing here for the *citizens*, not the Mayor or Aldermen. We can't have crowds of course, but we could play it out front and use the theatre audience. Bill wonders how to suggest the large crowd. A tape is the answer, but what do we hear? Shakespearian rhubarb would be fatal – 'Zounds, alack, and by my troth!'

We try the scene out front. Immediately much better.

I'm playing Richard very holy and wet. Bill says, 'Richard is going to have to act a lot better than that. He can't just suddenly change character completely. He's a famous man. These citizens know him. They see him every evening on the nine o'clock news launching ships and visiting armament factories. Everyone knows he's an angry, volatile character. His religiousness can't be soppy. He can't offer them another Henry VI. His must be a stern, chastising piety. He's right wing, he's Moral Majority.'

This solves a contradiction in Richard's public persona (violence and piety) which I hadn't been able to reconcile, and is a perfect example of those moments in rehearsal when the whole character suddenly comes into sharper focus. But building a character also involves leaving some ends untied, embracing the complexities of human nature.

THE OTHER PLACE *Camille.* It's increasingly difficult to concentrate on anything else other than Richard these days. As I sit reading the programme waiting for the lights to go down, my mind keeps drifting away to him and my face slouches into his. I glance up to find several people staring. I pretend to have something stuck in my teeth.

Ron's production is brilliant. It moves from salons to pastures as effortlessly as a film. Frances Barber is astonishing. Her cough is not a stage cough. You haven't heard it before – except in real life. You don't sit there thinking, 'Gosh, that's a good cough, wonder how the actress is doing that.' You fear for Camille's throat and lungs.

Meet her in The Duck afterwards. She's great fun, says, 'You and Branagh only have Laurence Olivier to follow. What about me? I've got Greta Garbo.'

Sunday 6 May

I have fallen in love with this eighteenth-century cottage Jim and I have in Chipping Campden. Julia's Cottage. I particularly love the view of her from the banked garden. The line of the tiled roof – it's grown soft from age and wear. Like driftwood.

At the other end of the garden there is a little raised stone patio with a tree which is still bare. This area looks like a set for *Waiting for Godot* in a rather twee production.

This is where I spend the day pacing up and down learning lines, being rather brilliant to the empty sunny garden, in the same way that in the bath I often sing like Pavarotti.

The *Sunday Times* magazine carries an extract from a new book about the Yorkshire Ripper, *Somebody's Husband, Somebody's Son*, by Gordon Burn. Fascinating. If an author was inventing this mass-murderer, writing a novel, would he *dare* make him work in a graveyard?

Plenty of fodder for Richard. The way Sutcliffe is ashamed of his body as a youth, and this description of him opening a coffin: 'He'd slide the lid back slowly until you could just see the face. Very carefully, he'd lift away the square of lace they used to cover it, and stare hard for about thirty seconds, concentrated, intent, like he was waiting for something to move.'

Monday 7 May

Jim takes me through the lines. They still haven't stuck. The *fear*. This isn't like me. Lines have never been a problem before. But Shakespeare's interweaving grammar is confounding me. And I can find no logic to why he sometimes uses a 'hath' instead of a 'have', a 'thee' instead of 'you', or vice versa. These little dents in the road trip me up constantly, making the journey rather nerve-racking. Part of the problem is having to learn the lines too quickly, so as to free my hands to practise with those fucking crutches.

Drive in, feeling very edgy again. I do a Monty session on myself in the car:

'What do you fear?' he would ask.

'I can't learn the lines,' I would answer.

Monty's face – gently mocking. No, not mocking, he would refute that. Gently amused. No, not gently. A *strict* amusement, a challenging smile to jolt me out of my indulgence. He would say, 'Do you *really* believe you've lost the ability to learn lines?'

'No, of course not.'

It's Bank Holiday and Stratford is wild, drunk and ugly. I had forgotten how this place can change character. Skinheads and punks day-tripping from Coventry and Birmingham, here for the river – to sail on, fall into and puke all over. Blaring portable stereos, the smell of beer, cider and cheap wine.

On the lawns outside the theatre, a group of punks all in ash-black. They look like charred people, survivors of some terrible explosion that has torn and frayed their clothes and has left their hair tinged with blue, red and green.

The theatre stands in the middle of this wild funfair looking totally incongruous.

VOICE CALL Ciss Berry, the RSC voice coach, is on holiday at the moment so I have a session with her assistant, David Carey. We look at the first speech. It's a shock to realise that I don't understand the first two lines. They are so famous you *assume* you understand them. Or rather, the first line is so famous you think it's a statement in itself: 'Now is the winter of our discontent'. But there is no full stop there. The sense is, 'Now is the winter . . . made glorious summer.' It immediately becomes easier to say now that it means something.

A disturbing talk with Mal. He has been increasingly distant and aggressively silent. It turns out that he's so excited about playing his first major part *in verse* that he wants us to stop imposing so much on the text. Now I understand why most of my suggestions have been greeted by 'It's not in the text.' This is a tricky area. It's my first big verse part as well and, God knows, I could profitably spend the next five weeks working exclusively on that, but I instinctively know that that wouldn't fully serve this play. A good production of *Richard III* (the Rustavelli for example) is going to thrill by being theatrical in the best sense of the word. Maybe I'm not being honest. Maybe it's more to do with the fact that, as a member of an audience, I find the classics difficult to watch and to understand. So I like them done by Brook or Adrian or the Rustavelli Company; I need them to be made vivid, illustrated to some extent. If Mal wants *Richard III* to be a purist's production we are going to fall out over this; it's really quite upsetting.

Tuesday 8 May

An oil slick on the river today, from the long weekend's abuse. In the morning sunshine it's as if a rainbow has fallen into the water and is being gently rubbed against the bank, washed and cleaned until it's transparent again.

Mal says, 'Take no notice of me yesterday. I was just in an argumentative mood. I've got a lot on my mind.'

He's moving house at the moment. A relief to know it's that and not more personal.

A bitty day. A pleasure to be watching for a change (scenes which don't involve Richard).

Pat Routledge's working method is fascinating. She keeps up a running commentary, as if she's cooking: 'I don't know, don't know yet . . . never mind, we'll find it, we'll find it . . . so I go over to them and say Ta-ra . . .'

Bill directing the three Queens —
Yvonne , Pat, Frances

GHOSTS SCENE (Act V, Scene iii) Bill gathers the actors concerned into a circle and encounters an immediate problem – the ghosts can't read it without corpsing.

Bill: 'Why is this scene so notoriously difficult?'

Roger: 'Could it be that the ghosts are usually drunk by this stage in the performance? I mean, Clarence has been dead for over two and a half hours.'

Bill attempts a rough staging and things get worse. The ghosts have slowly to gather in the middle of the stage and then swivel their prophecies from Richard at one side to Richmond at the other.

'It's not Wimbledon!' cries Bill. 'And you're wafting! I don't want to see any wafting! No ghost acting!'

The ghosts are going to come up out of the tombs, which have secret back entrances, so each new ghost joins the group from behind. This means the others have to sense his presence and make a natural parting for him. Inevitably, ghosts crash, trip, get tickled and goosed, Blessed burps and farts.

'English actors,' laments Bill afterwards, 'English actors are so self-conscious. There'd be no problem with that scene if you had continental or American actors.'

MOTHER SCENE (Act IV, Scene iv) We have a brief look at this vital scene. Bill has a nice image for when Richard calls for his drummers and trumpeters to drown her out: 'A petulant boy turning up the hi-fi.'

PRINCES SCENE After further consultations with Tucker, we have decided to abandon the piggyback ride and go for the Brando/gorilla version instead. The young York says, 'Because that I am little like an ape, he thinks that you should bear me on your shoulders!' . . . Richard's face goes blank, he rises slowly, pauses, and then defuses the tension with the gorilla act.

One of the older boys, Rupert Finch, says, 'Wouldn't it be better if you turned away so that we couldn't see what you're thinking? As if you were shunned. And then suddenly turn back and be the gorilla. It would be more surprising.'

He's quite right. It is much better. 'So wise, so young, they say . . .'

SOLUS The nightmare speech. Bill says, 'It's about fear in a very personal way. We mustn't talk about it too much. Anyway there's not a lot I can say. I know what it means to me, but it's got to be your personal expression of terror. We must just let it happen gradually.'

A stocktaking on the disability. As I'm coming off the book I'm experimenting more and more with the polio walk.

'Oh it's polio, is it?' says Bill. 'I've been wondering what you've been doing. Lucky we're having this discussion.' He feels it's *too* disabled, too extreme a difference from the speed and agility on the crutches. He'd prefer the disability to be less specific – he suggests bone damage caused by the difficult birth – but basically strong and capable.

I feel no sense of wasted research. Everything seeps together. The new walk, for example, immediately becomes slightly spastic, which I thought I had ditched as an option.

ARDEN HOTEL BAR With Bill and Roger Allam, who is a joy and one of the best verse-speakers in the Company. I call him The Voice Beautiful and he calls me The Body Busy (the other day he said, 'I wouldn't like to see you in *Whose Life is it Anyway!*'). I outline Monty's theory about Richard and his mother. Bill is very taken with this.

I.4

For false forswearing and for murder too:
Thou didst receive the sacrament to fight
In quarrel of the house of Lancaster.
FIRST MURDERER
And like a traitor to the name of God
Didst break that vow, and with thy treacherous
Unrip'st the bowels of thy sovereign's son.
SECOND MURDERER
Whom thou wast sworn to cherish and d
FIRST MURDERER
How canst thou urge God's dr
When thou hast broke it in s
CLARENCE
Alas! For whose sake did I
For Edward, for my broth
He sends you not to mur
For in that sin he is as de
If God will be avengèd for
O, know you yet He doth
Take not the quarrel from
He needs no indirect or l
To cut off those that have
FIRST MURDERER
Who made thee then a bloo
When gallant-springing brav
That princely novice, was struck
CLARENCE
My brother's lo
FIRST MURD
Thy brot
Provok
CLARE
If y
I a

Roger Allam

Wednesday 9 May
A bad day.

QUEEN MARGARET SCENE This morning Bill comes in and talks to the cast about finding more tribal/animal behaviour. Getting away from the stiff formality of history-play acting.

Bill has always been open about how uncomfortable he feels with improvisations, workshops and exercises. Unfortunately, for something like this, it's the only way. Instead Bill suggests running the scene, 'trying to be more bestial'.

The result is a disaster. Behaviour not from the animal world but the world of pantomime. Cackling laughter, food being thrown around, sinewy 'wicked' acting. Although I'm participating and probably responsible for some of the worst excesses, I can hardly bear to watch the others. Have to bury my head on the crutches for much of the scene. In one fell swoop there is a vision of how ludicrous this play can be if we don't get it right. The endless suffering, squabbling and cursing. Unintentionally, we've made it funnier than the Liverpool production, which was *trying* to be funny.

The rehearsal ends with extreme dishonesty. We all mutter the usual bullshit ('Well, we've got a good basic shape to work from') instead of sitting down and saying, 'That was terrible, that was embarrassing, we must never be so bad again.'

On to the King Edward scene (Act II, Scene i) and then the scene with Clarence's children (Act II, Scene ii), and worse and worse it gets. These are difficult scenes – people are dying left, right and centre, news of death being broken to brothers and children; wives and mothers in grief. So much *acting* going on. We're only at the beginning of Act Two and already every emotion known to man (or rather those unknown to man, but loved by actors) has been laid bare on the stage.

Feel very shaken by lunchtime. I fear that it's partly my fault. I've been *acting* too much too soon, starting with all that shouting at the read-through. People might be taking their cue from me: emoting instead of investigating. But we have also uncovered a dangerous trap in the play; it gives many of the characters A Big Moment. And, as actors, we love this – our chance to do a mini-Lear, Macbeth, Lady Macbeth, Coriolanus, Volumnia. That must be resisted or the story won't be allowed to flow. And anyway, we'd be laughed off the stage.

Find Bill and pour out all of this. His eyes glaze over, the flesh on his face drops at least an inch and turns to putty. He says, 'It wasn't that bad. You're over-reacting. You must allow everyone their own rehearsal process.'

I go away realising that this has been another symptom of the *fear*. The scenes were terrible, but there is no need for panic yet.

I must steady myself.

We are at that tricky stage: we're putting down the scripts, the lines are dragging in our heads rather than dancing. Everything feels exposed and faintly embarrassing. The scripts have been little shields up until now.

Blessed says, 'It's the time to be brave.'

Thursday 10 May
Go into rehearsals determined to take things slower, to act less, to question more, particularly the moments of horror.

The result is a much better day.

STRAWBERRY SCENE (Act III, Scene iv) Long discussion about what Richard does here. He has to burst into the Council Chamber saying that he's suddenly been bewitched, produce his withered arm as evidence and accuse Queen Elizabeth and Mistress Shore of witchcraft. Shore is Hastings's lover and so in this roundabout way Hastings is implicated and condemned to death. It makes no logical sense at all. It's pure bravado on Richard's part. Ironically, this does demand acting of the most spectacular sort, all guns firing, so impressive and so fast that no one has a chance to say, 'Hang on, you've always had that withered arm.'

It's generally agreed that the way we've found of doing this – smashing one of the crutches down on to the council table, Richard imagining this thing to be a withered arm – is effective in the way that the scene demands, and not ludicrous.

To increase the illusion of Richard being possessed, I suggest that he should come in vomiting – he's not above putting a couple of fingers down his throat for effect. But Bill feels that this would be going too far.

Thus we proceed with caution, step by step.

HASTINGS' HEAD SCENE The budget cannot stretch to another Tucker creation, but we are assured that the Prop Department will excel themselves. It will have the correct weight and floppiness of a freshly severed head.

How to bring it on stage? Bill A. suggests it is stuck on a pike, covered by a cloth which is then whipped off. This will surely get a laugh. It will be like a magic trick. His next suggestion is that it be uncovered on the pike dripping into a large tray underneath. Bill D. feels this will be too much like a kebab. He suggests one of the soldiers carry it on by the hair. Better.

What about the business of putting the head into the mayor's hands, and passing it about? This will definitely get laughs. Are they valid? Not sure. All I know for certain is that we must be able to shock when we want, make them laugh when we choose. My fear from yesterday's terrible rehearsals is us being laughed at.

BAYNARD'S CASTLE Still tedious. Why, why, why?

FIGHT REHEARSAL I hate to say it but I'm losing faith in the idea of the crutches. They get in the way so much. I can't reach for things or carry anything. They are very disabling (which I suppose is the point, but also a drag). Will it get easier with practice? More to the point, are the sodding things a good idea and worth pursuing or not? The main worry about losing them altogether is the point Charlotte made about the disability: it's *safer* when played on crutches.

We have all agreed that if they are to work they must be employed early on in the play as weapons. The earliest opportunity is the beginning of the Lady Anne scene when Richard stops the funeral procession and is challenged by the guards. Shakespeare doesn't indicate a fight here but, with a tiny snip at the text, one is easily contrived. It needs to be short and vicious. Richard's blows must be sadistic beyond the call of duty.

Stage violence is one of my bugbears. You hardly ever see it done well enough. Because the fights have to be choreographed so carefully and the blows pulled or cheated, a kind of balletic stylisation takes over. Most stage fights are rather graceful. They lack the scrabbling ugliness of real violence. Also a shorthand develops in playing pain. We often forget to consider the agony that a mere stubbed toe or bumped head can cause. Actors will take bone-crushing blows, do a token 'Argghh!', get up and stroll away.

But Malcolm Ranson is one of the best fight directors in the business. The usual problem – where to strike on the body? He devised a very effective metal backplate for Chris Hunter, as Oswald in *King Lear*, so that his back could be broken with a staff. One of the guards can have this. The target is large and I can swipe at it with full strength. With the

other guard we devise a jerky scrabble across the stage – when animals
fight those little charges and retreats are as vicious as the actual contact.
But then the problem is where to hit him? We are face-on so all the targets
are delicate areas. Eventually settle on a jab to his stomach. He can
catch the crutch as I swing it and then control the impact of the blow
himself.

The monks carrying the bier suggest that they could have crash helmets
under their cowls and I could lay them all out as well. Bill says that he
has no intention of playing the rest of the scene, one of Shakespeare's
most famous, among a pile of dazed monks.

Malcolm Ranson is disappointed to hear we won't be doing a big fight
between Richard and Richmond at the end. He wonders whether the
structure of that last section of the play doesn't demand a piece of action.
(Shakespeare does indicate a fight here.) But Bill is convinced that if we
can find the right image for a ritual slaughter of Richard, that would be
more effective.

LADY ANNE SCENE Excellent rehearsal. At one point Penny gets angry
with herself and says, 'I'm *acting* too much!' I could hug her. Bill being
very helpful to me today, curbing over-acting. Yesterday's fiasco is proving
valuable. He reminds me how dangerous animals are when they become
very still and poised.

At the end of rehearsals he whispers to me, 'Beware this scene doesn't
peak too early.' The instant rapport Penny and I have as actors is causing
things to fall into place too easily. What a pity there aren't more Richard/
Anne scenes throughout the play. He suggests we lay off the scene for a
while.

Poor Bill is in agony. He's done something to his back – someone said
it's the *Richard III* curse – and has to rehearse while clutching a hot water
bottle behind him.

I'm very pleased with my work today. I'm using my uncertainty with the
lines to be quieter, to investigate more, to think and feel. It's an unfamiliar
way of working, but rather good. Will pay dividends.

Friday 11 May
SOLUS Embarrassing doing these speeches sometimes. You feel like
you're auditioning.

We work on 'I do the wrong, and first begin to brawl'. Bill has a nice
image – it is The Story So Far. A lovely idea, but a light and jokey one.

Moving further and further away from the man's pain. There is still this basic contradiction to be solved.

KING RICHARD'S COURT SCENE (Act IV, Scene ii) This begins our second half. It's where Buckingham gets the elbow and Tyrrel is hired to kill the Princes. Bill's idea of having Lady Anne sitting there, white and semi-poisoned, is going to work marvellously. Shakespeare doesn't have her in the scene, but it will be a strong image – this silent, sick presence at Richard's side. Penny sits with eyes opened, but sightless. 'Valiumed out of her mind,' as she describes it. She also talks about a practice in Australian aboriginal witchcraft – 'pointing the bone' at someone to make them die (the power of suggestion). She says that Lady Anne has inadvertently done this to herself: in her first speech one of her curses against Richard was directed at his future wife.

Saturday 12 May
Driving into Stratford to meet the Bills for another visit to Chris Tucker's. A pink smoky dawn, mist billowing across an icy field of rape and up the side of Meon Hill where black magic killings take place.

Larry Adler is parked at the stage door. Bill A. hurries into the car with head down and jumper held over his face.

'What's the matter Bill?' I ask.

'I don't want Bill Kerr to see Larry driving me,' he whispers, 'he made me swear allegiance to him.'

'I doubt if he'll be up at this hour.'

'You never know. He's fiercely possessive. He once caught Terry Hands with Larry and it took months for them to make it up.'

We exit from Stratford with Bill A. crouched low in his seat.

CHRIS TUCKER'S Great excitement as we're ushered into the workshop. Squatting on the floor is a white plaster cast of my torso. And built on to it in grey clay is the deformed back. Brilliant anatomical detail – the skin bunched at the twisted hip, the vertebrae straining through the surface as if trapped. A magnificent shape, but bearing not the remotest resemblance to what we've asked for.

Despite the last thing we said to one another ('Are you sure you don't want a hump to one side?' – 'Quite sure') Chris has made the back scoliotic. When I ask why, he says that kyphotic humps are all much lower down. He produces medical books to prove it. I could produce the opposite evidence from my sketches made at Marylebone Library, but it's too late anyway. Or at any rate, he's not the kind of man to whom you could say, 'This is all wrong, please start again.' The Bills are perplexed as to why this is so crucial to me. The fact is, a severely scoliotic back like this would cause a twisting of the whole torso, displacing the rib cage considerably and causing the 'respiratory problems' so beloved of Tom 'Polio*myelitis*' Wadsworth. None of which I've been practising. Nor do I intend to. It would be painful and dangerous to sustain. Of course, the audience is never going to know all this – except for the odd orthopaedic surgeon – but I'm furious that my painstaking research has been swept aside like this.

The other alteration he has seen fit to impose is reducing the size of the deformity by about half and not building up the shoulders and upper arms at all. 'It would be pushing reality,' he says, producing the medical books again and pointing to the thin shoulders and arms of the victims.

'But with respect,' I say, my voice beginning to shake slightly, 'these people haven't devoted their lives to building up their strength and becoming dangerous fighting men.'

Chris shrugs and looks to the Bills. They are standing hushed. I feel very confused; his sculpture is magnificent but it would mean re-thinking everything. Unless we have an approximation of the diving-suit bulk, the optical illusion of wasted leg muscles won't be achieved.

He finally agrees to build up the arms, but he feels that to build up the shoulders would be, as he's fond of saying, 'pushing reality'.

He gets bored with the discussion and says, 'Come upstairs and see Bert.'

We're all rather relieved to end the session and troop upstairs to view his latest monster creation. It's for the film *The Company of Wolves* in which Stephen Rea has to turn into a wolf before the audience's astonished eyes.

In a drawing-room of inappropriate grandeur and elegance stand four gruesome figures, life-size and lifelike, known collectively as Bert. Each represents a stage in the transformation which begins with Rea tearing off his outer layer of skin and the wolf snout pushing through his face.

The Bert figures are stripped of skin so the muscles and fatty tissue are exposed. 'Looked much better, of course,' says Chris, 'when they were all wet and slimy and covered in KY.' They are worked by a variety of means, some muscles are moved by handles like beer pumps, others by remote-control. He is an expert in electronics as well as being skilled in chemistry, engineering and sculpture.

He's in his element now, a relish and pride that hasn't yet surfaced for our modest commission. He steps back with his remote-control device and starts punching buttons, looking like a cross between a child genius and a mad professor, and the models start to move. The naked muscles, blackish red like bad meat, begin to ripple. The eyes blink and cry real tears, pulses beat in the forehead, lips flicker into those twitching half-snarls wolves use to signal an attack.

We stand awestruck, our laughter becoming a little strained, as these repulsive creatures come to life. The necks stretch, the heads reach towards us, bloodshot eyes above salivating jaws that snap and bite at the air . . .

Bill D. looks round the splendid room and says, 'Imagine a burglar breaking in here and coming across these.'

'Wolves coming out of people's mouths, and he's talking about pushing reality!' says Bill D. as we drive back to Stratford with Larry silently at the wheel. 'There he is surrounded by all this fantasy, brilliantly conceived and executed, and he talks to us about pushing reality!'

We can all speak our minds now, safely away from Tucker's intimidating authority.

'We've been hijacked,' I say. Larry, misunderstanding, glances round. This makes Bill A. jump. He swings round too, expecting to find Bill Kerr hanging on the outside of the car, with explosives tied to his middle.

I continue, 'I'm afraid this reopens the whole question of the crutches.' Bill A. sighs deeply and gravely, and says, 'I'd be loathe to lose them.'

I am undaunted. 'More and more they become a theatrical effect with no medical justification. We'd worked out that Richard needs them because of his massive upper bulk. Now that's gone.'

Bill D. says, 'But I've watched you in rehearsals when you're not wearing any deformity at all and it still works. If you make something visually compelling enough, the audience isn't going to sit there asking questions.'

I say, 'But that's because we know what Richard is really supposed to look like. We've got the drawings in our minds. An audience isn't going to have that. Look, I really think we should use what's happened today to ditch the crutches. I've been thinking about this a lot. They raise too many questions. The idea lacks simplicity.'

Bill D.: 'No, that's crazy. We don't have to change. Tucker does. We just have to go back on Monday and tackle him again. Play the customer more.'

Bill A.: 'Isn't the problem with the crutches just one of familiarity? Give them another week and I promise you they'll get simpler. Simpler to work with. And thus simpler as a concept.'

Sunday 13 May
Second extract from the Sutcliffe book in the *Sunday Times*. He used to
go to a wax museum in Morecambe and, in a room nicknamed The
Macabre Torso Room, stare at Victorian models used for medical instruction: 'The Nine Stages of Pregnancy'. He was to reproduce these abdomi-
nal openings in the bodies of his victims. More and more like a work of
fiction.

Dickie and Bob [Robin Hooper, actor and writer] up for the weekend.
It's impossible for me to relax properly these days. They're taken on
compulsory country walks by Jim, while I go to the end of the garden on
to my little *Godot* stage and learn lines.

I'm exhausted by the evening, can't face cramming anymore. Lying in
the bath, the lights switched off, Mozart playing. Through the window
the nine o'clock sky is still a faint blue; the light rests in the bottles of
aftershave and bath foam, making their primary colours shine in the
gloom.

Monday 14 May
Four weeks to go.

Bill D. talking about Nicol Williamson in Peter Gill's production of
Twelfth Night (the last show Bill designed for the RSC), he says he was
'too relaxed in his talent'. This seems to me a perfect description of what
happens to some great actors. They develop their style and sit back in it.

Acting is just your view of other people. It must keep changing as you
do, growing with you, improving as you learn more. Of all the arts it is
the most *human*. So it must never stand still.

VOICE CALL Ciss Berry is back from her holidays. Small and soft like a
sparrow, hair like fine feathers. She's a brilliant teacher in that she
somehow communicates by spirit. That sounds pretentious, which she
isn't. Words are her joy, so how to describe her? Reassuring (the Company's mother in many ways), enquiring, modest. Often she will say 'I'm
not making myself clear', or 'I'm being so inarticulate'. But this is not
false modesty. In the next moment she will say, 'Richard doesn't fear
language in the way that he doesn't fear murder or anything . . . Oh, that
was a good thought!'

She listens to me doing the first speech and gently points out that I'm
singing the same tune, again and again returning to the note I started on.

We work at loosening it up. She makes me do it again, banging an
upturned wastepaper tin on each reference to nature – immediately I

Ciss

notice how many more there are in the section about his deformity.

She loves the idea of Richard as a tabloid journalist. We do the speech again, as if dictating to his secretary, relishing the purple phrases, the explicit descriptions of deformity.

Now she makes me do it while I sketch Richard at the same time. This is the most useful exercise of all. The diversionary tactic liberates the words and thoughts. Phrases that I've been shoving around like dead weights suddenly come to life. The pen bites into the hump and the bent legs. Interesting that by using something in which I'm confident (sketching) I liberate something in which I'm not (verse-speaking).

Ciss lays a lot of emphasis on observing the grammar. She points out that the first two sentences are four lines long, the third five lines long. She makes me try them in one breath each. Impossible, of course, but the exercise has planted in the mind the necessity to keep moving towards that full stop. She quotes Terry Hands, who says that in real life we always have enough breath for what we want to say.

She also sees the speech in three sections, the clue being in the opening two words of each section: 'Now is . . .' (the world like this); 'But I . . .' (am like this); 'And therefore . . .' (these things are going to happen).

They're building a rake in the Conference Hall to simulate the slant of the stage. This is another unknown factor concerning the crutches. Will I be able to manipulate them easily on an angled floor?

We're rehearsing today in the Methodist Hall down the road. Memories of a *King Lear* read-through here.

BOSWORTH SCENES (Act V, Scenes ii–v) A high silliness factor creeping in: we've run out of actors to man both armies. (At the Liverpool Everyman, one small group acted both armies by swopping their helmets back to front with different heraldry on each end.) At the moment, Richard's army is made up entirely of four generals. Since he has to arrive born aloft on his throne, they have to carry it. Which is somewhat undignified for high-ranking officers, and does not contribute to the growing sense of tragic doom.

Bill and Alison Sutcliffe set about scanning the cast list for potential soldiers, but it doesn't look promising. Everyone is either in Richmond's army, preparing to be ghosts, female, or too posh to ask.

Ciss with us in rehearsals constantly today, an invaluable new factor. Everything being sifted through her. I'm very self-conscious about her seeing the crutches for the first time. She's like Shakespeare's guardian in the Company. Not that she's a purist in any way – the opposite. But her responsibility is to the text, and the crutches are a massive imposition. Afterwards I cautiously ask her what she thinks of them. She says, 'Sorry my darling, I was so busy listening I wasn't really watching' – her tact is immaculate.

She has heard all these words spoken before and, I'm sure, so much better. Now I'm going to have to start some serious work on my voice. Something I've been happily delaying. One thing becomes clear immediately – Richard must be played in my own voice. I've been trying to press downwards into something deeper. But clearly I'm stuck with my own tenor range; I need every speck of variation it can muster.

Tuesday 15 May
Excellent day.

Bill full of aggressive energy. Unusual: he's normally too polite. He and Ciss set about me all day for over-stressing, and not heading for that all important word at the end of a sentence. Unless you hit it you can't pass it on to the next speaker or use it for your own momentum. Ciss's way of describing this is 'passing the baton' and 'climbing the ladder'.

Good changes are made all day: in the first scene of the play Richard can't possibly sit on the sidelines reaching for Clarence, pretending he can't get up. They are brothers; Clarence knows the full extent of his disability.

Moving Richard around immediately gives the scene a new vigour and tension.

And in the Queen Margaret scene, we finally abandon the idea of her wandering among us muttering her asides. Now that she can *enter* the scene there is the fresh impetus for us of seeing an old enemy whom we thought was safely in exile.

The scene is taking shape at last. The cackling, sinewy excess of that dreadful rehearsal has been quietly forgotten. No one has mentioned it since.

QUEEN ELIZABETH SCENE Bill says we must be aware of reducing this scene by resorting to modern English behaviour – reticence, impatience, and so on. 'This confrontation has no equivalent in contemporary England. Maybe in Amin's Uganda. The meeting between a mother and a man who's killed her children. A special intimacy, even beyond hatred. A dreadful intimacy. Maternalism versus Power.'

He says that Richard wins her round because he has a brilliant instinctive understanding of psychology. Queen Margaret, a few pages earlier, had been urging Elizabeth to bottle up her pain until it drives her mad. But Richard knows how to bleed her, to let her poisons out.

Also, Richard understands her fundamental materialism. Bill says that I'm doing the bargaining section ('The liquid drops of tears that you have shed shall come again, transformed to orient pearl') too prettily: 'Richard is saying to her, "Look love, I can turn your tears into jewellery."'

This gives the scene a much more disturbing quality.

Wednesday 16 May
VOICE CALL I wish I could remember exactly how Ciss put it: the ideas rest on the breath, both come out open and free. (She said it much better than that.) How the humour will be spontaneous that way, not planned or arch.

She makes me do the speeches sitting on the floor rocking. Says the voice instinctively goes to its proper centre that way, the breath coming from the diaphragm.

She makes Roger and me sing our duologue as an operatic duet.

Freeing, freeing all the time.

Ciss: 'In the last two or three years the R S C has started to underestimate audiences. Shakespeare is easier to understand spoken at speed rather than slowly spelt out.'

I'm developing a stiffness in the left hip. Is this from adjusting to the rake, or is it the deformed position itself? Will have to keep a careful check on this.

SOLUS 'Now is the winter' with Bill and Ciss. The main problem is the first section of the speech. Bill suggests doing it as if Richard is having to address a public function on behalf of his brother, the King, having to disguise his own feelings about peace. Then we try taking that one stage further, a kind of Jackanory treatment, 'Once upon a time . . .' I like this. At last something to grasp on to. And it has a kind of anarchic defiance: saying to the audience, 'I know you've all heard this speech before, so here we go.' But Bill thinks that is too dangerous to play, wants it to remain more enigmatic.

I do the deformity section full of aggression and self-hatred. Again Ciss says, 'You're telling us too much.'

I try the whole speech internalising the feelings, making the sections less distinct; in other words, *acting* less. Immediately feel the character coming through the lines unexpectedly, freshly, not being illustrated on top of them. 'That's more like it!' cry Bill and Ciss in unison.

This has been a breakthrough. We work on through all the speeches, everything now that much easier. For the first time tonight I didn't feel frightened by the soliloquies; more than that, I actually felt comfortable in them. What's happening is that I am surrendering to Shakespeare's Richard. He *is* funny.

A letter from Bob today with a well-timed quotation from Shaw about good Shakespearian acting. He's writing about Forbes Robertson as Hamlet: 'He does not utter half a line; then stop to act; then go on with another half line; and then stop to act again, with the clock running away with Shakespeare's chances all the time. He plays as Shakespeare should be played, on the line and to the line, with the utterance and acting simultaneous, inseparable, and in fact identical. Not for a moment is he solemnly conscious of Shakespeare's reputation or of Hamlet's momentousness in literary history; on the contrary, he delivers us from all these boredoms instead of heaping them on us.'

DIRTY DUCK I ask Bill D. when we're going to have a session in the make-up department to work out the facial prosthetics. He says, 'I'm not sure it's necessary any more.'

'What, you mean, no nose?'

'No nose.'

'Oh well, I suppose I was going off the idea too. Just the cauliflower ears then?'

'No.'

'What, you mean, no ears?'

'No ears.'

Bill D.

'All right, tell you what, how about eyebrows? Huge eyebrows meeting in the middle. Like yours.'

'No.'

'No eyebrows?'

'No eyebrows.'

'He's going to look like *me* at this rate.'

'Why not? Your image of the brute is for another actor. Anyway, isn't that how the Russians played him?'

It's a shock to realise that, in pulling away from Olivier, I was simply backing into the arms of Chkhivadze.

So we have agreed to use my own face. Richard is coming up from within now, not painted on top.

Thursday, 17 May

Thursdays at the RSC are a write-off. Matinée day, so most of the cast have to break at 11.30 a.m. to have their two-hour Equity break. Which means me doing more solus calls, or busking through scenes with perhaps one other actor, and Bill running round being everyone else.

But a chance to get to the gym again. The ache in the hip is less today. I'm sure it was having to adjust to the rake. However, it has been a warning. I must increase my fitness programme again. I've been neglecting it to give more time to learning lines.

CANTEEN Lunchtime. When you order your food they write it next to your name, then call you when it's ready.

Sebastian Shaw is in front of me in the queue. He gives his order to the girl and is about to go when she says, 'Sorry, what's your name?'

He stops in his tracks. Looks at her. Turns to us in the queue, says, 'She doesn't know who I am.'

The girl blushes. 'Sorry, I'm new here.'

'Sebastian Shaw,' he says, almost apologetically.

An odd, sad incident. He wasn't being arrogant. He's nearly eighty, has been with the Company longer than anyone in the building, and they don't know his name.

He's full of the most thrilling stories. At school, W. H. Auden played Katherina to his Petruchio. When he first arrived in Stratford for the 1926 season (he was playing Romeo, Hal and Ferdinand) he found the theatre had just burnt down. They had to play in a cinema. George Bernard Shaw used to sit in the front row making comments and causing the audience around him to giggle. Sebastian says, 'As far as my namesake was concerned, the world had only known two great playwrights. Shakespeare and Shaw. And he did not put them in that order either.'

As for Shakespeare, Sebastian says, 'Whenever I come up here for a season I like to go into Trinity Church, usually when there's no one else about, and stand in front of his tomb. Just stay there for a while. You know, in astonishment.'

MOTHER SCENE I come into the Conference Hall to find Bill and Yvonne Coulette cutting her long speech about Richard's birth and youth. I implore them to leave it intact.

Bill, grinning: 'And this is the man who sits me down in the pub every night and begs me to cut, cut, cut.'

'But not Richard's mother!' I say. 'The man's entire psyche is explained in this scene. Cut "Now is the winter" if you like, but not a comma from this scene.' I argue how brilliant Shakespeare was to reduce the scale to the domestic at this point.

Bill puts it better: 'It reminds us that Hitler was a baby in someone's arms, a little boy on a school playground.'

The speech goes back intact.

Yvonne's instinct, quite naturally given the lines, is to play the scene vehemently, aggressively. I feel it has to be odder than that. All the women in the play curse Richard. Water off a duck's back; the mother has somehow to turn him inside out. Bill agrees, and encourages Yvonne to be gentler, more maternal: 'Let him hear something in her tone that takes him right back into the nursery, a woman's voice singing gently, rocking him. That's the cruellest thing she can do to him now. Let her entice him into the curse. She's the spider now, he's the fly for a change.'

Building on this idea, Bill suggests that, once she has persuaded him to have the throne lowered to the ground, she should offer a hand and lead him gently on to the floor, to kneel together in prayer. He wasn't expecting to be moving about, so is without his crutches. Vulnerable. Now she can let rip.

Yvonne tries this version, but it's difficult – it means playing against the lines with all she's got. At the end of the curse her instinct is still to throw Richard's hand aside, or to go to strike him.

I beg her to try a kiss, a kiss implanted with the most maternal intimacy (I'm in fulsome Freudian mood now).

She looks to Bill imploringly, says, 'I feel she might want to, but she *can't*.'

Bill: 'What if she wants to, and *can?*'
Yvonne tries it. It is electric.
Monty was directing this scene.

Bill D. has been to Chris Tucker's today. He returns with polaroids of the enlarged arms, which look magnificent. He's given Tucker the go-ahead to cast it all into latex, without building up the back at all. He says, 'Following our conversation last night about normalising Richard, I think Tucker may have got it right.'

I have the evening off to pace my little *Godot* set and learn the last of the lines: the nightmare speech and 'A horse, a horse'. About the latter we made these two fascinating and irrelevant observations the other day: one, that it's the only bit of the play we haven't yet staged; two, that it's probably the second most famous line in the whole of Shakespeare ('To be or not to be' is probably in first place).

So now all the lines are learned. Roughly.

Friday 18 May
RICHARD AND BUCKINGHAM Bill, Mal and I spend the evening on the various sequences that make up this relationship. A marvellous relaxed evening, like old times with old friends.

All three of us have, I think, been behaving rather untypically in front of the new Company. Tension, I suppose. Bill and I have been sniping at one another, increasingly irritated by one another's weaknesses which we know all too well; Mal still tends to go into his aggressive silences.

But left on our own tonight, all of that disappears. Bill rushes around peering through an imaginary viewfinder and getting it wrong – holding it up to the closed eye – like he did in the telly rehearsals at Acton. Mal plays Buckingham very camp, flouncing around with hands propped high on his rib cage. It is an awesome sight – a camp Viking. I just stand there and laugh.

Good discovery for the Baynard's Castle scene: with the gentlest re-arranging of lines we contrive to bring Richard down from that upper window and hence break up the static nature of the scene. That's been one of the most cumbersome factors – Buckingham having to deliver his long speeches to a man behind and above him. Now Richard can be on stage level with the mayor and aldermen. This would also seem an ideal opportunity for him to function without his crutches for a while – increase his impression of harmlessness, vulnerability.

ARDEN HOTEL BAR Mal relates an interesting historical fact dug up in *Henry V* rehearsals: the two-fingered sod-off sign comes from Agincourt. The French, certain of victory, had threatened to cut off the bow-fingers of all the English archers. When the English were victorious, the archers held up their fingers in defiance.

This could be useful. The other day, rehearsing the 'Was ever woman' speech, Alison Sutcliffe suggested I count the pros and cons on my fingers to emphasise the audacity of what Richard has managed to pull off. He only had two things going for him and they're ironic ('And I no friends to back my suit at all but the plain devil and dissembling looks') so the idea was for him to use two fingers in a V-sign. Until tonight, I had dismissed the idea as being too modern.

Saturday 19 May
My favourite part of the day is the drive into Stratford. As you come up out of Chipping Campden you go over the brow of a hill. It's so beautiful I always risk crashing at this point, particularly as I try to time putting in the cassette at this moment. Today it is Delius. The world below is particularly spectacular this morning. The fields of rape – I will never tire of trying to describe them – are the gold at the end of the rainbow. The car roof open, a warm breeze blowing, a taste of summer, the magnificent copper beeches, white and red fruit blossoms.

PRINCES SCENE Richard and Buckingham's double-act at its most sublime. Richard sits back and lets Buckingham deal with each problem as it comes up – the Queen taking sanctuary, the boys' questions about Caesar, the interrogation of Catesby. Mal says, 'You keep passing the Buck and I'll supply the Ham.'

Lunchtime. I find Black Mac standing on the balcony overlooking the river, in fearsome mood. As someone passes us, he mutters, 'Thick as a Gurkha's foreskin, him.' And someone else is cursed from behind with a deadly 'Kipper!'

'Why Kipper, Mac?'

'Two faces and no guts, mate.'

Apparently the cause of this dark mood is the news that he might not be allowed to dress me. He's not normally a 'Mark One' dresser and his promotion is being opposed in certain quarters. 'Won't happen, mate,' he says looking mournfully into the Avon, 'won't happen till the Good Lord lays down his crook and fucks his flock.'

Black Mac

I tell him that the official explanation they've given me is that his daytime army job will prevent him being available for the crucial days of the technical and dress rehearsals. This is news to him and fills him with renewed determination: 'Righto mate. If that's their game, leave it to me. You want me, Animil, and I'm gonna be there!'

The afternoon is spent wandering around the darkening Conference Hall hammering in those 'hath's and 'thee's while thumping a rubber ball around, in the same way that I used to study for exams at school. *Merchant* is distantly on the tannoy. The applause at the end sends a tingle of excitement up my spine.

I think Richard is coming together. The major problem at the moment is a commonplace one – the *effort* of learning. It's the same when you approach any new skill or technique, from a dance step to driving a car. The effort of learning stops you, at first, from doing it well.

As for the crutches, Bill was right. They are easier to work with after a further week's practice. I have mustered my courage: I *am* going to use them.

Sunday 20 May
Tonight was the first time I couldn't get to sleep for excitement, rather than fear.

Monday 21 May
Three weeks to go.

Richard's army has grown. Paul Gregory, Brian Parr and Hepburn Graham have been press-ganged. My troops now number seven. We might win Bosworth at this rate.

RUN-THROUGH OF ACTS FOUR AND FIVE I shout far too much and give myself nowhere to go. Jim says afterwards, 'I feared for your voice and I mustn't.' Chris Ravenscroft (Richmond) has a beautiful spiritual quality. He fulfils perfectly the function of this character, in Bill's words, 'a breath of fresh air after hours of murder, mayhem and misery'.

At the end of the run Bill makes a very inspiring impromptu speech about Shakespeare. He's kneeling on the floor, his eyes very bright.

'The verse, breathing through you via the character to us, is in itself thrilling. It is seventy-five per cent of what this Company is about. It is our instrument and our challenge. It would be so easy if we were Russians and could have the verse roughly translated and then dazzle with images. We've got to dazzle with Shakespeare's language.'

V.3

And ample interchange of sweet discourse   100
Which so long sundered friends should dwell upon.
God give us leisure for these rites of love!
Once more adieu. Be valiant, and speed well!
RICHMOND
Good lords, conduct him to his regiment.
I'll strive with troubled thoughts to take a nap,
Lest leaden slumber peise me down tomorrow,
When I should mount with wings of victory.
Once more, good night, kind lords and gentlemen.

Richmond remains
O Thou, whose captain I account myself,
Look on my forces with a gracious eye;
Put in their hands Thy bruising irons of wr
That they may crush down with a heavy fa
Th'usurping helmets of our adversaries;
Make us Thy ministers of chastisement,
That we may praise Thee in the victory.
To Thee I do commend my watchful soul
Ere I let fall the windows of mine eyes.
Sleeping and waking, O defend me still!
Sleeps
Enter the Ghost of Prince Edward, son to
Sixth
GHOST (to Richard)
Let me sit heavy on thy soul tomorrow!
Think how thou stab'st me in my prime of
At Tewkesbury; despair therefore, and die!
(To Richmond)
Be cheerful Richmond; for the wrongèd souls
Of butchered princes fight in thy behalf.
King Henry's issue, Richmond, comforts thee
Enter the Ghost of Henry the Sixth
189

Chris Ravenscroft

The crutches that I will use in the show have arrived – magnificently
sculpted in iron to look like twisted wood, vaguely Arthur Rackham. The
new weight is a shock. Light gestures become heavy, my speed around
the room is halved. They are sent back for a re-think. I fear they will be
unusable.

Tuesday 22 May
Heavy rain; a bad day. We do runs of the Queen Margaret scene and Act
Two. All dreadful again. One long monotonous note of hysteria.

Ciss says afterwards, 'People have less emotions than actors think they
have. For much of the time we hide our emotions, we haven't time for
emotions. Our brains work so much faster than our emotions.'

Anyway all our emoting can't be right: these characters are tougher
than that, they've been through decades of Civil War.

SONNET CLASS A full Company workshop like this is a mirror – we can see ourselves, what this year's Company looks like, and the reflection today is not yet a flattering one. There's an air of cynicism and competitiveness, or else a lack of interest. One or two of the younger actors actually sit with their backs to Ciss, ignoring the class completely. Are they crazy? We're being paid for the privilege of being taught by her.

We get into a long and difficult discussion about the official RSC policy towards verse-speaking. Both Ciss and Bill refuse to be drawn. Bill says, 'It's like the English Constitution – there isn't one.'

At lunch Frances Tomelty asks Ciss why, in these group sessions, she doesn't just tell people to shut up and stop farting around.

Ciss goes very quiet, very focused. One of those really long pauses when you think you've offended her terribly. At last she says, 'Sorry darling, I'm just trying to think it through ... I think, what it is ... is that people must find their own way. Reach their own conclusions.' The essence of good teaching.

Down at the other end of the canteen, Harold Innocent is still demanding a definition of verse-speaking policy.

Pat Routledge says, 'There isn't one. Be told! We find our own way. It's an adventure.'

Harold: 'It's an adventure to jump in the river, but one might drown.'

Pat: 'If you start to drown my love, you will be thrown the prettiest waterwings the RSC can afford.'

They do tend to fence like this, these two, each giving as good as they get.

Pat: 'Mister Innocent, you need taking down a peg or two.'

Harold: 'No I don't. I like it up here.'

QUEEN ELIZABETH SCENE Another bad rehearsal. It's one of those days. We had really cracked this scene the last time we did it, but now Frances heads off in strange new directions.

Bill says, 'With every scene there are dozens of choices of how to play it. Unless we select one and stick to it until proven wrong, we will just flounder in chaos.'

The scene is extremely tricky for Queen Elizabeth. She has, apparently, to be won over by this man who's murdered her children, her brothers and, indirectly, her husband. She wouldn't even remain in the same room as him! Frances believes the answer is to become possessed by the devil. Which is why, today, it's like something out of Hammer Horror. I believe it's more chilling if the characters remain *human*. (I've bought the Sutcliffe book and am reading it at every possible opportunity.)

Wednesday 23 May

QUEEN MARGARET SCENE All morning spent on this. Unravelling, disciplining, simplifying and, best of all, *cutting* – immediately makes it easier to play.

One of the problems had been that the climax seems to be the confrontation between Margaret and Richard. Yet after this, Shakespeare has her cursing the others again. Most of this stuff gets cut. Pat loses a lot but takes it well and with good humour.

As he's racing against time with the morning schedule, Bill says to her, 'Let's just try to get to your exit Pat, get you off.'

She says, 'Yes please. I can imagine someone in the front row saying, "Dear oh dear, I thought she'd never go." '

She needn't worry. Her Margaret will be striking and original.

RUN-THROUGH OF ACT ONE Still the most difficult Act for me. And the thought of having to do that opening speech in front of the Company for the first time . . . oh God. Just before we start, I feel the *fear*, like a raging distant storm. I turn my back on it.

' "Now is the winter . . ." '

The run is thrilling. So many things fall into place for me. Richard's soliloquies and asides, which have seemed both bland and embarrassing in solus sessions, are actually enjoyable to do now. An audience at last – people to tell the story to. Get some encouraging laughs from the assembled cast and at other times the silences are palpable. (Contrary to popular belief in the profession, I feel that rehearsal laughs can be a useful guideline.)

Afterwards, Frances is very encouraging and Blessed does his wonderful machine-gun support: 'Bravo, 'kin marvellous, very exciting, very original, going to be sensational, 'kin terrific . . .' One or two other people pat my shoulder, compliment me on clarity and above all, speed.

If nothing else, mine will be the fastest Richard ever.

ARDEN HOTEL BAR Notes from Bill. He says, 'You can get some idea from today of the size of the part. That was only Act One. You have four to go. You will have to pace yourself very carefully. I would say from today's run you are still doing far too much, showing us too much too soon.'

Mal says, 'What was great about today's run is that you were serving the text and not doing a big number on it.'

The evening ends with Mal and me imploring Bill to cut more, and Bill staring glassily into the middle distance.

But we *are* in with a chance.

Thursday 24 May

A new confidence. It has become clear that Richard needs a basic neutrality, so that he can slip into his various acts without arousing disbelief from the other characters. Richard the actor is most important now, or more accurately, Richard the psychopath (the Sutcliffe book is proving invaluable).

My only secret worry is the mysterious problem with lines. In the flow of yesterday's run, they were mostly there. Or, at any rate, I could keep going on the rhythm of the verse, substituting synonyms when the actual words didn't spring to mind – Gielgud has said this is one of the pleasures of playing Shakespeare; nobody understands what you're saying so you can make it up when you forget – but today I'm drying and fluffing all over the place. For the first time I understand why older actors become so neurotic about their failing powers of memory. Each time I have to take a prompt it feels like a tiny humiliation.

Friday 25 May

RUN-THROUGH OF ACT THREE Again it is thrilling. Much laughter. But when it comes to the Baynard's Castle scene – which, comically, should be the high spot – the laughter stops dead. I'm confused about this. On the one hand, it's all right if the scene isn't funny – after all, the Crown of England is at stake. On the other hand, the laughter up until this point came out of Richard's outrageous manipulations – in which case, this scene should be a scream.

QUEEN ELIZABETH SCENE Scholars have puzzled over the outcome of this scene for centuries. Elizabeth doesn't actually consent to the marriage between Richard and her daughter. All she says is, 'Write to me very shortly, and you shall understand from me her mind.' This could be played as 'yes', 'no' or 'maybe'. Bill is very keen that it should be 'Yes, absolutely!'

Why does *he* have to write, when it's *her* answer he requires? What does she want him to write anyway? Does she want a postcard from Bosworth?

Bill says, 'She's just being very feminine. In one's youth one was always being plagued by women who wouldn't phone you until you'd phoned them.'

Frances's feminist hackles rise: 'How could you have been plagued by women who *didn't* phone?' The other women in the rehearsal room lean forward, Alison Sutcliffe, ASM Bridgette McManagan. Bill just blushes and grins sheepishly. Alert over. There is no sport here: he is the gentlest of men.

This leads to an interesting discussion about Richard's sexuality; Frances feels that this is what could win Elizabeth over in the end. Bill and I both feel Richard is probably asexual – can't or doesn't do it. Frances says to me, 'Well, watching you in the runs, Richard is very animal, which, I'm afraid, is rather sexy.' The old refrain – 'How many severely deformed people are regarded as sex symbols?' Bill says, 'It's all right as long as we can always see that he uses sex as just another weapon. One mustn't think that intercourse with this man would be champagne and Bolero. It would be the most savage, violent experience.'

We do the scene and Frances plays it beautifully again, the undisciplined chaos of the other day gone. Her need for Richard becomes rather moving. As Frances says, Elizabeth has lost everything, at least Richard represents a life-force, an energy, however twisted.

Saturday 26 May
CONFERENCE HALL Another Saturday afternoon in here, the light fading, rain on the skylights, *Henry V* on the tannoy. Jim takes me through the whole part, carefully listing each dry and fluff so that I can entrap them at last.

The new crutches arrive; knobbly wooden walking-sticks set into the iron tops. Although these are much lighter, there is a new confusing balance – iron at the top, wood below. I realise that Charlotte's old NHS crutches (battered and twisted after weeks of rehearsals) have become, without my noticing, the extra limbs we talked about. It's too late to change to anything else now.

I ring Bill A. who has retired for the weekend. Without hesitation he comes back to the theatre so we can sort out this nagging problem. Even if the NHS crutches are covered and disguised they will never have the gnarled and tapered look we imagine, or indeed the sound of wood. But he agrees we will have to use them in the show itself. Simply by living on them for five weeks, they are part of me now – with them I can turn on a sixpence and dance the old fandango. I think that if you pricked them they'd probably bleed.

Dying for a cigarette tonight. It's been seven weeks without one.

Sunday 27 May
JULIA'S COTTAGE Quiet, drizzly day.

Finish the Sutcliffe book. It's quite brilliant, written from a startling original viewpoint. There is hardly any violence or gore. What shocks you is the domesticity of it all. For example, after he is caught, his sister Jane has a recurring nightmare. He is handcuffed to her and has to accompany her everywhere. Then suddenly the handcuffs fall off and he says, 'I've got to do it again.' She wakes screaming. Your own brother – a nightmare creature. So Sutcliffe is demystified as a monster. He is 'somebody's husband, somebody's son' (the police's phrase used when they were frantically searching the country for that needle in a haystack) and Gordon Burn shows that it's so easy to overlook or excuse bizarre behaviour if it's someone close to you.

Nevertheless, towards the end, there is a growing sense among some of those around him that he might be the Ripper. And perhaps even a feeling in him that the end is coming. Wanting it to come? He cries suddenly towards the end. Like Richard, the frightened self breaking through.

Two quotations are interesting. One of his brothers on what he thought the Ripper might be like: 'I imagined him to be an ugly hunchback wi' boils all over his face, somebody who couldn't get women and resented them for that. Somebody with totally nothing going for him.' And a description at the trial: 'His face, even when discussing the most sordid details of his crimes, seemed constantly to flirt with the idea of a smile.'

This is the aspect of Richard that I have resisted most, the 'chuckling pleasure' Stopford A. Brooke referred to, with its melodramatic connotations. Yet the characteristic everyone remembers about Sutcliffe is a high-pitched giggle. So, perhaps a sense of pleasure then, a sense of delight . . . a sense of humour.

I've been quoting the book constantly in rehearsals. Some members of the cast have stated their disapproval that it should even have been written. Some of the women have expressed more – disgust and anger. What are they saying? They'd prefer not to know, not to understand? They'd prefer certain areas of life to be censored? Isn't that partly what breeds the Sutcliffes and the Nilsens?

Sutcliffe at 3, 11, 21 and 28.   27/6/84

Sutcliffe aged 3, 11, 21, 28

As we're leaving the King's Arms Hotel after Sunday lunch, I watch a beautiful white dove walking down the wet road. A car approaches and the bird accidentally turns into the wheel rather than away from it. A gentle crunch. The car passes. A shape like a discarded napkin left in the road. Still perfectly white, no red stains, but bearing no relation anymore to the shape of a bird. A trail of white feathers flutter down the road after the car. The suddenness is very upsetting. That gentle crunch.

Monday 28 May
Two weeks to go.

Another bad day on the early group scenes. We've all got different solutions to the problems in these scenes and no one can agree. Bill, the most democratic of directors, sits silently, looking miserable.

The current bone of contention is whether there should be outbreaks of violence in the court – the Margaret-mugging episode, Rivers and Dorset drawing knives on Richard's faction after Edward's death. I am very much in favour, others feel it's an intrusion on the text. Adam Bareham (Lord Rivers) says, 'The violence should be suppressed, these people should be able to sustain a politic decorum. Let's just use the text, not impose and demonstrate.'

I cannot let the matter lie. It seems too good an idea, that violence should always be a hair's breadth away. It says so much about the history of these people, the years of bloody civil war, the world that has bred a Richard.

Bill should decide this one, but he continues to sit obstinately on the fence, so it's left unresolved.

I go to the GBH to pump iron and deflate aggro. It's Bank Holiday in Stratford again. Morris dancers skip and drunk punks fall into the river.

BAYNARD'S CASTLE As an exercise, we try the scene for *real*. As if Richard was a genuinely honest and religious man and Buckingham was determined to make him King in order to cleanse the country of 'the corruption of a blemished stock'. It's the old problem of playing hypocrites and dissemblers. It's so difficult to enter into their play-acting with the emotional commitment they would be forced to use in real life. You are drawn like a magnet to the wink at the audience.

The exercise yields hidden treasures: how traumatic for Richard to have his family's dirty linen displayed in public, how savage Buckingham has to be to shake some sense into this man. Richard tries to clasp his hands over Buckingham's mouth or over his own ears, Buckingham wrenches these away, Richard weeps and sobs.

The discovery is so rich that we end up putting back most of what we'd cut.

And now that real issues are at stake the scene is also, at last, extremely funny.

Tuesday 29 May
It's the first sunny day for ages. The bright light makes you look around again and everything has changed. The countryside has turned green. That dusty, summer green I love (I suppose because of South Africa). Even the fields of rape are turning green now, so mercifully I can stop trying to describe them. Specks of white fluff on the air. Going over the bridge at Welford-on-Avon the river is a thicker, warmer brew today.

SOLUS We take stock. Almost all of the original plans for the character have changed. That's all right, that's healthy. Only by putting him on his feet (all four of them) could we really find out what works and what doesn't. The monster to strike pity and terror has gone; the new man has become funny and even a bit sexy!

'How many severely deformed people are regarded as sex symbols?' I ask for the last time, because Bill has found an answer: 'This is no ordinary severely deformed man.'

A rather upsetting incident involving one of the boys playing the Princes.

Bill and Alison Sutcliffe have had to choose an A-team and a B-team; the A-team gets to play the press night and schedules have to be worked round that.

For the A-team they've chosen a Prince Edward from one pair and a Duke of York from the other, which means separating the two sets of 'brothers' who have rehearsed together for all these weeks.

The demoted York freaks out and disappears. We assume this to be the behaviour of a diminutive prima donna, so he doesn't win much sympathy. Welcome to the big cruel world of theatre, kid. But as the hours pass, and Vera the child-minder and his parents fail to find him anywhere, the smiles start to freeze on our faces.

At last he does turn up, tear-stained and grubby. Our assumptions were all wrong. His despair is not to do with being robbed of the chance to play his York to the critics. It's because he's being separated from the boy playing Prince Edward with whom he's been working for weeks. He believes in their rapport: 'He *feels* like my brother,' the boy cries. Clearly he has the making of a serious actor.

The press night is starting to cause its special mayhem and claims an early victim.

Wednesday 30 May
Compromises are being reached on Court violence.

The tension of the other day is being defused almost single-handedly by Blessed, the rock on which this year's Company stands. With that massive smile and manic machine-gun delivery: 'Yes Bill, what d'you want me to do? You tell me, yes Bill, you tell me, I can take direction like the 'kin best of them! Yes you tell me Bill, where's John Barber going to be sitting, where's little Jack Tinker-Tailor?! You tell me Bill, I'm going for the 'kin reviews, me, you tell me Bill!'

He and I have developed a running gag – Hastings is always trying to be of help to Richard, getting him in and out of chairs, with a commentary under his breath: 'Copes well for a cripple doesn't he? 'Kin marvellous how he copes, never grumbles, there you go your lordship, you want to have a word with your mate Buckingham, off you go now, on yer holidays.'

'On yer holidays' has become a catch-phrase shared by a small group of us, to represent our enforced exile up here in Stratford. We greet by saying, 'Been down the arcade yet?', or 'I pulled a cracker in the Tunnel of Love last night.' Pat occasionally throws in, 'Breakfast is now being served in the Portofino Room', which she confessed doesn't just sound like an Alan Bennett line, it *is* one.

Blessed is a total anarchist; every line that he says is followed by a twinkling glance to Mal or me, as if to say, ' 'Kin daft innit?' The wonderful thing about his Hastings is that he's using this for the character and it fits perfectly. His Hastings is a man who doesn't take life seriously and so fails to notice that he's heading for disaster.

A solus session scheduled, but both Bill and I are bored with these – we need an audience now. It's a warm sunny evening so we cancel the rehearsal and head off to Lambs in Moreton-in-Marsh: the Bills, Alison and self. Discussion about the privilege of working at Stratford for the Company, how as students we all made pilgrimages here, hitchhiking, queuing for returns, sleeping-bags in fields, dreams of working here one day. We share a sense of wonderment that we should be directing, designing, starring here now.

The scoliotic patron again a source of intense fascination. As the evening progresses, and bottles of wine gather and empty, I become increasingly determined to speak to him tonight. Again a threatened exodus from the table. Bill D. says, 'I'd really rather you did this on a night when I wasn't here.' Bill A. says, 'It's completely bad form, like chatting up a waitress.'

Again, an argument rages about research. Where to draw the line?

Thursday 31 May

CORONATION SCENE Guy Woolfenden arrives to teach the cast the Gloria.

Guy is, of course, another RSC legend. He's been with the Company for decades and composed the music for three previous productions of *Richard III*. This makes me very self-conscious again. Like Ciss, he's heard all these lines spoken before, better or worse.

Bill's conception for the coronation is brilliant. Everyone is there – the congregation is made up of the living and the dead (ghosts of the early victims, Clarence, Hastings, Rivers and Grey). The ceremony is conducted by the clergy assisted by the murderers and Hastings' whores.

So the full Company is assembled (they'll be supplemented by a full chorus Guy's recording in London next week). I'm the only one who doesn't have to learn the Gloria. Sitting behind them all, sketching, I find

Blessed   Jim   Pat
Mal   Peter Miles   Brian Parr   Hep   Guy   Bill A.

it rather moving. The voices soar. So do my hopes for this production. I mustn't set myself up for disappointment.

People complain that the hymn has been set too high. Guy says he was watching the football on TV last night and was amazed to hear how high the crowd were singing 'You'll Never Walk Alone'. He says, 'I rushed to my piano and discovered they were singing a fifth higher than I bet any of them *thought* they could sing. The adrenalin supplies the boost.'

Bill fits the ceremony to the music. At the moment of climax, as the voices reach for that final 'gloria!', the throne bearers hoist me up as high as they can above their heads. A ripple of shivery sensations – it's like being shot out of a cannon. There is nothing more exciting than acting to live music, the make-believe at its most indulgent and its most thrilling.

The coronation is going to be a tremendous end to the first half. In fact, a hard act to follow.

Bill's idea is to echo it at the end – bring the congregation on again, perhaps singing, or a more violent chanting, for the death.

After the rehearsal Guy spots the throne we've been using for rehearsals and asks, 'Is that from an old *Julius Caesar*?'

'Looks more like a *Cymbeline* to me,' says Bill.

Jim and others are quick to join in, circling the throne, like a crowd of Arthur Negii on 'Antiques Roadshow':

'Or *Coriolanus* even.'

'Well, a *Titus* for that matter.'

'I wouldn't put a *Troilus* past it.'

'*Antony and Cleo*?'

'I don't know,' says Guy, 'the feet still have the look of a '72 Chris Morley *Caesar* to me.'

Black Mac's on board; he will be dressing me after all. He's using the two-week holiday due to him from the Army so that he can be here during the days of the technical and dress rehearsals.

'I told you Animil, if you wanted me, I'd be there!'

Friday 1 June
Despite a mogodon, I wake with the four o'clock gremlins. Today, the first run-through of the whole of our first half. Also the false back will finally arrive from Tucker.

RUN-THROUGH OF THE FIRST HALF The cast warm up on the coronation Gloria, while I limber up on the crutches. Feel very nervous.

A lot of the Company will be seeing it for the first time, also Bill D., the lighting designer Leo Leibovici, and Charlotte who has come up from London to pronounce final judgement on the safety of my deformed position.

Bill says, 'Right, we're starting in fifteen seconds' time . . .' I'm pacing around muttering 'Now is the winter' under my breath like a rosary. Bill's countdown is not helping: '. . . nine, eight, seven –'

'Has anyone seen Roger Allam?' asks Philip MacDonald, the stage-manager.

Everyone stops what they're doing and looks round the crowded room. No Roger Allam. The stage-managers hurry away to put out a call over the tannoy and to phone his digs. We wait poised. We can't start without him – the first Clarence scene is straight after 'Now is the winter'. Word comes back that he is nowhere to be found. Stage-managers are sent to his digs, we to wait in the Green Room. People who know him well say it is untypical of him to have misread the call sheet. Something more ominous is feared.

Waiting. At regular intervals he is called over the tannoy. But there seems to be some problem in pronouncing his name: 'Will Mister Allen go to the Conference Hall immediately . . . Mister Allung . . . Mister Annun . . . Mister Annum . . .' as if by trying different names it will miraculously conjure him up.

We wait an agonising half hour. At last Bill decides to proceed with Clarence's understudy, Andy Readman, who knows the lines and is prepared to have a go.

After all of this, the run is extremely tense. It probably would have been anyway.

Andy is quite stunning as Clarence. The character's fear and confusion are, of course, well served by the present situation. But even so, he plays with a speed and absence of emotional indulgence which we all could learn from.

I take until Act Three to relax and start enjoying myself. Earlier on, the feeling is dreadful – no laughs from the people seeing it for the first time, I'm trying much too hard, dripping with sweat after the first five minutes. I remember all the lines, but clumsily. Stumbling and paraphrasing.

Oddly enough it's the two boy Princes who get the first laughs and everyone relaxes around them.

Strange feeling afterwards. Exhausted, wet through, disappointed with myself, but also uplifted by the bits that have worked. Also a feeling of presumptuousness – the cheek of daring even to attempt this great part. Wanting to run away and hide, but having to put on a brave face, like after press nights.

Charlotte is very encouraging about the disability and gives it the seal of approval. She's never seen the play before, or even the film, and says it had her on the edge of her seat. That's good to hear. Jim also encouraging but says, 'You've got to find more of Richard's *intellectual* brilliance. You've got to be as agile with his mind as you are on the crutches.' Other reactions from Blessed – 'Going to be 'kin marvellous, very original, very exciting' – and Harold Innocent who says, 'Too long, too long.' I agree with this. It ran over two hours and people are still tending to play their moments rather than telling the story.

Bill has a rather charming weakness for note sessions. He launches into reams of detailed notes, forgetting until half-way through to make a general comment: 'Oh, by the way, it was very good.'

Roger Allam appears, looking ashen. He had simply misread the call sheet. He goes on his knees, and begins to crawl across the floor towards Bill.

Bill says, 'Roger, the worst punishment I can give is to tell you that your understudy's performance is rather brilliant.'

WARDROBE FITTING-ROOM With my heart in my mouth, I hurry over to see my back.

It's much softer than I imagined, lying on the floor like a big pink blancmange, a slice of blubber, a side of Elephant Man. I can hardly get my clothes off fast enough to hoist it on to my back. A crowd of wardrobe staff, the Bills, Alison, Charlotte, are gathered around. They gasp at the first sight. I view myself in a series of mirrors. It's magnificent from the side and back, moving with my body in a convincing and disturbing fashion. But nothing shows from face-on because of Tucker's refusal to build up a massive central hump extending on to the shoulders. A faint sense of disappointment that the bull is gone. But hardly time to register this as an army of wardrobe ladies descend with pins and scissors.

The back has arrived so late that they are now left with exactly one week to make all of my costumes. No doubt they've all been through anger and despair, but this evening there is an atmosphere of celebration. Everyone is grinning, laughing, chattering away. Again that sense of hope for this production is rather moving.

The deformity will be worn in two sections. The arms and knees will be sewn into a complete body stocking. The back will strap over this like a parachute.

Roger Allam seeks me out to apologise personally. He's looking so shaken I end up consoling *him*. He's been out and bought Andy Readman a bottle of Madeira wine called Duke of Clarence.

The Bills have disappeared to a lighting meeting, so I'm left alone for the evening. Exhausted and fighting back post-natal depression after today's run.

Luckily bump into Penny who feels the same, so we take one another to dinner at Hill's, Stratford's excellent new restaurant, and have a wonderful evening. She is terrifically constructive about today's run: 'It was too long, not because it lasted over two hours, but because the play is a classy thriller, no more, no less. It's got to go like the clappers.'

Saturday 2 June
Bill and Ciss give me notes on the run. Bill puts it vividly as always: 'You haven't learned the part yet. You've learned the lines, you played each scene well, but you haven't got the shape of it yet. It's like you're surfing this magnificent wave, but you're not content to lie on the board and enjoy the ride. You're paddling furiously with your arms, expending lots of energy, but not affecting the progress of the journey in any way.'

Ciss points out that Richard has no set-backs in the early part of the play, nothing to jolt his sense of confidence. Success with every step he takes. She talks of me overworking my voice and it lacking a lightness of touch, but is always careful to add, 'It's only a question of degree, darling.'

I request that we run the whole play at least three times next week. I've got to be able to treat it as just another play, de-mystify it. In Shaw's words, I'm still too 'solemnly conscious of Shakespeare's reputation'. In a way, I've got to get a bit bored with it.

I mention cuts and the discussion immediately disintegrates into a tense monologue from me. Everyone felt the run was too long, why is Bill the only person who can't see it? I resort to a few blows below the belt, suggesting that by refusing to cut, he's making my job harder, forcing me to overwork in the effort to drag this deadweight along.

Bill's tactic is to sit very still, stare at the floor and not enter the discussion at all. It's very effective. I run out of steam and begin to pack up for the weekend.

He suddenly says rather formally, 'I just want you to know that I think you're doing smashing work on this.'

I'm taken aback. He never normally says things like this to me, but expects me to know for myself when things are working well.

I say, 'Thank you. And I'd like you to know that I think you are too. And it sometimes occurs to me that you think I've lost faith in you.' (Very pleased to have had the chance to say that.)

'Oh no, no.' He blushes, we shake hands in a curiously formal way and part for the weekend.

Feel shattered with exhaustion as Jim drives us back to Islington. Sleep most of the way, half waking as we come into a sunny London evening. Horse chestnut trees, coral and white, through the sun-roof of the car. A glimpse of myself in the wing-mirror. Unshaven. Heavy eyes. Arriving at the house, that hazy sense of waking from or falling into a dream. The house so familiar and yet the garden wildly overgrown. Branches, vines, firethorn and pink roses pouring in from both walls, giant hollyhocks leaning about, the grass long and silvery . . . an ice cream van plays 'O Sole Mio'.

London feels like it's on another planet.

Sunday 3 June
Impossible to relax without Richard, yet essential to leave him alone for the day. A long swim at Dickie's club, the RAC. The Victorian/Egyptian swimming-pool is beautiful. Floating face-down at the deep end, hanging in space.

Monday 4 June
Only one week to go.

Evening rehearsals are interrupted by an emergency RSC policy meeting. There's a feeling at the top that shows are being over-designed, made over-elaborate. The Bills are rather nervous that some of our set might get cut as an example to the others.

WARDROBE FITTING-ROOM Normally the designer would be present at every fitting but because of the meeting I have this one on my own.

They have made a rough of the first black costume to try over the false back and arms. It is a shock to see how the deformity disappears under a black covering. Of course that colour is famous for its slimming powers. The muscular arms don't register at all, the hump only just. I dare not say anything, but watch with a growing sense of despair as the wardrobe ladies pin and snip round me. My first instinct was right – Tucker's scale has been too small, it's filmic. The costume itself looks good. The wardrobe ladies are delighted and hurry away to start some serious stitching.

I return to the Conference Hall with heavy tread. Something will have to be done. And tonight.

The Bills are looking relieved. Our set is intact. They got away with a light ticking-off. Their sense of well-being is about to be shattered.

'It can't be right!' I blurt. 'We may have changed a lot of our early ideas, but we were still expecting something of the deformed brute. Instead we've got a man with a slightly bad back!'

Rehearsals are cancelled, the wardrobe staff are alerted and we hurry back across the road.

Maurice Robson, the head cutter, has a fearsome frown on her face.

'Well, here we are again,' I laugh nervously.

'Yes,' she says murderously.

'Right,' says Bill D., and like a sculptor sets to work on me. He calls for a spare pair of Tucker's arms and stretches them over the ones I'm already wearing, doubling their size. Grabs some grey foam rubber and shoves this between my back and Tucker's, trebling its scale.

The costume will have to be started again. Only six days to go. I suggest we ditch altogether the idea of a second, heavily brocaded costume. This will lighten the workload. Everyone agrees. Maurice smiles gratefully and I feel slightly safer now as she wields her heavy scissors round my neck and groin.

Afterwards, in the pub we give vent to our anger with Tucker, but also with ourselves. We knew it was too small and were too frightened to confront him.

'It was those wolves,' says Bill D.

Tuesday 5 June

QUEEN MARGARET SCENE We still can't agree on certain aspects of the scene and are very much the 'wrangling pirates' Queen Margaret calls us. Bill suddenly says, 'Right. We're obviously not going to agree, so you'll have to accept that I can see better from the outside than you can from in there. *This* is how it will be . . .'

I've never seen him do that before. The problems are sorted out within five minutes.

FIRST FULL RUN-THROUGH Bill's brief is, 'Tell the story, serve the story.'

I go at it lightly and softly. My aim is just to get through it.

For the Woodville dinner in the Queen Margaret scene, stage-management have set real food for the first time, but, forgetting how much the tables are thumped and jumped on, they've used oranges and apples. All our agonising over this scene is forgotten as it turns into a farce of rolling fruit.

In the Princes scene, when I bash the crutches together, one breaks. This is a sad development. The NHS crutches which have lasted six long weeks of battering are not, as we thought, invincible. Bill D. blames the Tory party and the NHS cuts. Another metal will have to be found.

The second half feels much better. I've always been more comfortable with the neurotic Richard rather than the supremely confident one.

It runs about three and a quarter hours. With an interval, that will be three and a half. At the end, Bill says there are only three people who can't go any faster – Mal, Frances and self – everyone else can and must. Yvonne Coulette gets very upset. She feels she can't go any faster and has been constantly volunteering cuts.

In the pub I am supported by Mal, Roger and Penny in begging Bill to cut. He stares at the carpet. The problem gets more serious with each day. Already people will be heartbroken to lose their favourite bits. Which is why it would have been better to cut before rehearsals began.

Bump into Harold Innocent who says, 'Too long, too long. There are scenes in our production never witnessed before on the English stage. I've only ever seen the Queen Elizabeth scene once before and has *anyone* ever seen the Clarence children before?'

Wednesday 6 June
SECOND RUN-THROUGH Bill's brief is, 'Go for the humour, the lightness.' He has done a few little snips and everyone does take it faster. In all, we cut about eight minutes off the first half.

I take a plunge at the part, well a gentle plunge, and the first half does feel better. But the humour of the character is still a mystery and one which only a live audience can solve.

Something happens early in the run to help me get closer to the character. For the Woodville dinner, stage-management have – unbelievably – set oranges and apples in the bowls again, and inevitably they start rolling around again. In the middle of some immortal couplet I break off and say, 'Fucking hell, right, excuse me a moment', carry the bowls with the remaining fruit to the front of the rake, throw them off, and return to continue with the scene. I'm not really that angry but everyone thinks I've had a 'turn', and the room has gone very quiet. For the first time I get some sense of the danger Richard should engender among those around him. It is very liberating for me, and the rest of my performance has an unpredictable edge as a result.

Bill has picked up one of the apples that I threw out, and sits munching it. At the notes session afterwards he says, 'You won't be seeing fruit in that scene again. Something today convinced me that the Woodville family are exclusively meat-eaters.'

I am pleasantly surprised by the strength of my voice throughout the first half; then, on the big 'If?' in the strawberries scene, I stupidly over-strain it and live to regret that piece of overacting – there's the whole of the second half to get through. But my voice holds. Just. A tin of Nigroid voice tablets is carried with me throughout.

Without my noticing too much, I sail through the lines with only one or two stumbles and generally the whole affair passes off without too much effort. A step forward. The part at least felt within reach today.

WARDROBE FITTING-ROOM Again the atmosphere is bright and good-humoured in the face of impossible odds. Today is the fortieth anniversary of D–Day after all.

A new rough has been stitched together to try over the enlarged back and arms. I could weep for joy – we're there at last. An image that goes back to the early sketches. The beast, the bull. And the massive upper bulk again creating that optical illusion of wasted legs and tiny feet.

The new weight of the enlarged deformity raises the problem of how to support it. The obvious way is attaching it like a parachute with the crotch as anchor, but I went through all this with the harness for the Fool and my manhood almost never recovered. They will try cross-fastenings on the chest.

THE DIRTY DUCK A thrilling discussion about Shakespeare, with the Avon drifting by at our elbows and the evening turning pink, blue, mixing to purple. Bill, Penny and I vow to do a production of *Merchant* in the future. Bill wants to try cutting the whole last Act. Who cares about those sodding rings after the trial scene? I'm delighted – imagine having no rows with Bill over the length of the play!

Thursday 7 June
Grateful for the bitty, matinée day.

NOTES SESSION On yesterday's run. Bill very skilfully finds a word of individual praise for everyone. He says the run was more thrilling than he thought possible with a play he knows to the point of boredom.

The new crutches arrive, made of the metal they use for racing bikes and circus trapezes. The weight is comparable to the NHS crutches. We bash them together and they appear to be indestructible, not even denting slightly. But in appearance they are exceptionally ugly. Dead straight and rather thick. The shape has no movement or grace at all. I shall think of them as a last resort. Waiting now for the titanium crutches.

Doing bits with Ciss on stage. I love working in this huge space without an audience or the need to perform. The holy magic this place has in repose. A few working lights throwing shafts across the heavy red folds of the *Merchant* set, but mainly a feeling of darkness, of coolness.

We do some voice tests and then Ciss makes Penny and me do the Lady Anne scene running around the auditorium between the seats, me trying to catch her. Whenever Ciss does voice workshops in here she loves getting the actors off the stage and into the auditorium.

She says, 'We have to give words space, let them float out. The words and ideas are more important than what anyone can do with them. They have to be allowed to live in the air.'

Back in her little office a solus voice call. I sense she is worried by my voice from the two run-throughs. Not its staying power, but my inexperience with the verse. But I also know she wouldn't be driving me so hard at this stage if she wasn't quite confident in my basic grasp of the role.

She talks about freeing the vowels. 'Vowels are what we spoke first.'

'You mean as babies?'

'And as we evolved as human beings. Vowels carry the shape, the weight, the meaning of the words.'

She asks me to remember the first poem or rhyme I learned as a child, to recapture my first joy of musical language. My brain aches with the effort of going back that far. 'Jack and Jill' is all I can think of. She makes me recite it on the floor, rocking. Then 'Now is the winter' in the same way. She is sitting on the floor as well, cross legged, her head cocked, eyes alert, as if the sounds may actually be seen or scented in the air. She says, 'We're on to something. Can you feel it?'

'Yes . . . sort of.'

It sounds mystical as I write it down like this, but as Alison Sutcliffe says later, 'Ciss is teaching something profound, not handing over some glib method.' If it is sometimes confusing it is because you are reaching inside for a new sensation. Try and define it and it remains elusive. Allow yourself to feel it and it will come. Not immediately, but suddenly without trying in a few days time. In a run-through or rehearsal, you are suddenly aware of the words coming out freely, 'living in the air'.

It's happened in the past, will happen this time.

SOLUS Nightmare speech. Bill makes me do it very slowly, exploring each thought: 'Let Richard think for the first time like an ordinary man, not like an express train. Like any of us asking "What do I fear?" ' He says if we can get sympathy for Richard at this stage it will be a considerable achievement, but it's a sympathy which should make the audience want him killed quickly. Not out of revenge for what he's done, but to have him put out of his misery. Bill says, 'We enjoy the early Richard because, for most of us who aren't like him, it is such a strain being good!'

LONG LARTIN MAXIMUM SECURITY PRISON Ciss does regular workshops here. I've asked if I could do one, hoping it might throw some new light on Richard. We've decided to do it on the Lady Anne scene. When we met this evening to drive out to the prison, Penny said, 'You do realise that everyone in that room will have murdered or raped at least one person.' She is wearing very tight jeans which can only be removed, she assures me, with the latest laser equipment.

We are led through the prison grounds which look quite friendly in the sunny evening light, rather like a university campus. But eerily deserted. And yet the gates buzz and spring open just as you reach them. Big Brother is watching.

In the classroom the sunlight streams through the bars on the window as the prisoners file in, smiling and nodding at us, a bit awkward.

Ciss seems unusually nervous as she begins the session. She gets them on their feet. 'All hum,' she instructs them. 'Mmmmmm' go the hefty cons, 'Mmmaaa ... Mmmooo ...' Ciss yells over the din, 'Pat one another's backs!' Penny joins in gamely, bounding into the throng. 'And chests!' calls Ciss. Penny disappears momentarily in the rush.

We read the scene. They are a wonderful audience. Our visit seems to be a form of nourishment to them. They listen with rapt attention, almost like blind people do, hearing each and every syllable.

Afterwards, a discussion rages. I find the arguments difficult to follow because they're all studying sociology, psychology or philosophy. One of them is particularly witty and charming. He is doing English Literature and talks about Brook's *Midsummer Night's Dream.*

The usual dilemma crops up: why does Lady Anne give in to Richard? 'Easy,' says a quiet and rather beautiful young man. 'Evil is erotic.'

Another says, 'Shit, Richard the Third would have made a good crook, wouldn't he?'

As they're leaving, they each come up to shake hands. The charming man who talked about Brook's *Dream* asks Penny if she would do him a special favour. He wants her to send him a photo. Just of her hands.

He's the only one accompanied back to his cell by a special warder, who has been standing just outside the door throughout. The rest troop away noisily in a group.

I feel rather like I did after those visits to the spastics' work centre and disabled games evening. Uplifted by the courage on display.

Evil might be erotic, but, from the evidence of this evening, it's also quite invisible.

Friday 8 June
VOICE CALL Ciss is inspiring as always, but her worry about my voice is beginning to communicate to me. I'm starting to listen to myself speak. Fatal.

THIRD AND FINAL RUN-THROUGH We won't be doing the whole play again until next Wednesday's dress rehearsal. Today's run is, in a way, the summation of the seven weeks' work in the Conference Hall. Next week we move into the theatre and a new phase begins.

Bill and I are alone, waiting for the others to come in. He says, 'What should you go for in this run?'

'Can't think of anything. To tell you the truth, I don't really feel like doing it at all.'

'Good. We said you should get bored with it.'

And precisely because I am a little bored, we have the most extraordinary run-through.

Malcolm Ranson, the fight director, is watching for the first time. Perhaps because his job entails devising ways of maiming and killing, he has a rather dark sense of humour and starts giggling early on. This communicates first to Bill, who also starts, then to me and finally to the whole cast. I play the whole of the first half on the crest of a corpse. Sometimes I am able to control and use it – with this much hysteria in the room waiting to explode, one can achieve electrifying effects by holding it down or throwing it back in their faces.

But at other times the hysteria claims me as the most helpless victim and things get steadily worse until, half way through the Baynard's Castle scene, I'm unable to continue. The whole room is full of shrieking people, like an asylum.

The atmosphere is so dangerous. On many levels. Another director or one of the older, more 'professional' members of the cast, could at any moment jump up and scream, 'Will you stop it!' But the discovery is rich. The anarchy, the disrespect for the *final* run-through unleashes my performance from the caution of seven weeks' rehearsal and sets loose the character at last. Although I didn't realise it, or plan this to happen, I needed to behave this disrespectfully as an actor to make the final leap into Richard's amorality and discover the true nature of his humour – Stopford A. Brooke's 'chuckling pleasure' and Peter Sutcliffe's high-pitched giggle.

The consequences for the second half are valuable too. Gone are the soliloquies, the asides, the manipulations, the plottings, and Richard's delight in all this. As King, the man becomes serious, paranoid, starts to disintegrate. Our run-through audience are dying to enjoy themselves like they did in Part One, but there are few opportunities. Their regret that it's not as much fun as before is directly linked to Richard's own sense of frustration and nostalgia for those joyous days. Events move nervously and horribly towards the inevitable end.

I have understood something about the whole part today. At the end I am not too drenched, the voice tired but still there. Inside, I'm deeply, deeply happy.

Bill says to the assembled cast, 'Well, we've done three good ones now. Don't know what to say . . . I'm terribly excited really . . . You're working together as a Company in a very generous way . . . Christ, I'm not going to make a ra-ra speech. You can all feel the potential of what we've got on our hands. Have a good weekend, and thank you.'

The word spreads like wildfire and it's encouraging the way people from all around the theatre keep coming up to say, 'I hear it went terribly well.'

Jim says, 'You're getting better and better each time. I think you might be on to something a bit special.' His eyes bright.

WARDROBE FITTING-ROOM The first costume is finished. A queue of people waiting to try their creations on me. Debbie with the crowns and hat, Julian with the gloves and shoes, and finally Pam with the hair-piece. This has been made to match my own curly hair and perfectly fills the gap between my head and the hump. It's rather flattering – light years away from the Hermanus head – but looks so natural we decide to leave it as it is and ditch the spiked, punky look.

With everything on for the first time, I rotate, feeling the new shape from every angle. Suddenly I spy my shadow on the wall and get a shock. As I tell Bill A. later: 'Even though we've gone for a different shape, a different costume, different hair, the crutches, twisted knees, I looked at my shadow tonight and saw Laurence Olivier in the part.'

Bill says, 'That shape, that famous outline – that's not great acting, that's great writing.'

Saturday 9 June

The titanium crutches arrive – they make jet engines out of this metal. The weight is fine, lighter than the NHS ones, and they're beautifully slim, which would mean we'd be able to cheat a tapering effect. But a few bangs together and they start to dent.

We've run out of time. Can't experiment anymore. We are now faced with a clear decision – whether to stick with the NHS crutches which I have worked on for weeks but which we know can break, or do we go for the horribly thick bicycle metal? Bill D. wants the former, says we can have spares in the wings in case of breakages. I can't make up my mind. Could I do each performance with that constant risk? What if one suddenly broke on a fast exit or the leap down from the tomb? On the other hand, the bicycle metal is so solid and ugly. Bill A. puts me out of my misery: 'Let's put safety before beauty.'

The bicycle-metal crutches are rushed away to the Prop Shop to be disguised as best as possible.

SOLUS On stage. Exhaustion from the heavy week catching up with me now.

Ciss is working on 'Now is the winter', making me gesture on each of the open vowels. I am getting muddled, can't separate the sounds from the meaning anymore. Finally have to say, 'Ciss, I can't do it. It's too late for this kind of elementary work.'

'It's the perfect time for it,' she says, gently insistent, 'you understand the meaning, now rest on the sounds, let them do some of the work.'

'It's unnerving me.'

'It shouldn't. You mustn't worry, darling. It will happen gradually.'

'But that's what's unnerving to hear at this stage. I don't want to be waiting for something to happen gradually. I've got to be there now.'

I feel awful rejecting her of all people, but it's touching on a big worry – is my voice good enough for this part? The instrument itself. If it isn't, I mustn't dwell on it at all.

Now I just have to go with yesterday's discovery. A kind of fuck-you-all attitude: fuck off Shakespeare, fuck off the-proper-way-to-speak-verse, fuck off snapping tendons and Laurence Olivier.

JULIA'S COTTAGE Night. Treat myself to a bottle of Mersault and write up the week's events. It's useful this, helps me to get some perspective on a period of my life that is increasingly dream-like.

Much later, go out to sit in the garden. Dark, rich country night. A silhouette of dangling willowy branches. There were children playing in the shadowy garden next door, but now they've gone to bed. I can hear a stream, lambs bleating – a rather ghostly sound – and just once, heels on the pavement.

This time next week I will be standing in front of one and a half thousand people . . .

Sunday 10 June
Richard has his ghosts, his 'babbling dreams', I my four a.m. gremlins. Awake very edgy. Having to introduce two major new factors next week – heavier crutches to get used to, and wearing the deformity for long periods of time with whatever discomfort or heat exhaustion it causes. How has this happened? Almost the first thing Bill and I agreed was to have the deformity to wear throughout rehearsals, and to make the crutches second nature.

Sundays are the hardest days to get through anyway. Time to stop and think, which I don't really want to do. Refuge in the Gielgud book, *The Ages of Gielgud*, only to come across John Mortimer's lament on modern verse-speaking. I snap it shut as if killing a bug.

Mum rings from South Africa. Finally she asks, 'And Richard the Third?' like she's been doing ever since she decided Trevor Nunn really meant it, back in Joe Allen's. But today the question is resoundingly casual. She is trying to underplay her great anticipation and excitement.

'Fine,' I answer.

'Good!' she instantly replies, before I can elaborate at all, 'I've certainly never heard you so calm before an opening.' She so wants this to be true, so wants to send strength and courage through the telephone.

To the King's Arms Hotel for lunch, but I'm terribly restless. Keep thinking back to a similar lunch here two years ago, with Gambon before *King Lear* opened. We chatted and joked as always, but he wasn't quite with me. A man with something else on his mind. I think the only people who can know this feeling are those in the performing arts, sport, bullrings and death row.

Jim senses my tension and suggests a long walk. It's baking hot again. We set off along the side of Dovers Hill. A single path through waist-high wheat fields, still an unripened green. We walk for miles like this. At last a field of barley, light and silvery. The day changing. Shadows of clouds. A breeze skimming across the field, flowing shapes, ghosts departing.

Monday 11 June
The set isn't ready for us to start the technical rehearsal, so a change of plan: Guy and his orchestra move into the Conference Hall and we spend a happy day working through all the music cues, fitting them to the play. Acting to music again. I realise why it's so enjoyable – you feel like you're in a film. In fact, Guy's music is very much from a thriller. Which worries me slightly. I'm still not certain that the play will work on as simplistic a level as that. But a lot of the music is quite breathtaking. Richmond's theme, like Chris's performance, is a veritable gale of fresh air. It makes you sit bolt upright, inspired to slay dragons by the herd. And the coronation music, with orchestra and full (recorded) choir supplementing the cast, is a magnificent piece of ornate ritual. He has unashamedly borrowed from *Carmina Burana*.

Today is also Richard's coming-out day. It's a chance to get used to wearing the deformity as well as the new crutches. So I get dressed up in it all – Tucker's creations and full costume – and, feeling about as foolish as is possible, creep into the back of the Conference Hall. Everyone else, of course, is in normal clothes and there's me looking like something from the closing-down sale at Biba's. But all the comments are positive and encouraging and my bizarre appearance is quickly absorbed into the day's work.

Spending hours like this helps to make up for all the lost time. The discomfort is minimal, but the heat factor is impossible to gauge without performance energy and stage lights.

The bicycle-metal crutches have been covered in black leather (which makes them sound surprisingly like wood) but still look solid and ugly and disappointingly like modern crutches. I'm just going to have to learn to

live with them. I fear we've passed the point where any further requests
from me to produce something better would be welcomed. However, the
new weight is quickly adjusted to.

For the Bosworth scenes the battle horses are brought into the Conference Hall for Chris and me to practise mounting and dismounting. They
are most impressive to look at – two awesome, huge skeletons in gold and
black. Mine isn't quite finished yet and has an ear missing. Mal says that's
why it didn't come when Richard called 'A horse, a horse'.

Tuesday 12 June
Actors' nightmares tumbling over one another. In one, I am desperately
trying to learn the first speech before the first entrance. In another, Bill
and I are trying to select speeches for the end; new material has been
discovered about a Russian presence at Bosworth. I awake in a cold sweat
after making the immortal utterance, 'I think Brezhnev's speech is rather
good and I just can't see why you won't let him keep it.'

THE TECHNICAL REHEARSAL Cue to cue, lights, music, sound effects.
I love techs – the show without acting – and I think I'm rather good at
keeping the atmosphere light. There's a great deal of laughter all day. Bill
remains patiently good humoured throughout, despite the pressure. The
atmosphere is buoyant: Leo and the lighting team at their control panel
in the stalls; Charles waving and calling 'Coo-ee' from his perch in the
dress circle; Guy using the front of the stage to scribble a new fanfare
('The cue's coming up Bill, just as soon as the ink's dry').

There are a group of cleaners watching from the back of the upper
circle – the shows that they must have seen . . .

The routine problem as props and furniture and bits of the set arrive,
failing to resemble what we were expecting or had requested. Much
bashing of square blocks into round holes.

Sometimes the enforced alteration can be an improvement. At the
beginning of the scene with Hastings' head, the front screen flies out and
was to reveal me sitting on one of the tombs – the moment in the play we
eventually found to climb up on them. But the screen proves to be too
close to the tomb to allow me to sit on the edge in safety. The compromise
is to stand on the tomb astride the carved figure, which everyone says
looks even more effective from out front.

The set has worked magnificently. The tracery walls are a lighting
designer's dream, and Leo is not missing a trick. Shafts of light smudged
with incense fall across the ghost-white tombs. But some of the costumes

worry me slightly, rather like some of the music did yesterday. We're on a dangerous tightrope. There's a very thin line between the imagery of morality plays and that of picture-book Shakespeare and Hollywood medieval epic. But many are splendid – Harold Innocent is looking marvellous in acres of blue satin and white ermine out of which stick rotting bandaged hands; Jim's Tyrrel costume is one of the best of all, in that it looks like clothes that have been well lived-in, making him so seedy he's unrecognisable. The Queen Margaret image has worked terrifically as well. As Pat wanders by, wrapped in yards of Lancastrian flag, Blessed says, 'I see Margaret's popped over from France for her holidays, pity her parachute failed to open.'

Many problems with hats – something else we should have been rehearsing with for a while and not at the last minute. Blessed has hidden his ('I look enough like a 'kin sofa already'). My hat – a huge ornate Bosch creation – has a life of its own. It's like wearing a live octopus. Also, it tends to lodge on the hump so that when I turn my head it stays pointing forwards.

A long day.

Jim waits to drive me home although he could have left hours ago. I couldn't have done without his support over the last few weeks. Slump gratefully into the car.

The countryside is lit by a brilliant full moon. In forty-eight hours I will actually have *done it* in front of an audience. How like sexual exhibitionism that sounds – and how like it this business is. With that thought, a peculiar mixture of fear and excitement begins its slow, spidery crawl up my spine . . .

Wednesday 13 June
A letter from Bob with this quotation from a letter that Chekhov wrote to his wife: 'Art, especially the stage, is an area where it is impossible to walk without stumbling. There are in store for you many unsuccessful days and whole unsuccessful seasons, there will be great misunderstandings and deep disappointments . . . you must be prepared for all this, accept it and nevertheless, stubbornly, fanatically follow your own way . . .'

The strange way tension and exhaustion manifest themselves – reading it makes me cry uncontrollably for about five minutes. Because, of course, it's about the possibility of failure . . .

THE TECHNICAL CONTINUES Today more jagged and tense. Partly

because Hastings is dead and thus no Blessed filling the theatre with that
warm generous spirit.

But there's always Black Mac, swearing and cursing, but gentle as a
lamb. Strapping me into the false back: 'This is an evil contraption, Animil.
You've gotta be a martyr to be a Mark One, either that or fokkin daft!
Mark One spastic more like.' Never has my nickname, Animil, been more
apt than it is for me as Richard. He goes through some of the other names
he's coined over the twenty-one years he's worked here: Peter Hall was
Chief Sitting Bull; Ian Holm was the Dwarf; Norman Rodway was the
Bog Hopper; Patrick Stewart was Bald Eagle; Richard Griffiths was
Hippo; John Wood was Two-b'One ('If he stood sideways he'd be marked
absent'); Blessed the Gorilla; and Nureyev, whom he dressed one year (a
mind-boggling thought) when the Ballet was up here, was Big Balls. 'Vy
you callst me Beeg Ballst?' Rudi had asked. ' 'Cause that's a canny set of
tackle you've got there,' came the answer, causing the great dancer to
send out immediately for a dictionary of Newcastle slang.

The throne – bearers are all developing back trouble. I've been saying
for weeks they need some professional advice, from a weight lifter and/
or a theatre physio like Charlotte. Now, with the constant repetition of
sequences that inevitably occur at a tech, their backs are starting to give
under the weight. A local osteopath is coming in to see what they have to
do and advise whether it's feasible and safe. If we have to lose the image
of Richard being born aloft it will be tragic.

It's my bugbear, born of my own accident, but when it comes to matters
like these, theatre in this country is totally amateur. Actors busk their way
through the fights, dances, pratfalls and crippled distortions asked of
them, without knowing half the time what they're risking.

After much haggling the RSC have finally agreed to pay for me to have
a massage before each performance – something else that Charlotte
recommended as a precaution to avoid injury. These are proving to be
wonderful rest breaks in these hectic days. The masseuse is a small, sweet
lady called Jenny who looks about seventeen, but has fingers that could
split bricks apart.

We get hopelessly behind schedule and it becomes apparent we aren't
going to make the dress rehearsal this evening. Since photographers from
all the national newspapers have come up expecting a full run-through,
we have to hurriedly improvise a photo-call for them. Which means getting
into make-up. I find myself sitting in front of the dressing-room mirror,
wondering what to do. Unusual for me. I end up doing some functional

stuff for the large theatre – outlining the eyes, slightly shading the bone structure – which in the old days would have been called 'basic juvenile'.

Sit staring at myself in the mirror. Richard is definitely not a character job after all. He looks and sounds very much like me. I'm rather pleased. Maybe this is what Postlethwaite meant when he talked about me eschewing the predictable way I would play the part. Strangely enough, of all the things that various people have said, his comments have haunted me most.

Thursday 14 June
Despite two mogodon I wake at 6.30 a.m. Fresh, not too frightened. Today – the dress rehearsal and the first public preview – will be too chaotic for fear. I think I function better under pressure.

Get up and practise the lines. This is still my greatest worry, a fear so private that I hesitate to write it even here. At yesterday's tech 'the Breton Richmond' came out as 'the Briton Wretchmond', and 'to make the wench amends' became 'to make the mench awends' (the first Jewish Richard?).

It's my birthday today. Yesterday, somebody asked how old I'd be and I didn't know, genuinely didn't know whether it was thirty-four, thirty-five or thirty-six. Suppose that first blurred birthday happens to everyone eventually. I've worked it out – I'm thirty-five today. Happy Birthday.

By chance I overhear the Radio Three news this morning for the first time in weeks. It would seem that the outside world does still exist. And it's relatively relaxed – the coal strike continues, a new divorce law, voting for the European Parliament, the cost of living either highest or lowest in Bradford, a football tour, cricket. Only at the Royal Shakespeare Theatre in Stratford-on-Avon does a brave little group face Armageddon.

At the theatre a pile of cards – birthday and good luck combined – await me, as well as a mysterious pink box and telegrams from South Africa. Mum and Dad's says, 'Hope you find your horse, keep your Kingdom, and conquer the world.' Normally I find their overblown sentiments embarrassing, but today they're oddly touching. The excitement they must all be feeling back home. Also messages from Esther, Randall, Verne and, unusually, Joel – which instantly makes me cry. The pink box opens to let a helium balloon float out with 'Dickie III rules OK' scrawled on it by Charlotte. Also a card to the Animil from Mac. Another with love to Richard III from Dickie I. And Sara Kestleman has sent a beautiful print of an engraving of Richard III. The trouble she must have had finding it moves me terribly. I sit in my dressing-room and again am unable to stop crying. I'm hopelessly tearful these days.

THE TECHNICAL CONTINUES Racing against time now. A problem
with the death. How to get into the best position for Chris to slide in the
Boar-sword – there's a small gap in the armour to take it, and a metal
sheath inside to keep it well away from my own back. He's behind me, so
I can't tell when he's there.

Guy: 'Can't you take a cue off the music?'

Me: 'Can't I'm afraid. I'm tone-deaf.'

Bill: 'Well, when the singing stops. Even you must be able to tell the
difference between singing and instrumental.'

Me: 'Bill, we've worked together long enough for you to know I'm so
tone-deaf I can't tell the difference between music and silence.'

Chris: 'Look, I'll nudge you with my toe before I stab you.'

Me: 'It's all right, Bill. Chris is going to nudge me before he stabs me.'

Guy: 'A killer and a gentleman.'

Everyone says the slaying looks excellent from out front. Bill has ditched
his idea of having the full cast on stage, but seems to have achieved a
coup de theatre similar to the coronation, with just two people, music and
lights.

Odd that I've never been as self-conscious about 'A horse, a horse' as
'Now is the winter'. I think it's because the former is so rooted in my
concept of the whole deformity: the man simply can't run away, he needs
that horse desperately. So it's never seemed like a famous quote.

The osteopath has given the go-ahead to the throne-bearers, as long as
they are supplied with weight-lifters' support-belts and padding for their
shoulders.

DRESS REHEARSAL Bill and I have agreed that I should take it very
quietly and gently if I'm to have anything left for tonight. He assembles
the cast to warn them not to let this reduce their own energy.

The run-through is basically smooth. Miraculously everything from the
last few days slots together. I sweat fiercely – Blessed said that, by his first
entrance (five minutes into the play), it was like acting with a portable
shower unit. As the afternoon progresses it gets worse. Black Mac bears
the brunt – dripping wet clothes don't lend themselves easily to quick
changes. But despite the heat, it's pleasurable strolling through the
performance using a normal voice. Have to hold myself back from the big
moments towards the end, such a temptation to have a go at them, but
have to keep marking through. A useful discipline and exercise – these
great parts need mapping out like this. Rest camps on the side of Everest.

Hastings' head finally makes an appearance. Despite all our discussions it *is* just another prop head, bearing only a passing resemblance to Blessed and having no weight at all. The poor thing doesn't even have ears. I fly into a totally unprofessional rage backstage, screaming and swearing while dressers and actors look on bewildered. Afterwards, I am doubly ashamed of myself when I am told the man who was making the head had been rushed to hospital and this was the best they could do in the circumstances.

Now it's over, we have the two-hour wait till 7.30 p.m.

We're going to do it, we're actually going to do it.

I feel a restlessness that is almost uncontrollable. Try to eat, but, as at lunch time, no appetite. Half a bowl of soup is the most I can manage. Energy is being supplied by the sportsman's protein mix that Blessed recommended – a mildly repulsive drink made up of protein powder, milk and a banana – which I just manage to down. Try chatting to people and find that helps, particularly if I can joke and seem relaxed to them. Acting in real life helps quell the screaming voice inside – 'Help me, let me go, let me escape please!'

Selecting a tape for my massage I come across the opera choruses from that drunken, lazy day on a beach on the other side of the world. I lie there watching the polite Avon drift by, remembering how improbable it seemed then that I should come back to England and play Richard III.

Jenny, the masseuse, says, 'Your body is bursting with energy today.' Says it transmits to her through her hands, so that by the end of the session she is buzzing as well.

FIRST PREVIEW At 6.45 p.m. Mac and Pam O'Halleron arrive to dress and bewig me. Pam is another friend from my previous season here, which is a comfort. Joking with them helps calm me again. When Pam has gone, Mac says casually, 'It's gonna be a good show, mate. You can always tell. They're talking about it round the theatre. Like they did with your Fool. It's gonna be a fokkin hit, you mark my words.'

Bill never comes round to actors' dressing-rooms. Very unusual this. It is routine for the director to pop in before, after and sometimes during first nights. But I think his way helps to defuse the tension. No token good wishes before and token congratulations afterwards.

But tonight, surprisingly, his voice comes over the tannoy in the manner of this-is-your-captain-speaking: 'Hello everybody, this is Bill . . . just want to say uhm . . . good luck, have a good time and uhhh . . . that's all. Right. Thank you.'

I ask Mac to leave me alone for a while. Put on some perfunctory eye make-up, muttering my rosary, 'Now is the winter . . .' Will I remember the lines? In the profession it is considered a joke that outsiders always ask the question 'How do you learn all those lines?' This is a joke that I will never again find remotely funny.

Tannoy: 'This is your Act One beginners. Mister Sher, this is your beginners' call please. Elecs and sound operators stand by. Musicians stand by for cues one and two. Stage staff stand by on OP and Prompt Side doors. This is your Act One beginners . . .'

Waiting in the wings I feel completely calm. Peeking at the audience. Familiar somehow. Just another show.

But as the house lights dim, I feel the heat correspondingly drain from my veins. I have to give myself a little shove. Mutter 'Come on,' like a parachutist launching himself into mid-air. Forcing myself to do something that human beings simply were not intended for.

Scurry on stage and take up the sunbathing pose. Eyes closed. Hearing the music change, feeling the lights warm on my face. Open my eyes. There they are. One and half thousand of them. A wall of people. In Dame Edna Everage's immortal phrase, 'hanging off the picture rails'.

' "Now is the winter –" ' horrifying sense that if I pause at all here they will all join in and finish the line in chorus so, hurriedly – ' "of our discontent made glorious summer by this son of York." '

Feeling calm again. The rush downstage revealing the crutches produces an audible gasp. Teasing them with the profile turn, knowing they're straining to see the hump.

To my surprise, when Blessed comes on I realise my face is quite dry. As I exit from the scene, a polite round. In with a chance.

The Lady Anne scene goes well. Just before her spit, on the spur of the moment, I slide one of the crutches under her skirt and between her legs. Normally, I would never dare try something like this at a first performance but Penny and I have always had a special rapport in this scene. Nevertheless it shocks both of us as well as the audience, creating a rather wonderful moment. Another exit round. But I am starting to feel exhausted already.

Sucking Nigroid voice tablets as I dash round to the entrance on the other side. Nigroids are planted everywhere, even on the upstage edge of the throne. But the voice is feeling strong and whip-like.

In the Queen Margaret scene – the old problem scene – things start to go wrong. Sense a restlessness in the audience. However, Pat gets a round on her exit.

From then on, the first half is up and down. Another round after the Clarence scene. But something is wrong. Am I trying too much for the comedy, showing too many cards? Or is the play itself darkening as it should? Or is it simply too long? Should Bill have cut more, or should we be playing faster?

Win them back on Baynard's Castle and they certainly seem to like the coronation – the interval applause is thunderous.

I'm soaked through as though a bucket of water has been poured over me. Mac supplying endless pints of Coca Cola with ice – I drink about ten during the evening. Later when I pee it's the colour of Coke.

The second half is very good. My voice holding out well. Feel they're with me now. I'm playing the humour much harsher, less sycophantically than before, making them enjoy it on my terms.

During the Richard/Buckingham bust-up I bash Mal fiercely on the chest and spend the rest of the scene worrying about it. Try to apologise with hand contact, but I feel terrible, getting out of control like that. I seek him out afterwards. He says he didn't notice a thing.

Jim's Tyrrel takes a terrific leap forward in front of an audience. He had been experimenting with different accents, but doing him posh now adds to the seediness.

Queen Elizabeth scene excellent. Frances is very moving in the speech about losing her children and starts to cry for real. In my current emotional state I feel my own eyes filling. Have to fight against it. Would hardly be like Richard. In the screaming, Hitlerian 'cannot . . . will not be avoided' section I do too much and feel the voice give way. Come off, cursing myself. The whole of Bosworth and the oration to go. Popping Nigroids till I risk overdosing.

The Nightmare speech is unfelt and technical. Different funny voices coming out. I had hoped it might release in performance, but not yet. Afterwards, in the Ratcliffe scene ('O Ratcliffe, I fear, I fear!'), my failing voice cracks badly, giving me a terrible fright. Fear that it won't last and the relief that we're coming to the end produces a flood of real tears. I stop it instantly for 'play the eavesdropper'. Real emotion is so useful to act with – wish I had more access to it.

Disaster in the arming ceremony. My soldiers accidentally get the two arms of the armour the wrong way round; I can't bend them at all. In between my lines, I mutter 'Help me, twist them round', but neither they nor I am sure what has happened or how to solve it. Can hardly get on to the horse. A feeling that I could break an arm with the strain of trying to bend against the armour joint. When I do struggle on to the horse I can hardly gesture at all. This, combined with no voice, turns the oration into a spectacular non-event.

The applause at the end of the show is vaguely disappointing – a respectable success perhaps. At least I remembered the lines.

Penny and Frances have bought birthday champagne for the dressing-room afterwards. Then to The Duck where Pam has picked the most beautiful rose from her garden and put it in water in a brandy glass. 'Like I did for your birthday two years ago,' she says, presenting it to me.

Driving home, on a quiet country road, I take my foot off the accelerator and let the car gradually slow and stop. Sit there staring at the full moon. Exhaustion like I've never known.

Friday 15 June
Almost before I'm awake, I try little voice tests: 'Mmmaaaa, mmmoooo . . .' Surprisingly it's mostly there, except for medium-high notes which are dry, vaporous sounds.

My brother Randall phones from South Africa. 'Hi, howzit going?' Very casual. But again I can sense their excitement, their hope for this one.

'I think it went all right.'

'Just all right?' He laughs, but you can hear the disappointment. As Mum's telegram indicated yesterday, they were hoping, at the very least, my Richard would conquer the world.

VOICE CALL Ciss and I agree that, because of the vocal strain of the part, when/if the show transfers to the Barbican, we'll both request it never plays twice a day. The problem doesn't arise up here in Stratford because there's always a change of play between afternoon and evening shows. This is so that a tourist coming up for a day of culture can have a different menu at each sitting. This doesn't apply to the Barbican. Jacobi sometimes played Cyrano eight times a week, twice on Thursdays and Saturdays. An opera singer asked to sing a comparable role as often as that would simply laugh.

Lunch time. I beg Bill to make some cuts or to get the show moving faster. It's up to the rest of the cast now. I'm going as fast as I can, which maybe is why I keep stumbling over lines. He agrees, but when it comes to Company notes, does nothing about it at all.

SECOND PREVIEW I'm much more nervous. Having to do it all *again*, without last night's adrenalin.

There are less laughs and the first half drags terribly. The lighting computer has a nervous breakdown, so the audience witnesses several total eclipses in the middle of scenes. One of these happens in the Princes scene and I fear for the kids. But they're much calmer about it than we are. They simply hold their lines until standby lights come on and then continue as if nothing had happened.

My voice holds out well, growing stronger as the evening progresses – until the big shouting moments at the end when it deserts me. But in many ways it's better paced than last night. However, the lines are less secure and at one point I dry completely – before the line 'The sons of Edward sleep in Abraham's bosom'. After a long, long pause it comes out as, 'The sons of Abraham sleep with Edward's sons', causing Freud and Shakespeare to exchange sideways glances in their respective graves.

The show ends at 11.05 p.m. The audience are too tired to clap properly. And they're not pleased at having missed both their last buses and last orders in the pub.

An awful, flat feeling.

Ciss pops into my dressing-room. She is worried about my voice: 'We must be very careful now darling.'

In search of Bill A. We're so close to having a good show, but he must, *must* cut now. He's not in The Duck. I buy a bottle of wine and set out to find him. Roaming the dark streets, feeling like a gunfighter.

Back at the theatre I find Sonja Dosanjh, the Company Manager, switching off lights in the offices. She rings round possible numbers, Bill's digs, the theatre restaurant, but no sign of him.

I wander into the wings. That cool darkness. A figure standing alone on the set. It's Bill D. looking wrecked and grey after days of strain.

Almost as one we say, 'He's *got* to cut.' Apparently he's been badgering Bill A. for days as well. We set off together, resolved to sort it out once and for all. As we head out of the stage door Bill A. bursts in: 'I know what you're both going to say! It's all right, I'm cutting two whole scenes.' The Clarence children scene and the one in which Elizabeth flees to sanctuary.

We sit down on the floor and, passing the wine bottle around, consider the implications. Both scenes unfortunately involve the Duchess of York which means Yvonne losing about a third of her part. Bill A. is worried what effect this will have on her. But tonight's performance has finally convinced him.

Even his notes on my performance tonight – 'By the way, I thought

"Now is the winter" and the speech in the Elizabeth scene were quite dreadful' – can't wipe the grin off my face.

He also says he's never seen me dry before and found it fascinating to watch. It's a relief to have this secret fear out in the open at last. Maybe this will lay the jinx.

Saturday 16 June

Arrive to find Bill A. looking like a ghost. Says he hasn't slept at all. Yvonne is coming in at eleven when he'll break the news to her.

We do notes on the early scenes, but he's hardly concentrating and generates a ghastly tension. Makes some general comments on the Lady Anne scene and then asks if Penny and I want to go through it quickly. I say, 'I'd rather not spend the time. There are so many other things that need sorting out.' Penny suddenly starts to cry. Says she is suffering from terrible stage fright – having to deliver the goods right at the start of the play, no warm-up, no second chances. It's one of those parts in Shakespeare, famous but tiny. I realise that I've misjudged the situation completely. Because of our immediate rapport I assumed she shared my total confidence in the scene. But I've been overlooking certain facts – it's her first time on that great stage, and coming from another country the reputation of this place is that much more awesome. I know how she feels.

Nevertheless, the fact remains that the scene has always been excellent and time spent on it now would be wasted. These working days during the previews are almost the most valuable in the whole process. The audience teaching us what does and doesn't work.

She assures us that she'll be all right, and feels better for having shared the problem.

We're all cleared out of the Conference Hall and Yvonne is called in. Nobody else knows yet. I pace around the balcony, watching the Avon drift by.

Five minutes later we're called back in. Bill looks ten years younger and is glowing with relief. Apparently she took it very well and he was more upset than she was.

I seek her out to offer condolences. She says she has sensed it all along and that's why she has been constantly volunteering cuts. Says she was much more worried for the kids playing the Clarence children (who've lost *all* of their lines). But apparently the little girl just shrugged and said, 'Well, that's showbiz.'

On stage. A lighting effect, which is being tried through one of the upper cathedral windows, reveals a spider's web spun overnight, glinting delicately. The Bills and I stare up at it in delight. A good omen – the bottled spider.

Outside the theatre on the lawns, a group of university students are reading the entire works of Shakespeare non-stop, as a stunt to raise money. There are about four of them and a pile of cloaks, hats and wooden swords. They have been at it for over forty-eight hours. Currently on *Much Ado*, they are already staggering and giggling, voices gone, heavy eyes – drunk on Shakespeare.

THIRD PREVIEW The cuts help enormously. Paradoxically, although they give me less rest breaks, they make the first half much easier to carry. The audience is noticeably gripped.

Towards the end, in the middle of the Bosworth scenes, I'm waiting for an entrance, hunched forward on the crutches. The green cue light comes up earlier than expected, startling me and causing a fart of quite remarkable resonance. Scurry on stage with my little army all suppressing hysteria, only to find that one of my first lines is, 'I will not sup tonight'. This renders everyone helpless. Simon Templeman (Catesby) is forced to desert the stage before he has been given the crucial instructions, summoning Lord Stanley's army. The scene is almost ruined, but this relaxation and anarchy has been lacking in the past few days and is welcomed back.

We finish at 10.50 p.m., fifteen minutes shorter than last night! The audience continue to clap after the house lights come up, demanding another call. A few of us run back on stage. Some of the audience are on their feet, but whether out of enthusiasm, or simply caught leaving the theatre, is hard to tell.

No voice at all by the end. Ciss visits the dressing-room to say, 'You're going to have to make a decision about next week darling, you're risking permanent damage now.'

Try not to think too much about this. It's lucky the RSC *didn't* give me any more Shakespeare biggies. I'm clearly not ready yet.

THE DUCK 'Was it all right, aside from the corpses?' I ask Bill. He grins and shakes his head in disbelief.

Our first chance in ages to do some stocktaking. The production has turned out so differently from what we both intended. But, as Bill says, that's surely part of the creative process: 'When you set out to do a painting you don't know how it's going to turn out. It grows.' I mention how some of the music and costumes have worried me. The tightrope that we're walking. Last night's show felt silly and trivial, a pantomime. Tonight was something weirder, richer.

'Exactly the same as *Molière* and *Tartuffe*,' Bill says, 'the balance between comedy and nightmare.'

Bill D. puts it lucidly as always: 'What we've got is a comedy-thriller in the best sense of the words. Vintage Hitchcock, if you like.'

I think I've understood something about it tonight. It *is* a young writer's play. It *is* a young director's production. It *is* a young Shakespearian actor's performance. It has the crude vitality all of that implies.

As I'm leaving the pub, putting on my jacket, someone says, 'Don't move! There's a spider on your shoulder.' That's the second spider today. We turn the jacket inside out, examine my shirt, but no sign.

I can't help smiling – the bottled spider has, at last, been absorbed.

Sunday 17 June
Disappointing little piece on me in the *Sunday Telegraph* magazine. Rotten photo and uninteresting comment. We've hardly had any publicity at all, there's little anticipation of this production. I keep telling myself this is a good thing. If we're successful, it will be nice they didn't spot it coming. If we're not, it'll be better not to have had a big build-up.

Of course there is always the other depressing option – the production might just be regarded as run-of-the-mill, middle-of-the-road Shakespeare. Early on in rehearsals, the publicity department asked me if I had any ideas on angles they might take. Various editors had already expressed a lack of interest in 'just another production of *Richard the Third*'. That hurt me a lot.

The day is spent in monk-like silence, resting the voice. And making first-night cards for the Company – individual cartoons. It's relaxing using sketching to make this dreaded Sunday fly by.

Monday 18 June
FOURTH PREVIEW In the dressing-room, Black Mac is laying out my costume and deformities, while I'm practising one of the speeches under the shower.

He says, 'Clever, henny, clever, must be clever to remember that fokkin bollocks.'

But this is just Black Mac bravado. Later he confides to me: 'The shows I've seen here mate, the memories I've got, and I've viewed them from angles no other bugger has ever seen, no fokkin critic, not even the directors have seen them like I have, from my special places in the wings.' He taps his forehead, says, 'They're up here mate. Special memories.'

Tonight's performance is done on three large bottles of mineral water at room temperature instead of gallons of iced Coke. Ian MacKenzie (Ratcliffe and understudying Richard) told me that Coke wasn't very good for one, and iced Coke positively bad. The vocal chords are muscles, and to be constantly doused with icy fluid when they're overworking isn't a good idea. I am grateful but puzzled – I thought understudies were meant to push you down stairwells, not recommend ways of keeping you going.

Mark through the performance very lightly, particularly vocally. Very unusual sensation this, holding back in front of an audience. But I've got four performances to get through this week and, however much I try to pretend tomorrow night isn't special, I'm determined at least to be in good voice.

So, a feeling of being once removed from my performance tonight, once removed from the whole experience of being on stage. Looking out calmly at that beautiful black space, the green exit signs like jewels on black velvet. During the Richmond scenes at Bosworth, when the lights are down on my side of the stage, I sit staring at the wall of people. How bizarre it is.

The nightmare speech remains a disappointment to me, shared, I know, by Bill. He has always regarded it as one of the finest speeches in Shakespeare. He said earlier today, 'The trouble is, you're playing it exactly like the rest of the part. But a new man is born there. It's as if T. S. Eliot has thrown a speech into a Shakespeare play.'

Maybe tomorrow night . . .

Two mogodons to sleep without thinking about the opening night tomorrow.

Tuesday 19 June
I wake with that feeling, that sickening feeling. It only lasts as long as I lie in bed. There are still the last cartoons to be drawn. Sadly, I run out of time and fail to do ones for Alison Sutcliffe, Charles and the rest of stage-management.

The day is warm and thick like treacle. 'Twill be a storm . . .

Entering the stage door, the first signs of hysteria. Flowers, cards, presents already piling up. A carnation from David Troughton with a card written as Bouton to Molière – 'Master, have a glorious summer' – starts me crying again.

Rehearsal on stage with the coronation cloaks. Apparently, on several previews the naked hump (or 'The Money' as Bill D. has taken to calling it, because of Tucker's astronomical bill) hasn't been fully revealed when Buckingham disrobes Richard. Endless suggestions – change the fur to silk so it will slide off better, weights in the hood to drag it down. After an hour of rehearsing this, Mal says he's now more nervous about this responsibility than playing Buckingham.

The whole day feels like someone has their finger on the fast-forward button. Dashing into town to buy booze for tonight's party and presents, dashing back for the afternoon call, the stage door now looking like a florist's and greeting-card shop.

2.00 p.m. Conference Hall. The cast in a circle. Bill asks us to speak the play quietly, stopping one another if there's a word or phrase we can't understand. Very useful to hear the story again. Atmosphere sober. Blessed bubbling and twinkling as always, but I resist the temptation. Important for this exercise not to disintegrate into corpsing. Hope my whispering seriousness is not misinterpreted as nerves, which I don't feel yet.

4.30 p.m. On stage with Ciss. All of us standing in a circle ('A circle is always aggressive,' she says, 'use it to get rid of tension'), humming, rocking, chest-patting. Words from the play exchanged across the circle. Animal words, religious words. The atmosphere very similar to the end of the play – an army gearing themselves up.

5.00 p.m. Now the two-hour wait. No sickening nerves yet. Maybe they won't come this time.

Jim's first night present is beautiful – a huge joke-shop spider in a rather elegant Victorian perfume bottle.

Massage. Doze off to *Don Giovanni*.

THE OPENING NIGHT 6.00 p.m. Cold shower. Muttering 'Now is the winter . . .'

6.15 p.m. Mac arrives, relaxed and chatty, bearing piles of cards from downstairs. The heat of the evening is intense. As he advances with the hump I say, 'I don't think I can bear wearing that tonight, Mac.' He says, 'Righto mate, I'll go and tell them Richard's got better.' Phone rings. Bill, sounding stiff and formal: 'Just want to say have a good one.'

6.40 p.m. Fight rehearsal in the Conference Hall. The tension backstage relatively low. 'Good luck, good luck' is the constant greeting as people pass one another. Some of my cartoons have been opened and are being passed round, making people laugh.

6.45 p.m. Dressing-room. 'Give me ten minutes alone, Mac.' Strolling around doing 'Now is the winter . . .' Oddly calm.

6.55 p.m. Beginners' call over the tannoy. Look at myself in the mirror and say aloud, 'Right, let's go and play Richard the Third.'

6.57 p.m. Waiting in the wings with Allam, Paul Gregory, Jonathan Scott-Taylor and Guy Fithen. We peer at the audience through the tracery walls of the set.

'Come on, you buggers, get into your seats.'

'Look, the critics are writing already.'

'Tony, when your crutches first appear, expect a cacophony of scribbling.'

7.00 p.m. Graham Sawyer arrives from front-of-house to give the final clearance. Philip mutters into his mouthpiece 'Going', and the house lights start to dim. The music crashes and I scurry on stage. Get into position and feel the lights change. Open my eyes.

' "Now is the winter . . ." '

The first thing that strikes me is that the audience might be in more of a state than I am. Waves of tension that you can reach out and touch. How stupid first nights are! The frosty passivity of the critics ('We're not actually here, we're just observing') mixed with the nervous supportiveness of friends, relations and theatre staff. It's like playing to a dozen audiences at once. The laughter is muted and only starts about a third of the way back, behind the scribbling heads. A feeling that there might be some real people, ordinary members of the public, out there somewhere.

I underplay moments, overplay others, in an attempt to reach this totally untypical jumble of spectators. I dry briefly in the Lady Anne scene and have to do one of my Shakespearian rewrites. Later in the same scene I'm horrified to hear my line 'I'll have her' come out as 'Oil 'av 'er!' Still, there is an exit round, albeit rather token.

Better from here on in. Realising that I'm expending too much energy in trying to sort this lot out, I calm down to the point of indifference. Whenever I go backstage, worried faces loom out of the dark to whisper, 'How's it going?' 'Extremely well,' I keep replying and take a perverse delight in their expressions of surprise. Know they're thinking, 'Well, he's not getting the laughs he got at the previews.'

At the coronation the big moment comes – Mal comes to disrobe me. We share a smile and I whisper, 'Your big chance Mal, go for The Money.'

Don't know whether he managed it or not. Forget to ask afterwards.

The second half is much better. The audience appears to have decided it's not at all bad. They're more relaxed and confident and therefore so am I. Who's in charge here?

My voice lasts well and, thank God, I've got some big guns left for the oration. But no breakthrough on the nightmare speech.

Curtain call. The applause is disappointing, but I'm told there were some bravos and we are called back for another one. Blessed, Mal and I yell to one another over the applause, 'Well, you're on yer holidays!' Glimpse the scribblers scurrying up the aisles, dashing to their deadlines. Wonder how they find enough telephones?

Great relief backstage. People surround me, hugging and patting, Blessed sweetly saying, ' 'Kin marvellous performance, inspiration to us all, great triumph.'

In the dressing-room, a race to get out of the drenched deformity and into the shower before people start arriving.

Standing naked under a stream of water, shampoo, soap, stage blood, running mascara – the most beautiful feeling. I survived.

A knock on the door and, through the rushing water, a familiar hoarse voice: 'Tone, where are yer?' Gambon!

Lots of other faces from the old Company: Chris Hunter, Monica McCabe, Ludo Keston, Dusty Hughes. How wonderful that they should have come all this way.

Now the dressing-room full of RSC hierarchy. Suddenly Trevor Nunn pushes his way through and 'Trevs' me. I've heard a lot about this 'Trevving', but never had it done to me. From what I'd heard, a 'Trev' is an arm round your shoulder and a sideways squeeze. But this 'Trev' is a full frontal hug, so complete and so intimate that the dressing-room instantly clears, as if by suction. I'm left alone in the arms of this famous man wondering whether it's polite to let go.

He says, 'When this show moves to London there are going to be queues round the block. It's going to be one of those.'

A flash of a night in Joe Allen's some millennia ago.

At last alone. Step outside on to the little balcony, gasp at the fresh air. The storm never happened. It's a gloriously warm, almost Mediterranean night.

At The Duck, Pam whispers that the word is good and nods towards a table where they sit: Billington, Coveney, Tinker and others. These crazy evenings in The Duck after an opening night, when we all pretend we don't know one another – us and them. I miss James Fenton because he used to cross no man's land and offer you a drink.

Mal and I sit with Gambon and his companion, Lyn. Try and recapture the patter of two years ago, but there is something melancholy in the air. Beginning the descent. Gambon starts to talk about how strange it was driving into Stratford tonight, and his eyes fill.

We go to the party. It has been arranged by Steve, Jonathan, Guy and Hep. They have floodlit the garden of their digs. There is a barbeque and a Richard III cake to cut. Something which has happened, invisibly, over the last couple of weeks is that the Company has cemented together round this show. The cynicism and indifference are gone. There is a new enthusiasm for the work. I think that's one of this production's triumphs.

The only wet blanket this evening seems to be me, sitting alone at the back of the garden, forcing myself to eat although I still have no appetite. The exhaustion is massive, preventing me from having even one wild night of celebration.

Eventually find Bill. He has slumped alone in the living-room. Looking as wrecked as I feel. We smile at one another. Nothing left to say.

Later, I'm glad to have the opportunity to tell Gambon that at last I understand why he felt so disparaging about his great performance as Lear. At the time his behaviour seemed like destructive modesty. But Shakespeare's great parts are humiliating to play, or at least, humbling. You get to meet his genius face to face.

Leave the party early. Have to do it all again tomorrow and then again on Thursday.

Walking through Stratford on this warm, clear night. Not a soul about, just the beautiful timbered buildings, which often you can't see for the crowds. Late at night, this place looks like any quiet country town.

Jim and Lyn fall behind as Gambon and I stroll along Waterside saying very little. It means a great deal to me to have him here tonight. Lear and Fool. Where this chapter of my life began.

August 1984

Summer again. A glorious summer. As you come up over the hill from Chipping Campden, the world below has turned the colour of straw. One of the worst droughts in years, but droughts are in my blood, so I love these dry, bright days. The countryside is baked and cracked; sheep pant in little shaded groups under the trees.

Much has changed at the theatre and yet somehow it remains the same. *Hamlet* is in rehearsal now, and so the Green Room chat is about that: when the question of ghosts comes up now, it's Hamlet's father; when a head is passed around, it's Yorick's skull.

But the days following the opening were, for me, some of the worst I can remember – dominated by the news that a friend had been murdered. Drew Griffiths, writer, director, actor. We worked together in the early days of Gay Sweatshop. He was murdered on the afternoon of Saturday, 16 June, and they still haven't found the killer.

This, together with the usual post-natal depression, made these days very bleak.

As far as I can see, the only disadvantage in not reading reviews is that they can't help to fill these horrible days. They don't supply a new charge, fuel for excitement or fury. Suddenly – time on your hands. Suddenly – nothing on your mind.

But it does become apparent that we have a success on our hands, perhaps even a big success. Without reading reviews, you have to rely on other signs: now the applause at the end is rapturous, we are regularly called back for a third time, people stand and cheer.

Celebrities start flying in to see the show. And I am asked whether I'd mind if they came round backstage afterwards. If I'd *mind?* Michael Caine, Douglas Fairbanks Jnr, Peter Brook, Donald Sutherland, John Schlesinger, Charlton Heston ... *Charlton Heston?* I was making plasticine models of him when he was in *The Ten Commandments* and I was in nappies. Best of all, Mum and Dad are in the audience that matinée and are invited to have tea with him during the interval. Dad goes round for days afterwards shamelessly name-dropping, telling everyone that he had tea with Moses.

Michael Caine should have the last word on the reviews: 'What about those reviews then?' he said.

'I don't read them.'

'Don't read them? You *wrote* them didn't you?'

The Richard III Society descends in force. Most of them celebrate our production and write thrilling letters, but one or two are less enthusiastic: 'I read in the papers that you are yet another actor to ignore truth and integrity in order to launch yourself on an ego-trip by the monstrous lie perpetrated by Shakespeare about a most valiant knight and honourable man and most excellent King.'

As soon as we opened, the lines ceased to be any problem at all. Now they all come out effortlessly to the last 'thee' and 'hath'. I have not become prematurely senile, I have not lost my powers of memory. It was simply this show's special gremlin.

Otto Plaschkes has successfully raised the finance for Snoo's *Shadey* film. So this gentle character, this little misfit whose only ambition is to change sex, will live alongside my psychopathic bottled spider for a few weeks in October and November, as I commute between Stratford and London.

Busy, full days, in what I thought was going to be such an empty year.

The dollar is strong. Americans invade. Stratford gets so full it might be sick. It's a perfect time to be far away in Chipping Campden in a beautiful cottage, dictating a book to a lovely lady called Ainsley Elliott, who plays her typewriter like a piano.

We work with the French windows open to the garden, the dry lawn, the drooping, still trees. With one hand we have constantly to fend off wasps and bees, with the other we encourage ladybirds to land and bring us luck. Or money spiders. There are spiders everywhere these days. Every known species seems to be spinning webs in the garden, or under the eaves, or all over this room. Each morning I come in to find new running, glinting lines tying everything together, the furniture to the ceiling, the windows to the doors, the grandfather clock to the table on which lies a pile of notes and sketches from this past year, my battered copy of the play resting, in pride of place, on the top.